Dante's
Cure

Dante's Cure

A JOURNEY OUT OF MADNESS

by
Daniel Dorman, M.D.

OTHER

Other Press • New York

Copyright © 2003 Daniel Dorman

Production Editor: Robert D. Hack

Text design: Kaoru Tamura

This book was set in 10.8 pt. Minion by Alpha Graphics, Pittsfield, NH.

10   9   8   7   6   5   4   3   2   1

Library of Congress Cataloging-in-Publication Data
Dorman, Daniel.
    Dante's cure: a journey out of madness / by Daniel Dorman.
        p. cm.
Includes bibliographical references.
    ISBN 1-59051-101-8 (hardcover : alk. paper)
    1. Penney, Catherine Louise,–Mental health.   2. Schizophrenia–Treatment–Case studies.   3. Psychotherapy–Case studies.   I. Title.
    RC514 .D67 2004
    616.89'82'0092–dc22

                                                                    2003022675
                                                                    Rev.

To the memory of Ivan A. McGuire, M.D.

This is a true story.
Some names have been changed.

Contents

ACKNOWLEDGMENTS

I want to thank my patient, Catherine Penney, for wanting her story told, and for spending many hours articulately describing why she became insane, her experience of madness, and how our relationship led to her recovery. All members of Catherine's family generously invited me into their homes for interviews. I am grateful for Joyce Engelson's help as development editor. Her critique of an early draft was a private writing course. Thanks to Sheila Baird for reading several versions of the manuscript and her always-helpful feedback. Laurie Johnson provided superb editorial help. Many thanks to all the people at Other Press, especially Judith Gurewich, the publisher, for her interest in schizophrenia and her appreciation of the psychotherapeutic process.

One

ALONE IN A DARK WOOD

I went astray
from the straight road and woke to find myself
alone in a dark wood. How shall I say
what wood that was! I never saw so drear,
so rank, so arduous a wilderness!

Dante Alighieri, The Inferno

CATHERINE LOUISE PENNEY, AGE seventeen, knelt on the floor of her bedroom in front of her grandfather's antique Spanish dresser. On its yellowing marble top she had placed two wooden figurines—one of the Virgin and the other of Jesus standing with his arms stretched forward. Above the little altar hung three pictures in simple black frames: St. Thérèse of Lisieux, St. Bernadette, and St. Rose of Lima. St. Thérèse, a Carmelite nun, had seen Jesus floating above her, and died in 1897 from tuberculosis, at age twenty-four. Her kindness was the envy of the other nuns. St. Bernadette, a French peasant, had had a vision of the blessed Virgin at Lourdes in 1870. She chose to become a bride of Christ at age seventeen and drew the envy of the Mother Superior who made her clean the toilets and scrub the floors at the convent. St. Rose of Lima was reputedly so beautiful that a sailor, catching a glimpse of her through a window, demanded to marry her on the spot. To remain pure, she scarified her face with sandpaper.

Catherine, her skeletal hands clasped in prayer, knelt motionless in the shadowy stillness of her bedroom. Only her lips trembled: "Hail Mary, full of grace, the Lord is with thee. Blessed art thou amongst women and blessed is the fruit of thy womb, Jesus. Holy Mary, Mother of God, pray for us sinners now and at the hour of our death. Amen. Hail Mary, full of grace . . ."

"I'm a sinner," she whispered. "I have bad thoughts. I want to be good in His eyes. God will love me. Hail Mary, full of grace, the Lord is with thee. . . ."

Florence Lindner, Catherine's mother, squeezed open the door. "Cathy, you've been in here all day. Come to dinner."

"Okay, mother."

"You haven't eaten anything today."

Silence. Catherine froze.

"We're having dinner," Florence said again. "Please come on."

"All right."

Florence had married Joe Lindner in 1956, six years after Chester Penney, Catherine's father and the real love of Florence's life, died in Korea. Catherine was nine months old when her father was killed. The Lindners lived in Tustin, California, one of many bedroom communities surrounding Los Angeles. Their house, on a cul-de-sac at the end of a two-block-long street of one-story stucco homes, shone with a fresh coat of off-white paint. The garage door was usually open on weekends. Inside, built-in cabinets and neatly arranged tools hung on the wall above a workbench.

Catherine joined the rest of the family—Florence, Catherine's younger sisters Cindy, Bunny, and Theresa, and Theresa's twin brother Michael—at the dinner table. Joe lay sprawled on the couch in the living room. Most of the time he was too drunk on grapefruit juice and vodka—which he began sipping at ten o'clock in the morning—to even stand by dinnertime.

"Cathy," Florence said under her breath, "Won't you have some meatloaf?"

"I'm fine, mother."

"Get serious, mother, really," Cindy, age sixteen, drawled.

"Cindy, don't upset Cathy."

"Don't upset her? Don't *upset* her? She's *already* upset. Look at her— she's a bag of bones!"

"Cindy—"

"Are you *blind*? She just pushes her food around on her plate! After we're gone she sits there for hours staring at it. Why don't you *do* something? Cathy, what's *wrong* with you?"

Bunny, age ten, so named because she hated for anyone to call her Mary Beth, settled in for another round of dinnertime fighting. Theresa and Michael, age eight, glanced at each other. Florence's most definable characteristic, aside from her cerulean blue eyes, was her tentativeness, which she conveyed by cocking her head and hesitating before she responded to others in conversation. Often, she clutched her hands together in her lap as she spoke in her soft, flat voice. Florence shifted uncomfortably in her seat. "Let's be nice," she said to everyone and to no one.

Nice, thought Cindy to herself, staring at her mother. *Be nice. Not another word. If an elephant walked across the table, she'd say it wasn't nice. I should be nice. Take Cathy with me. With my friends. Really. She just slinks around, follows after me. Look at her: sweet Cathy. Shit. Never any trouble from her. Sits there and mumbles to herself. Stays in her room for days. What's wrong with her? Crazy, that's what. She's crazy as a bug. And mother never says anything about anything. Except when she fights with Dad. Then she rants and raves. Pathetic, that's what this place is. Sixteen years old. Two more years 'til I'm outta here.*

Cindy slammed her fist on the table. "You're all *so* pathetic," she spat, rising from her chair.

"Cindy—"

"Yeah, I know, mother. It's not nice," she said to the table behind her as she stalked off to her room.

What *was* wrong with Cathy? Florence believed that her eldest daughter was just shy. During her elementary school years, Catherine did occasionally talk to one friend on the phone, but she never brought anyone home or spent the night at slumber parties. Sometimes she even seemed afraid to spend the night in her own room. She would knock softly at her mother and father's open bedroom door and whisper, "I'm afraid, mother." Florence usually replied, "Well, come and get into bed." Joe snored away while Catherine slipped into bed on Florence's other side.

When Catherine was sixteen—a junior at the local public school, Tustin High—she came home one day after school with a friend, Terry. Florence told Joe, "Maybe she's coming out of it." Catherine and Terry had been classmates during the sixth, seventh, and eighth grades at Old Mission Catholic School, located next to an original California mission, in San Juan Capristrano. During the hour-long ride in the yellow-and-black school bus from Tustin to the Old Mission school, Terry had tried to fend off taunts directed at Catherine by pimply faced boys at the back of the bus. Alan Serty and Harvey Claremont were the worst. As Catherine and Terry boarded the bus, one or the other would shout, "Hey, witchy." Their sycophants hooted and howled.

"How's it going, bug eyes?" A chorus of laughter.

"Leave her alone," Terry commanded from her seat next to Catherine.

"Aw, she's S-T-R-A-N-G-E and you know it. What does Frankenstein have to say?"

"Ignore them, Cathy," Terry whispered.

On a bet, Harvey moved up and sat behind Catherine. "I just want to get a closer look at the freak," he said, smirking. Catherine stared straight ahead, rigid in her seat.

Terry turned around and glared directly at Harvey. "You are a slime ball," she said. Harvey grinned and then got up and strode toward the back of the bus, his head bobbing like a bantering rooster. His little show ignited snickers from the group.

After Old Mission, Terry had attended a different high school as a freshman. The next year, she and Catherine found each other in gym class on the first day of school. "My sister!" both declared in unison, and immediately made plans to get together. The two girls attended some afternoon pep rallies for the Tustin High Tillers football team and some games with nearby rivals. They ate dinner together once or twice a week at Terry's house—Joe's drinking made eating at Catherine's impossible. They met daily in the school cafeteria and went to movies on weekend nights.

One Saturday, as they were drinking iced tea together, Terry asked, "Why don't you wear some makeup, Cathy? You have such beautiful eyes." Catherine's eyes were even more watery blue than her mother's, and looked slightly more prominent, perhaps because of her angular face and long eye lashes. But with her thick, slightly wavy, black-brown hair, light olive complexion, and five-foot-five-inch, 132-pound frame, she had potential. "Maybe some mascara and a little eye shadow," Terry coaxed.

"Maybe I will," Catherine replied. "You think it would be okay? Really?"

"Let's go try some, over there, at Long's." Terry nodded toward the store across the street. "They have a whole counter," she said, gleefully. The two girls dashed over to the store. Terry played makeup artist, experimenting with samples and finally declaring, "This is it." Catherine looked at herself in the mirror—and smiled. She bought some Maybelline mascara, eyeliner, shadow, and blush. Terry squealed, "You look great!" Catherine spent the night at Terry's house, where the two girls crowded into the bathroom, giggling in front of the mirror.

"Yuck, this eyeliner won't go on straight," Catherine laughed, pulling at the skin at the side of her eye.

Terry jumped up to show her how to apply it. "You need some shadow and blush, too. Let's see . . ." After two hours Terry pronounced Catherine "done."

"Wow," Terry told her. "You sure look different. It's great. Do it tomorrow morning, before you go home."

"How do I get this off?"

"Cold cream," Terry replied. "Gobs of cold cream." She slid three fingers into her mother's cold cream jar and slopped the cream onto Catherine's hand and face. They both laughed. "You look like a ghost with black eyes," Terry giggled.

Late the next morning, Terry's mother dropped Catherine off at home. She walked in the door just as the family was finishing lunch, and preparing to leave for twelve o'clock mass.

"What's that shit on your face?" Joe growled in his gravelly voice.

Catherine stopped dead in her tracks. "Dad—it's just some makeup."

"Makeup? You look like a whore." Joe had kept his military haircut—cropped close on the sides and flat on top. He wore his pants crisply pressed and his shoes spit-shined. His son Michael addressed his father with "Yes, sir" or "No, sir," and had to place his shoes outside his bedroom at night for inspection.

"Joe," Florence pleaded, "don't—"

"Don't interfere, Maggie." He turned to Catherine. "Wipe that shit off your face."

Catherine retreated to the bathroom and removed her makeup.

"Not a word from anyone, you hear?" Joe announced, glaring at his family from the head of the table. "No daughter of mine looks like that."

Later that week, Terry convinced Catherine to go with her to a party—

music and dancing at Anne Bradford's house, a friend of hers. "You need something to wear, Cathy, something sexy."

"Oh . . . you know, my father won't let me."

"Friday evening, how will he know?" Terry asked.

Catherine admitted that her friend had a point, and the two went shopping the next night. "You've got great legs," Terry told Catherine. "Long, not stumpy like mine."

"You always look good, Terry."

"It's the clothes. You need a miniskirt. A hip-hugger."

"He'll kill me."

"No, he won't. Everyone wears them."

Years before, Joe had been an active-duty Marine Corps officer. He had flown recovery aircraft, picking up satellites and the remains of missiles launched into the Pacific Ocean from Vandenberg Air Force Base on the California coast, north of Los Angeles. After he retired in 1964, he worked for Holmes and Narber Engineering Company, doing the same thing. He typically arose at four o'clock every morning to go to work. Sometimes he was gone for days. Usually home by two o'clock in the afternoon, he was rarely awake at eight o'clock in the evening. On the night of the girls' party, he was sitting dazed on the living room couch when Catherine tried to sprint past him wearing her new navy-blue hip-hugger miniskirt, a gold short-sleeve tank top, and blue two-inch heels. And her makeup.

"Just a minute, young lady!"

"Dad, it's a party. Everyone—"

"Don't 'everyone' me. Where are you going, up on Sunset Boulevard with the rest of those whores? That skirt is so short you can see your cousy, you little tramp."

He arose, unsteady on his feet, just as Florence moved in front of Catherine. "Let her be, Joe."

"You bitch."

"God damn it, Joe!" Florence screamed. "Don't call me a bitch, you drunken, stupid slob! You're making life miserable for all of us! Why can't you leave the kids alone?"

Joe moved closer and brought his fist up to Florence's nose. Florence stood her ground.

"You fucking cunt. A house full of cunts," Joe grumbled as he staggered to the bathroom. Catherine slid out the front door.

"Whew!" she told Terry. "What a scene. You know, he's always like that, especially on weekends. I worry about mother, though. She really loses it."

"What do you do if he doesn't stop?"

"Sometimes we all just go over to Aunt Jane's house. Mother, the kids, and I stay there until he's in bed."

"How awful." Terry shook her head. But then she brightened. "Sounds like you need to have some fun."

Anne's mother welcomed Catherine—she hadn't seen her since the girls attended the Old Mission school. "Why, Cathy, aren't you the grown-up young lady!"

"Thank you, Mrs. Bradford. It's all Terry's fault."

"You girls look so cute. Come on, there's a crowd downstairs."

Catherine and Terry descended a narrow staircase to the Bradford's basement activity room. A crowd of sixteen- and seventeen-year-old boys and girls milled about. A neon-lit jukebox pumped out Smokey Robinson and the Miracles' "You've Really Got a Hold on Me." A few couples gyrated out on the floor. Terry introduced Catherine to a group of girls, then plunged into an excited conversation with her "best platonic boyfriend."

One girl, Hillary, had been dubbed "Miss Personality" by her friends. "Come on, Cathy," she said. "I'll introduce you to William Pembroke. He's really, really cute."

The two walked over to the chip-'n'-dip table.

"William, this is Cathy."

"Hi," replied the tall boy. He wore a Beatles haircut—straight, black hair cut evenly below his ears—and sported a black jacket without a collar, known as a Nehru jacket, and flowered pants. A silver ankh pendant dangled from a chain around his neck. "I haven't seen you around before."

"This is my first time here," Catherine replied.

"Would you like to dance?"

"No, thank you."

The two stood in awkward silence for a few moments.

"Well, see ya," he said, and walked off.

Catherine stood alone, nibbling on potato chips and watching the crowd. Hillary spotted her and ushered her back to the group of girls. "Having a good time?"

"Yes." Catherine answered. "I am."

For the rest of the evening, Catherine didn't budge from the chair at the edge of the little group. She agreed that government and economics were boring classes. She said that drama was her favorite, and that she had just signed up for private flamenco lessons one day a week after school. She told the girls she had Spanish ancestors.

Catherine spent that night at Terry's house. "I'm an alien," she said to Terry in the darkness of the bedroom, each girl on her back, side by side in twin beds.

"What are you talking about?"

"Oh, that boy, William. He asked me to dance."

"Well, why didn't you? You dance real good. I've seen you in your room."

"No, I'm hideous. I'm ugly."

"Cathy—"

"My eyes are too big. My nose is too big. I have horrible hips. My father calls me 'hippy' and 'fatty Cathy' all the time."

"I wish I had your figure."

"I should go on a diet."

"Cathy, you don't need to lose one ounce."

After that night, Catherine and Terry began to see less of each other. They still talked on the telephone three evenings a week and met in the school cafeteria for lunch. They even went to some school basketball games, now that the season had begun. But no more parties, and no more talk about clothes or boys.

Once or twice a month, Catherine drove her mother's car, often accompanied by Cindy, to the desert to visit the girls' grandmother. Catherine loved the iridescent purple-blue of the mountains on evening walks with Nana through the desert scrub. Cindy just grumbled. When Nana wasn't staying at her trailer in the desert, Catherine visited her at her home in Long Beach, drinking tea in the living room or on the patio.

Catherine thought that Nana looked elegantly Spanish, with her large brown eyes and olive skin, and her gray-black hair pulled back tightly in a bun at her nape. "You look like Lupe Valdez," Catherine told her, comparing her to the 1930s and 1940s Spanish actress. Catherine never tired of hearing Nana retell the same stories of her Spanish ancestors, who immigrated to the West Coast before California achieved statehood. The remains of the original family land grant still stood in San Fernando as the Lopez Adobe, a state historic site.

"Tell me about my father," Catherine asked again during one visit, and Nana told how he was "the light of my life." Chester Osgood Penney had attended Jordan High School in Long Beach, California, the same school that Florence had attended. After graduating, he was admitted to the United States Naval Academy in Annapolis, Maryland, where he received a degree in engineering and his commission as a lieutenant in the Marine Corps. He was assigned to China and Guam, where he served out his time. He then enrolled in petroleum engineering courses at the University of Southern California and worked part-time as a petroleum engineer. He met Florence at Yosemite National Park, where both were vacationing with friends. They married four months later. Six months after that, when the United States entered the Korean War, Chester was called up as an active reserve officer.

Photographs of Chester adorned the living-room walls and hallway tables. The house had belonged to Nana's parents. Her mother's bedroom, hardly touched since her death in 1964, also contained a shrine to Chester— Nana had displayed his postcards and letters on the bureau. She had also mounted photographs of her son, many of them showing him as a baby and young boy, in serried arrangements on the walls. Alone on a small table stood a printed pamphlet, opened to a section titled "Penney's Hill." It read: "Lieutenant Chester Penney went forward alone to reconnoiter and returned to spearhead an assault by C platoon on Hill No. 1305 with his pistol and knife. He killed seven Chinese before he was killed by a grenade."

"You look just like him," Nana told Catherine. Nana talked again about how she could not sleep well for six months after two Marines appeared at Florence's house with the news that Chester had been killed in action in North Korea, two months after his reactivation. Her daughter-in-law, Florence, now alone with Catherine and two months pregnant with Cindy when she lost her husband, cried every day for five years after the news came.

On February 12, 1967, Catherine's seventeenth birthday, Nana gave her a delicate gold-chain bracelet and a small green leather diary with a brass lock and tiny key. In the diary, Catherine wrote: "Today is my birthday. I received this diary and a bracelet from my grandmother. I love them both. I am watching *The Blob* with Steve McQueen on television. Yum, yum, he sure is cute. Now I have decided to be a great flamenco dancer, like Carmen Amaga. She is my idol."

That afternoon, after the birthday party, Catherine peered at her face in the bathroom mirror. "I hate my eyebrows," she muttered. She concentrated on her left eyebrow, plucking out one hair at a time with her mother's tweezers. She plucked until she had abolished the entire eyebrow. She then set to work with an eyebrow pencil, tracing out a thin line where the eyebrow used to be. She left her right eyebrow alone. At dinner that night, Cindy snickered, "Your eyebrows, what did you do?" Catherine retreated to her bedroom in tears. The next morning, she added liner to the plucked area, but still was not satisfied. Complaining that she did not feel well, she stayed home from school. The next day, Terry helped her mitigate the damage by plucking away some of Catherine's other eyebrow.

"3/3/67. Dear diary: I did my improv of Amanda in *The Glass Menagerie* in drama class. I hate to watch myself on the monitor. I'm so ugly. Received a letter from Nana today. I'll write her tonight."

"3/4/67. Dear diary: I went to my flamenco lesson and learned some new steps. Tomorrow is Sunday. I must go to confession because I am a sinner."

That week, Catherine bought a calorie book and called it "my bible." She determined to eat only 1,000 calories per day.

"3/13/67. Today is a good day. I stayed home from school. I have not stayed on my diet. Tomorrow I will."

"3/15/67. Going to Nana's for Easter. I feel so lonely at times. Grandfather died a year ago. I miss him."

"3/17/67. On a church retreat today. I am very depressed. I hate me and everyone else in the world. All nature works against me. I might even commit Hari Kari. DAMN SHIT HELL. How do you like that?"

"3/20/67. I feel halfway human. I am too fat. I must cut down. It makes me sick to see all these articles about priests and nuns leaving their orders.

It makes me sad to see how and why He died when hardly anyone follows Him. I am not too Holy tonight. I am the worst sinner of all but I still love God. Always will. He is my first love."

" 3/22/67. If I don't lose some weight, I'll kill myself. I babysat twice today. I got my hair cut. It looks pretty good."

"3/23/67. I want to go to a convent and live with the sisters. I'm so depressed. I wish I were not so sinful. I need more patience and grace."

"3/30/67. I wish something would happen for the good of me. I'm not too happy."

"4/2/67. Took Cindy and the kids to the beach."

"4/5/67. Today was a beautiful day. I'm going to take coed volleyball. I like swimming."

"4/9/67. I've gained weight. I will kill myself."

"4/19/67. Last night I went to the movies with Cindy and mother. I saw James Coburn. He is sexy."

"4/20/67. I was in a play contest. Our class put on *The Pencil*. I played a Mexican housemaid who was supposed to be hysterical. She kept running to the head of household, screaming 'Señor Larry, señor Larry!' We got lots of applause. Mrs. Archer said I have real talent."

Catherine began dieting with draconian severity, eating the same foods every day. She had half a doughnut and half a grapefruit for breakfast, some days substituting the doughnut with a bowl of Grape Nuts cereal topped with skim milk. For lunch, she always ate one apple and one hard-boiled egg. She usually fixed herself dinner at four-thirty in the afternoon: a slice of steak between two pieces of bread, and a scoop of cottage cheese. She rarely sat down to eat dinner with the rest of the family. If she kept to 1,000 calories a day or less all week, she treated herself to a slice of custard pie on the Fridays that Joe brought one home from the pie shop. By the time summer vacation had arrived, Catherine's weight had dropped to 105 pounds. Florence decided she had to "do something," so she made an appointment for her with the family's general practitioner.

Dr. Charles Stoner, a kindly fellow with white hair and white mustaches, examined Catherine and told her, "Now Catherine, I've known you for a long time. You don't have enough meat on you. I'll give you vitamin B-12 shots once a week, and I don't want you to lose any more weight. Okay?"

"Okay," Catherine replied.

Dr. Stoner told Florence that Catherine had agreed not to lose any more weight and that she was otherwise in good health. He gave Florence some mimeographed papers with suggested foods for a 1,500-calorie diet.

Catherine dieted even more fiercely. She reduced her calorie intake to 800 a day. She had stopped making diary entries, but on 6/15/67 she wrote: "Everyone is talking about how thin I am, but I am still too fat. Today is Monday. I'll have some cottage cheese and nothing else. On Tuesdays I can have my bean burrito. On Wednesdays, my tuna salad on bread. On Thursdays my steak, and on Fridays I'll have my reward—pie. God, I'm tired."

For the rest of the summer, Catherine spent each afternoon in the backyard, stretched out in the sun on a lounge chair in her one-piece swimsuit. The endless sparkling of water from the kidney-shaped swimming pool obliterated thought, providing her with a respite from the sin and ugliness that she felt she could not escape.

At four o'clock, she would pad inside to watch "Dark Shadows," a soap opera about a vampire disguised as a country gentleman. One day she watched a show about bulimia, a psychological disorder in which people throw up to lose weight. She slid two fingers back along her tongue until she gagged; then, in the bathroom, she pressed down hard. She vomited.

I deserve that, she thought to herself. *I ate too much cottage cheese.*

"Cathy, are you all right?" Florence called.

"I'm okay, mother."

"I'm worried about Cathy," Florence confided to Joe on a Sunday morning, before he had had his first drink. "Have you seen her in the backyard? She looks like a skeleton."

"I'll talk with her," he said. Joe walked to Catherine's room and knocked on the door.

"Yes?" Catherine had just built her little altar. She rose from the floor.

"Can I come in?"

"Yes."

Catherine was sitting on her bed. Joe sat down next to her.

"How's doing, kiddo?"

"Fine."

"Your mother and I have been talking, Cathy. She's worried, you know? You're too thin. You shouldn't worry her."

"But Dr. Stoner is giving me vitamin B-12 shots."

"Yes, but if you don't start eating more, we'll have to take you to see a specialist. I think we should do that anyway. Would that be all right?"

"Okay," she answered.

"I'll get the action going," he replied, patting her on her back lightly with the tips of his fingers. "Is there anything bothering you?"

"No, Dad."

"Okay, honey. So long."

Down, I'm going down, she thought to herself day after day. *I am like a monk in a cave on a diet of rice and nothing else.* She sat for hours with her chin resting nearly on her chest. To commune with God. Deeper and deeper. *I am in control,* she thought. She imagined food sliding down inside her. *I am inside my stomach.*

In the dim light of evening, or early in the morning, Catherine began sneaking outside and sinking to her bare knees on the crushed stone surrounding the pool. She thought about the penitents marching on their knees over tessellated pavement before the Basilica of Our Lady of Fatima, in Portugal. "Holy Mother, full of grace . . ." When she stood up, blood trickled down both shins.

In August, the Southern California sea breeze withers and gives way to a stagnant brown haze before the September Santa Ana desert winds broil the air and ignite the land. One early September evening, Catherine sat in her room staring out her window at the sunset. She heard a whisper, then another whisper, or was it a word? "Who . . . ?" She listened, straining. Silence. Then, she heard it again. Shivering, she dropped to her knees, and clasped her hands in prayer.

On the first day of school, Terry almost shouted at her. "Cathy! What *happened*? You've lost so much weight!"

"Yeah," Catherine replied. "My mother is worried about me."

Terry's brow furrowed. Then she asked, "Do we have any classes together?" The two girls compared schedules. "All right, dreaded American history at ten o'clock. I'll see you then."

"See ya."

No more C's this year, Catherine told herself. She buried herself in her books. An "A" on her American history quiz. A "B" in algebra. In English literature class she could identify the poet, Robert Burns, from the opening verse:

Green from the rashes, O;

    Green from the rashes, O;

The sweetest hours that e'er I spend,

    Are spent among the lasses, O.

She studied so intensely that her head began to pound.

Joe grew suspicious of Catherine's trips to the bathroom after meals. She would sit at the table after the others had left, most of her food still on her plate. Then she would get up and head for the bathroom. One night, Joe followed. He listened at the door while stealthily turning the knob, then suddenly pushed open the door. He saw Catherine scraping food from a crumpled paper plate into the toilet.

"Dad!"

"Catherine, you've gone overboard. We're taking you to a psychiatrist."

William Barber, M.D., had been practicing psychiatry for fifteen years. He looked the part in his tweed jacket and his Freudian mustache and beard. During Catherine's appointment he weighed her. She weighed eighty-nine pounds. He took a detailed history. What did she eat? Did she count calories at every meal? Did she force herself to vomit?

"Yes," Catherine admitted.

"This is anorexia nervosa," he declared to Florence and Catherine. "I suggest a hypnosis session and group therapy. Any questions?"

"You can help her?" Florence asked.

"Alarming increase in anorexia," the doctor mused. "Too much emphasis these days on being thin. Every young girl wants to look like Twiggy. Have to reprogram them. And the group helps; she can see she's not alone."

"All right," Florence said.

Catherine arrived the next week for her hypnosis session.

"Just lie on the couch," the doctor instructed. "Close your eyes." Catherine complied. "Do you hear the ticking of my clock?"

"Yes."

"Concentrate on it."

Catherine listened to the cadence of the pendulum clock in a glass-fronted wooden case on the wall near the couch. She felt her arms and legs go limp.

"You are feeling relaxed," he intoned. "Listen to my voice. You are feeling more and more comfortable."

The clock ticked on.

"Catherine, look in the mirror. You see a lovely, curvaceous young lady weighing a hundred and twelve pounds. You can't wait to eat."

Catherine visualized herself in her bathroom on her knees before the toilet, throwing up. *I want to weigh eighty pounds*, she thought to herself. The doctor instructed her to wake up.

The therapy group met at the doctor's office at seven o'clock on Thursday evenings. Mickey Swarthmore, about forty years old, introduced herself as the "facilitator."

"Group, this is Catherine, our newest member."

Hello's and hi's around the circle of three men and three women.

"Let's go over the rules for our group," Mickey said. "We don't discuss what is said here with anyone outside the group. Each of us has a right to privacy. Without privacy, we wouldn't feel free to speak openly. We refer to each other by our first names."

Catherine took a seat.

"Perhaps each of us will tell Catherine why he or she is here. Robert, would you mind?"

"Oh . . . no." Robert was twenty-eight years old and always wore a suit and tie. He seemed stiff and awkward, and stuttered—though not so much in the group, he said. He also became nervous easily, often urinating in his pants.

Barbara, also twenty-eight, had strawberry-blond hair swept up on top of her head. She was a hairdresser. "You look like you might have anorexia, honey. I have a sister who died of anorexia. She only weighed seventy-five pounds. Well, we'll talk." Barbara was "not in love" with her husband. He was "real sweet," but she had no interest in him sexually. She thought about having an affair.

Janet, thirty-one, came because she drank too much. Janet applied her bright-red lipstick beyond the edges of her lips, and wore lots of dark-blue shadow around her eyes. Her curly hair dangled in ringlets over her ears and one eye. She made a point of saying that it wasn't her fault she drank so much. Life was "stressful." Her husband was no help. Her friends were not "supportive." Catherine detected a slight slurring of her words as she spoke.

Alan, forty-one, was "depressed." His wife was leaving him, for no apparent reason. He worshiped her. He had sacrificed everything for her and their two daughters. She told him he was boring and weak. She needed a "real man."

John's pants were wrinkled. His socks drooped to his ankle bones, and the laces of one shoe dragged on the ground. He had urination-control problems, too. It was "all those guys lined up at the urinals" in public restrooms. He just couldn't get his stream started.

Finally, there was Anne. "I'm in my forties," she said. "Suffering bothers me. There's just too much suffering. I need a break."

Catherine told how she had lost more than thirty pounds. She still felt fat. And, she had only one friend.

As the meetings continued, Mickey tried to get Catherine to talk more—with little success. Mickey also asked questions designed to get at what was really bothering each member. Did John feel self-conscious in places other than restrooms? What suffering was Anne talking about? Her own? Or other people's? One day, Anne blurted out that Catherine's suffering was getting to her and that she might leave the group.

Catherine fared better with Barbara. She even agreed to let Barbara "do" her hair. The hairdresser bubbled at the idea. "Sure, honey, let's do it. The salon is just in Santa Ana."

Catherine made an appointment for the following Saturday, during which Barbara gave her a short, chic haircut. The hairdresser eyed her new client and pronounced, "Very cute. It looks better short." Catherine offered to pay but Barbara wouldn't accept. "It's on me, honey. Come down early next time, and we'll go out for hamburgers at the A & W."

Two weeks later, Catherine made another appointment at the salon. She didn't eat all day so that she could treat herself to a hamburger and a slice of lemon meringue pie.

"If you don't start eating, honey, you'll die. Why don't you come visit me in La Jolla? You can meet my twin daughters."

"That would be fun," Catherine said.

"How about this afternoon? You're my last customer. We could leave right now." Catherine drove behind Barbara to her home in La Jolla. They walked on the beach at La Jolla Cove, Barbara's seven-year-old girls laughing and skipping in front. They ate lunch on the patio of the La Valencia Hotel, watching the fog merge with the horizon over the blues and greens of the ocean.

Back home that evening, as she sat in her room, Catherine sensed she was not alone. The whispers had returned. Catherine listened. Yes. A word. Repeated. A voice, out loud.

"Suicide," it said. "Suicide."

Catherine cowered. "What is that? Who *are* you?" she whispered back. She sat paralyzed, trying not to listen. "Suicide," the voice said again, more insistent this time. Catherine walked down the hall toward the living room. Cindy, Florence, and the twins were watching "I Love Lucy" on television. Their laughter muffled, but did not extinguish, the voice.

Later that night, before Catherine turned back her grandmother's quilt on her bed, she dropped to her knees to pray. Even as she said her rosary, the voice spoke: "Suicide. Kill yourself, kill yourself." Her eyes squeezed shut, she mouthed the words, "I'm bad, I'm bad, I'm bad . . ."

Catherine's drama class at school and her weekly flamenco lessons were all that stood between her and the horror of the voice. In the evenings and on weekends, she began to hear a chorus of voices, and whispers, too, jumbled and disembodied.

"Kill yourself. Suicide. Kill Theresa."

"Theresa?" Catherine exclaimed.

"Kill Theresa," returned the voices. "Kill Theresa, kill your mother, kill—"

"Kill!" Catherine finally screamed.

"Cathy, what's wrong?" Florence asked, knocking softly and opening the door.

"I fell asleep, mother. I had a dream."

"Oh. Why don't you come and watch TV with us? You've been in your room all day."

"All right, mother."

At the group meetings, Catherine sat quietly with her head down, the muscles in her neck occasionally twitching. The group members, except for Anne, who now missed two out of three meetings, were all worried about Catherine.

"What's wrong, honey?" Barbara said. "This is the place to let it all out."

"Don't push her!" Janet interjected. "Can't you see she's in pain?"

"Catherine will speak when she's ready," Mickey answered. After the meetings, the members frequently went for coffee at the White House, a hamburger joint nearby. Catherine went, too, and from time to time talked about her drama class and events at school. She also told them about her dance classes, portraying an arrogant flamenco dancer, swirling and clicking her castanets, to spirited applause. "Why, you'd never believe it," said Barbara. "With you so quiet and all."

One day, Mickey took Catherine aside at the White House. "Catherine, I can see that you're drowning. Perhaps you'd like to talk with me alone?"

"That would be nice."

"Good. Here is my phone number. I'll be away for the Christmas holidays, so call me in January."

"Okay."

In December, and January, too, you can see the horizon all the way from the Tustin Hills to the San Bernardino Mountains. You can even see the snow on Mount Baldy. It must have been this way all year long a hundred years ago, before automobiles disgorged their toxic gases on the freeways. Catherine spent every vacation day in the backyard, trying to get away from the voices. But they followed her. Even when they were quiet, she could feel their presence. She visited Nana in the desert, and walked among the mesquite bushes and spidery ocotillo with their now sleeping red-orange flowers, in full bloom for only a few weeks each April.

On Christmas morning, she smiled weakly and thanked Florence and Joe for the black and red flamenco skirt they gave her.

"Great hunk of ham, Maggie," Joe remarked at Christmas lunch. "Troops, that's why I married your mother. Ham and sweet potatoes. That's what she is, nothin' hi-falootin about Maggie."

The others sat silently.

"Why is everyone so quiet?" Joe said. "Cathy, don't just mash your food around. Hold your head up! You, too, Michael. Sit up straight!"

"Um-hmm," Michael mumbled.

"What'd you say?"

"Yes, sir."

"What do you say?"

"Yes, sir!"

"That's better. I'm tired of the goddamn Mickey Mousing around here."

"Yes, sir!" Michael said again.

"And you, young lady," he said, looking directly at Cindy. "We'll have less of your slamming doors and listening to that . . ."

"Just say it, Dad. 'Jew bitch.' Streisand." Cindy returned his glare.

"Joe, don't . . ." Florence pleaded. "Not today. It's Christmas."

"Christmas, shit," Joe said as he got up and shuffled off to the living room, where he flopped down in his chair.

Catherine's pounding headaches made it hard to study, but she kept at it. Memorizing made the voices recede. *Nathan Bedford Forest, confederate raider, was promoted to major general for defeating the Yankees at the battle of Cedar Bluff, Alabama, on May 3, 1863,* she thought to herself. *John Wilkes Booth, President Lincoln's assassin, was shot on April 26, 1865, by Yankee troopers who had found him hiding in a tobacco shed south of Fredericksburg, Virginia.* Grades were mailed at semester break, the third week in January. Catherine made straight A's.

The voices now sounded constantly. Catherine called Mickey. They would talk at Mickey's home, in her library. "I see clients here," Mickey told Catherine. "But I don't want to charge you."

"I'm sure my mother would pay you," Catherine answered.

"No. Tell me, what's bothering you?"

"I think something is really wrong with me."

"Are you worried about your weight?"

"Well, yes, but . . . I think that's the same. I haven't lost any more weight in months. I'm still eighty-nine pounds."

"What is it, then?"

"I have terrible headaches. Maybe I have a brain tumor. But—there is—I hear something in my head."

"What do you hear?"

"Voices."

"Voices?"

"Yes."

"What do the voices say?"

"Well," Catherine said. "One voice started out saying 'suicide, suicide, suicide,' over and over. Then it said, 'Kill Theresa . . . and mother.' Then more voices, then more, like birds chattering when I was alone in my room. Screaming, yelling, blasting my ears. Now it's happening all the time. I can't stand it! They are—"

"Catherine, have you told your mother?"

"No. I'm bad. I'm evil. I should be punished."

"I think you may be sick, sweetheart. You need to have a medical workup. Would you mind if I called your mother?"

"Well . . . okay."

Mickey called Samuel Johnson, a neurologist, who agreed to see Catherine. But based on Mickey's description of Catherine's symptoms, he thought she should be hospitalized. Mickey then telephoned Florence. Catherine was admitted to St. Joseph's Hospital on her eighteenth birthday. That afternoon, she was wheeled to the electroencephalogram suite, where a technician inserted needles attached to wires into her scalp. Tiny wire-like pens mounted in a stainless-steel cabinet vibrated wiggly lines onto a large sheet of paper. "Lie still, please, and close your eyes," the technician said. Catherine closed her eyes and listened to the faint hum of the machine.

At seven o'clock the next morning, the doctor tapped on the door as he strode into her room.

"Catherine, hi, I'm Dr. Johnson."

"Hello."

"I'd like to examine you." Catherine sat on the edge of the bed. The doctor rapped her knees gently with a small rubber mallet, which made her lower legs swing forward. He tapped the insides of her arms at the elbows and above her heels, which made her forearms and feet twitch. He rolled a tiny wheel with a row of sharp teeth lightly over her skin, first on one side of her body, then the other.

"Do the two sides feel the same?"

"Yes," Catherine replied.

The doctor asked her to stand with her feet together, her eyes closed, and her arms at her sides, to observe whether she swayed. He had her touch her nose with each index finger, starting with arms outstretched.

"This afternoon, we're going to do a pneumoencephalogram," he announced. "I'll need to put a small needle in your back. Then I'll inject some air into your spinal canal. This will let me see your brain on the x-rays. I'll see you this afternoon." Catherine started to answer, but he turned to leave.

The pneumoencephalogram was painless except for the needle stick in Catherine's back as she lay on her side on the cold x-ray table. It was all over in thirty minutes. But afterward her head hurt so bad that she thought it might explode. The nurses cautioned her to lie still for twenty-four hours.

As she lay in bed that afternoon, Terry peeked into her room. "Cathy?"

"Oh, Terry, you're here." Catherine remained motionless on her back, as the nurses had ordered.

"What are they *doing* to you?"

"Sticking needles in me, everywhere."

The two girls talked about school. Terry was impressed that Catherine had made straight A's last semester. She told Catherine that she had been to a Seeds concert at the Santa Monica Civic Auditorium, and chattered about her exploits with boys. "We haven't talked enough lately," Terry said as Florence arrived. "I'll call you. Bye."

"Bye-bye."

Dr. Johnson arrived promptly at seven o'clock the next morning. "Catherine," he said, "I've found nothing medically wrong to account for your headaches. I think the problem is psychiatric, so I've arranged for you to see Dr. Ganz. He'll be by tomorrow."

That afternoon, Joe showed up. He stood silent for a moment at the end of her bed. "Hi, honey."

"Hi, Dad."

"You okay, honey?"

"Yeah."

"I know today's your pie day. I brought your favorite—custard."

"Gee, thanks, Dad."

"You know I'm not so good at chit-chat, Cathy. I just feel so bad for you." He wiped his eyes with the backs of his fingers. "We'll get this thing under control, you hear?"

Dr. Ganz, the psychiatrist, muttered his name by way of introduction as he walked into her room the next morning. Short and balding, he reminded Catherine of the television cartoon character Elmer Fudd, with his pasty white face and pug nose, and his tendency to trip over his own words. He took notes as he asked Catherine about her weight and diet.

"Do you hear voices?"

"Yes." Catherine wanted to tell him how they clamored and screamed inside her head. But he raised his eyebrows over his round wire-frame glasses and looked at his watch—he had been there fifteen minutes. "I'm sorry, but our time is up," he said, and walked out.

"Schizophrenia, undifferentiated, and anorexia nervosa," he wrote in the hospital chart. A nurse called Florence to tell her that Catherine would be discharged. She urged Florence to call Dr. Ganz. Florence obeyed right away. The doctor informed Florence of his diagnosis and told her he had prescribed Thorazine, an antipsychotic medication. He would see Catherine and Florence in his office in a month.

Catherine tried to override the voices by repeating, "cottage cheese, burrito, custard pie; cottage cheese, burrito, custard pie; cottage cheese . . ." But the voices screamed even louder in protest. She tried to escape them by diving even deeper within herself: down, down, down into nothingness. She thought she had found another dimension. When that didn't work, she went back to repeating the names of foods, over and over. But the moment her attention lapsed, the voices were upon her again. *Concentrate*, she thought. *Sit still. Don't move. Don't even breathe.*

The outside world became an intrusion on her efforts to control her mind. Attending to her schoolwork grew impossible. In the early weeks of her last semester in high school, she managed C's on quizzes in California history and home economics, and received D's and F's in her other courses.

She randomly marked "true" or "false" on test questions, and on essay exams she wrote nothing at all.

Drama class was different. Catherine came alive. Or so it seemed, since she usually sat motionless with her chin buried on her chest, waiting her turn. But she became animated when practicing the part of the Wicked Witch of the West in the *Wizard of Oz*:

"Hee, hee hee, my little pretty! You thought you would get the best of me, didn't you? Well, I've got news for you, my little pretty. I'm going to get rid of you *and* your little dog Toto, too!

"Oh, what's that? Water! No, don't throw the water! Oh, I'm melting! I'm melting!"

The realistic quality of her solo portrayals sent shivers through her classmates. Some even thought that her improvisations could win the contest for a drama scholarship to be held just before graduation. But Mrs. Fitzpatrick, Catherine's drama teacher, was concerned. She thought Catherine might be taking drugs. She called Florence. "She is taking medication," Florence informed her. "She is also seeing a doctor."

A month passed. Florence took Catherine to see Dr. Ganz again. Afterward, Florence told him there had been no change. Catherine still sat quietly in her room every day after school, Florence explained, often in a seeming daze. She rhythmically nodded her head, or sank to her knees, praying. "Does she still hear voices?" Dr. Ganz asked. "Why, I don't know," Florence replied. "She never says anything about that." The doctor recommended adding Stelazine, another antipsychotic medication.

At breakfast, Florence said to Joe, "Why is he talking to me? Catherine's the one who is sick."

The two drugs made the voices recede slightly. But they also made her tongue feel thick, and left her with the sensation that she was walking on the angled floor of the fun house in an amusement park.

Some of Catherine's other teachers also called Florence. She was failing all her classes, with the exception of drama. Florence met with the assistant vice principal and told her of the doctor's diagnosis. She consulted with the principal, who told Florence that Catherine would be given barely passing grades and allowed to graduate, even though she had stopped participating in class and handing in homework.

Catherine told Florence that she had decided to stop the group therapy. "They are all nice people, and they mean well, but . . . I don't say anything. It isn't doing me any good."

On the day of the drama contest, Catherine performed the Wicked Witch. She then played Carmen Amaga dancing the Ferruca, an amalgam of male and female roles. She had continued her weekly flamenco lessons and had mastered the castanets. She stomped and swirled, to a standing ovation. And she won—a full-tuition scholarship to the School of Performing Arts in Colorado Springs, Colorado.

But Joe had been fired. Federal Aviation Agency blood-alcohol and liver-function tests revealed the extent of his drinking. "We just don't have the money, Cathy," he told her. "We can't pay for you to live there. I'm worried about keepin' up to snuff around here."

"It's okay, Dad. I don't think I could make it there, anyway."

"I think I've got a job lined up at Lockheed. Not flying . . . we'll see."

In June, a boy in drama class, Mark Hamilton, asked Catherine to the senior prom. On the day of the dance, Barbara fixed Catherine's hair. "Your first date? Oh honey, I'll make you sooo beautiful! What are you wearing?"

"I went shopping with mother. It's silk."

"Oooh!"

"It's blue and has a high neck, and long sleeves . . . and it's flared at the knees."

"Is it form-fitting?"

"Um huh, it is."

"You'll look great, honey. I know you'll have a good time."

Mark drove up promptly at six o'clock. Cindy peered at him from behind the living-room curtains as he walked up to the front door. He wore a rented tux and carried a bouquet of red roses. *How did Cathy swing that?* Cindy marveled to herself.

Florence answered his ring, and stood admiring the tall young man and his dark hair and energetic eyes.

"Hi, I'm Mark Hamilton," he said.

"Hello, I'm Cathy's mother. Come on in."

"Hi, Cathy," Mark said. "You look real pretty."

"Thanks."

Florence felt relieved as she watched her daughter get into Mark's car. *Maybe this will all work out,* she thought.

Mark had made dinner reservations at Five Crowns, an upscale restaurant in Newport Beach. Catherine forced herself to eat spaghetti with meat sauce. Mark ordered filet mignon. "It's too bad you can't go to Colorado," he said. "You're not going to give up on drama, are you? You're really good, you know."

"Gee, thanks. I'm going to sign up for drama at Saddleback College later this month."

"Wow, that's great."

The prom was held in the ballroom of the Hilton Hotel. Catherine and Mark sat with Melissa and Tom, both from drama class. Catherine excused herself from the fast dances, but she felt comfortable with the slower ones. She and Mark left at one o'clock in the morning and drove home. "Cathy, I had fun," he told her as they pulled up in front of Catherine's house. "Maybe we can go out again?"

But he never called. For weeks after the prom, Catherine rarely emerged from her room. She missed her graduation ceremony. Her diploma arrived in the mail.

Florence thought Catherine needed prayer. She called the parish priest, but his receptionist told her the priest did not do "that sort of thing." A neighbor told her of a lady who would "pray the devil" out of Catherine. Florence made the arrangements. Catherine did not object.

The praying woman had graying, frizzy hair springing from the sides of her head. She examined Catherine with piercing black eyes. Her darkened room was bare but for a mostly empty bookcase, a card table, and a straight-backed chair. "Sit down, my dear." Catherine obeyed. The woman placed a Bible on the table and placed her left palm on it. With her right hand, she grasped the top of Catherine's head. "Leave her!" the woman ordered. "Leave this child!" Her hand tightened on Catherine's scalp. "This daughter will be made pure! Whole!" The woman shut her eyes. "The devil will leave. The Lord is my shepherd. I shall not want. No evil shall touch her. Evil will leave her!" She removed her hand. "Go now, and pray."

In the weeks that followed, the voices screamed day and night, mocking the effort to silence them. Catherine forced herself to register at Saddleback

Junior College. She signed up for four courses: English composition, introduction to biology, algebra, and drama. But when classes began, she could not stay focused on her work. She tried to make her mind blank, to shut down the voices. And the drugs made her drowsy. She sometimes remained in her seat long after the professor had dismissed the class. One day, as she sat on a concrete step waiting for class to begin, a young man with a long ponytail approached and asked her if she was "suffering."

"I am," she answered.

"I used to be on drugs," he confided. "Then the Lord saved me." He invited Catherine to join his prayer group, which met in Laguna Beach.

Florence objected. Once was enough.

"I *know* praying is the answer," Catherine pleaded. "That woman, she was strange. But these are good people. He said he could help me."

Florence assented, as long as she could drive Catherine there and wait for her. The address in Laguna Beach was an apartment in town, just behind a string of art galleries lining Pacific Coast Highway. Al, the student she met, welcomed her. "Brothers and sisters, this is Catherine." Voices in unison sounded from a circle of kneeling youths: "Welcome, Catherine."

They look like hippies, Catherine thought to herself.

Sarah, Al's girlfriend, said, "Welcome, sister." Alice, Suzanne, and Samuel nodded. Catherine joined the circle. They all grasped each other's outstretched arms.

"Oh, Josanna, Josanna," prayed Al.

"Josanna," the group intoned.

"We shall be saved," Al said. "The Lord is abundant. God makes a divine connection. God dropped faith into our hearts. Are you with me?"

"We are with you!" Cries of assent rose from the group. Sarah started shaking and mumbling. Alice shouted—not a word, something guttural. Suzanne fell forward on the floor. Al clutched a Bible, eyes raised to heaven. "From the book of Daniel, 'They that lead many souls to righteousness shall shine as the stars.' We pray for our new sister."

Suzanne and Alice got back on their knees. All knelt quietly, with bowed heads.

"Will you join us next week?" Al asked Catherine. She nodded, tentatively.

Alice walked up to Catherine and put her hand on her shoulder. "The end of the world is coming. California will slide into the sea. You will be saved."

Back in the car, Florence asked, "What happened?"

"They prayed. I guess I'll try going back next week."

At the next meeting, Al played jazz on his violin. The others hummed, clapped their hands, and shouted, "Amen!" They all sang "Down by the River," then Al invited Catherine to join the group permanently. A small donation, he said, would help support the meetings.

"I don't think I'll be back," Catherine told him.

"Oh. Well, take care, daughter," Al replied.

Catherine's efforts to paralyze herself caused her mind and body to ossify. In drama class, her teacher had to call her name two or three times to shake her out of her stupor. In the middle of July, she finally withdrew from school. At home, Catherine fixed her own meals on her own schedule, rarely joining the family for dinner. She spent hour after hour in her room on her knees, praying. By September, Florence decided to talk to her. "You can't just sit in your room every day and do nothing. What do you want to do, Cathy?"

"Drama," Catherine replied.

Florence called the Veterans Administration and found that Catherine, because her natural father was killed in Korea, was eligible for education benefits. She called drama schools and found an approved one that would accept the VA tuition payments—Madame Moleska's School of Theatre Arts on Wilshire and Crenshaw Boulevards in Los Angeles. Florence, Catherine, Theresa, and Michael all drove up for Catherine's enrollment. Florence helped Catherine register, then spent the day at the Santa Monica beach with the children.

As one of her first assignments, Catherine was to play a scene from a fairy tale. She picked "Mary Had a Little Lamb," and her performance won applause from the class. After class, her teacher asked to talk with her.

"Are you on drugs?" she asked.

"No, I'm taking medication."

Catherine drove to Los Angeles every day for class. She declined a role in the class production of Ibsen's *A Doll's House*. She mostly watched the class, occasionally doing an improvisation she had done before. A class-mate, a man in his thirties, asked her out. "My mother won't let me," she answered. "But thank you." Others tried to cheer her up: "Hey, put a smile on that pretty face." "You're going home after class? You gotta be kidding." "C'mon, we're all gonna go out, have some laughs." "Are you okay?"

Florence thought she had to do more to help Catherine, but did not know what to do. She talked to her neighbor, whose son, Art, was coming home from basic training at Camp Pendleton, just north of San Diego. Perhaps Catherine would like to meet him? "You are eighteen," she told Catherine. "You should date." Catherine agreed to meet the young man, so Florence called the friend. The two women arranged the date.

On the following Saturday evening, Art arrived. He was exactly Catherine's height, and not bad looking (Catherine thought)—despite his Marine Corps recruit's shaven skull. They went to the Long Beach amusement park. Catherine tried to beg off a ride on the roller coaster, but finally gave in. After the ride, she confessed that it was fun. They ate hot dogs on sticks and got their fingers gooey from cotton candy. Art nailed ten out of ten little clowns with a BB gun, and gave Catherine his prize: a pink and blue bear. And he won a stuffed alligator at shuffle board, sliding wooden disks down an alley into numbered holes. At her front door he told Catherine he had had a good time and would call her when he next had leave time. He leaned over and kissed her lightly on her lips.

"Oh my God, it was awful," Catherine wrote of the kiss in her diary, neglected for over a year. "I'm bad. And I went off my diet. I'll starve my-self tomorrow."

Florence began to despair. Every evening now, she sat for hours in the dark living room, downing one or two martinis. "Are you sad, mother?" Catherine asked.

"Yes, dear, I am. I don't know what I can do for you. I'm going to call Dr. Ganz again. He has to do something."

Dr. Ganz thought Catherine should be hospitalized for two weeks on the psychiatric ward of St. Joseph's Hospital, so that he could regulate her medications. Catherine agreed, so long as she would be permitted to attend her drama classes each day in Los Angeles. So, at the end of October 1968, she was admitted. The hospital looked like any other, except that patients milled about in a large room with couches, card tables, and a television set. Group therapy, led by one of the nurses, was held every evening—Catherine just sat and listened. The doctor, as before, spent just a few minutes with her each morning. She reported that the increased drug dosage left her dizzy and made her arms and legs feel stiff and heavy.

"That's the proper medication effect," the doctor opined.

When the two weeks had passed, Dr. Ganz told Catherine she could go home. "Keep taking the extra Thorazine and Stelazine," he said, dismissing her with a glance.

Today, yesterday, and tomorrow merged into an unchanging timelessness. There was no time. Just numbness. No wakefulness, no sleep. Nothing above or below. Catherine floated, drifting, within the miasma of her mind.

Months passed. Or was it years? Or days? The voices now shrieked through a loudspeaker in her head: "Kill your mother, kill your mother, kill your mother, kill your sister!" Over and over and over. Catherine thought, *Where is the old Cathy? Jerk your head up! Get out! Come up!* Florence noticed the spasmodic twitching of Catherine's neck muscles, and saw her head bobbing up and down. Catherine would lower her head; then, with a sudden jerk, her head would come back. Then, she would lower it slowly again. Even when she walked about, that fitful motion continued.

Christmas came around once more. Florence went about making cookies and decorating the tree. She prepared Christmas dinner. Ham and sweet potatoes again, Joe's favorite. The family sat around the candlelit table. A sprig of mistletoe hung in the doorway to the kitchen.

Suddenly Catherine stood up. "I can't stand it!" she screamed. She ran to the bathroom and reemerged clutching the bottle of Thorazine. She poured the entire contents into her hand and put her hand up to her mouth.

"Cathy!" Florence shouted, jumping up from her chair.

Catherine hurled the Thorazine to the floor, where the capsules bounced and then rolled to a stop. Joe left the room.

"I won't take any more of them," Catherine announced. "They're not helping. I feel worse than ever! I'm crazy! I'm a goner!" She turned and fled the room.

February, March, April rolled by. How long had it been since drama class in Los Angeles? Last November? And flamenco? Her last dance lesson came and went just before graduation—Catherine wasn't there. May, June, July, August. The thermometer, hanging outside on the shady side of the house, read 100 degrees. It must be summer. No matter. Cindy would be getting married next month. She had met Allen on her graduation trip to Europe, two months ago. No matter.

Catherine tried to descend, away from the voices. Down into a clammy, mucoid darkness. She felt a jolt. Not the jolt of trying to jerk her head back up yet again. An electric jolt, and then a feeling of current running through her entire body. And again, and again. Only in sleep did that electric current and the screaming voices cease. Why not sleep all the time?

Death is near, Catherine thought one night, standing at her bedroom window. *He is out there, stalking me. I can feel him. There he is!* The apparition beckoned, and then vanished. The voices chanted, "Suicide, suicide, suicide, kill yourself, kill yourself," all through that night and the next day.

At six o'clock the next evening, Catherine walked into the kitchen, where Florence was preparing dinner.

"Goodbye, mother."

"Cathy, where are you going? We're having dinner."

"I don't want any. Goodbye."

Catherine walked outside, got in the car, and backed out of the driveway. She drove toward Irvine Park, where the road ended on a cliff. But at the last minute, she bypassed the park and drove to Mickey's house instead. It was seven o'clock. Catherine knocked on the door.

"Catherine! What's wrong?"

Tears streamed down Catherine's face. "I . . . I can't stand it anymore," she sobbed. "I almost drove off a cliff in Irvine Park."

"Oh, sweetheart!" Mickey folded Catherine into her arms. "Is it the voices, still?"

Catherine nodded.

"You look so much thinner since I last saw you, too. How much do you weigh?"

"Eighty-eight."

"Catherine, you really *will* be dead if you keep on this way. Are you seeing a psychiatrist?"

"No. He put me in the hospital. It was a joke. I just sat around. He gave me medication that just made me worse, so I stopped taking it."

"We've got to do something. Will you let me call your mother and get you an interview at the UCLA Neuropsychiatric Institute?

"Mickey, I'll try anything. Go ahead. Call."

Two

A Desolate Chasm

*And I found I stood on the very brink of the valley
called the Dolorous Abyss, the desolate chasm
where roils the thunder of Hell's eternal cry,
so depthless-deep and nebulous and dim
that stare as I might into its frightful pit
it gave me back no feature and no bottom.*

Dante, The Inferno

THE UNIVERSITY OF CALIFORNIA at Los Angeles hospital is a medical magnet for the entire Los Angeles area. Like hospitals attached to university medical schools in other cities, UCLA has the reputation of offering up-to-date diagnosis and treatment. The waiting room of the admitting and evaluation department of the Neuropsychiatric Institute is large and practical with institutional couches, bare walls, and a metal check-in desk.

Today, some of the patients sat there stiffly. Others tapped their feet or paced. They looked frightened. Many were just nineteen, twenty, or twenty-one years old—the age when mental breakdown tends to occur.

I walked up to the admissions desk. "Your patient is over there," the clerk informed me. "The one looking down at the ground."

"Hello," I said, as I approached Florence and Catherine. "I'm Dr. Dorman. I'm a resident in psychiatry."

Florence rose slowly. "How do you do?" she said as we shook hands. A high-pitched "Hello" came from Catherine on the couch.

"Would you mind coming this way?" I asked. Florence and Catherine followed me to a consultation room. I took one of the straight, hard-backed chairs and turned to Catherine. "Can you tell me what's wrong?"

"I'm sick."

I waited, but she did not elaborate. "How long have you been ill?"

Catherine did not respond. She sat hunched over, her chin resting on her chest—I could see only the top of her head. Strands of straight, dark-brown hair hung like a curtain over her face. Thin legs protruded from under her loose-fitting, red-and-yellow-flowered cotton dress. Her nylon stockings pooled about her ankles.

"Could you tell me what has happened to Catherine?" I asked Florence.

"Catherine has not been well for a while," she said softly.

"Can you tell me for how long?"

"A long time. Let's see . . . she's nineteen now. . . . Well, it's been a long time."

"What do you mean by 'not well'?"

"She's been getting worse."

"Did her doctor give you any information for me?" I asked.

"Yes. Catherine's therapist, Mickey Swarthmore, told me to give you this." Florence handed me a sealed envelope. Mickey had telephoned Catherine's doctors and had typed a two-page summary of their findings. She had also enclosed a copy of the St. Joseph's Hospital records.

The brown canvas suitcase Florence had placed on the floor next to her answered my question as to whether she wanted Catherine admitted to the hospital. I addressed both women: "Catherine, I do think you need to be in a hospital. You've lost a lot of weight, and I'd like to begin intensive treatment. But under California law, you cannot be admitted to a mental hospital against your will, unless your life is in immediate danger or you are a danger to someone else."

"I would like her hospitalized," Florence broke in. "We've tried everything else."

"Catherine," I asked, "are you agreeable?"

"I need to be in a hospital," she said.

I directed Florence to the admitting office, where she filled out financial-responsibility forms. Joe's retired military officer's insurance would cover Catherine's expenses. About forty-five minutes later, I found Catherine and her mother sitting in the large waiting room. I escorted them to the ward.

"You can spend as much time here as you wish," I told Florence. "I would like to talk with you before you head home. Perhaps I can arrange to interview your husband, too? Maybe tomorrow morning?"

"Well . . . my husband . . . yes, that would be fine."

"Good. Here's my office number. I'm down on C floor. I'll see you there at, say, one o'clock?"

"Okay."

The psychiatric wards are located on the fifth and sixth floors of the ten-story psychiatry building, which in turn is a part of the larger general-hospital complex. The hospital is adjacent to the medical, dental, and nursing schools, in a corner of the peaceful, tree-shaded university campus. The ivy-covered, red-brick buildings and quiet walkways contrast with the busy commercial center opposite the hospital.

When Florence, Catherine, and I arrived on the ward, Ruth Sargent, the head nurse, met us. All the patients gathered around to meet "the new girl." Ruth introduced them, one by one, as Catherine stood by, looking at the floor with her arms held stiffly at her sides. She offered only a timid "Hi" to each patient's name. It was Ruth's job to get a general impression of new patients so she could discuss treatment ideas with the nurses. After an attendant showed Catherine to her room, Ruth told me, "Whew! She's sicker than anyone I've seen in my three years here. Her nutritional status gets my first priority."

Catherine and her mother sat down at opposite ends of a small couch and fell silent. Catherine looked down at her lap, and Florence looked at her daughter. To me, their silence did not look forced, nor did either woman appear uncomfortable. I had the feeling that their silent togetherness was not unusual.

Florence finally rose and said, "Well, goodbye, Catherine. I'll see you this weekend. What about other clothes?"

"I don't think I need anything."

Catherine got up, too, and followed her mother to the door. Florence kissed her lightly on the cheek. Catherine stood motionless. Florence seemed eager to leave. "Goodbye," she said again. Catherine did not answer. She stood rooted to the spot and watched her mother's back fade down the long hall.

The ward to which Catherine was admitted contained sleeping quarters and a day room, a large general-purpose room. The day room had four frayed couches, a card table surrounded by some marred wooden chairs, and a variety of easy chairs; the room looked used, but clean. At one end was a glass-enclosed nurses' station. Two long hallways stretched in opposite directions, away from the room. The sleeping quarters, segregated by gender, were off the halls. Most rooms were doubles, but at the end of each hallway was a larger room accommodating eight patients. In the rooms stood metal beds with thin mattresses, and scratched wooden bureaus. Each person had a narrow closet.

Typically, patients lounged in the day room. They played cards, or dozed, sprawled out on the couches; some sat and stared at the always-on television set. The one spark of life came from the lively ping-pong games that some people played in the corner.

A dining hall, served by a cafeteria line, bordered one side of the day room. It, too, had a well-used, clean, institutional look. Long, pale-green formica-topped tables and the inevitable scratched chairs filled the room.

To ensure that patients would not harm themselves or others, the upper half of one wall of the dining room consisted of glass, through which the nurses and other staff members could watch the patients. Moreover, all the exterior windows of the ward were covered with a steel meshwork screen—not as secure as bars, but strong enough to prevent someone from jumping out a window.

The first evening, in the dining room, Catherine sat with her hands folded in her lap, looking down at her plate. Occasionally, she pushed some food around with her fork. When the other patients had finished and drifted into the day room, Catherine got up and shuffled to her room.

Linda Freylich, a popular nurse on evening duty, discovered Catherine kneeling beside her bed, her hands clasped in prayer.

"Would you like to join the others?"

"No, thank you."

"Would you like to talk?"

"No, thank you."

"I'll check in on you later," Linda said, and withdrew.

Catherine stayed in her room the entire evening. Linda told me that she peeked in on Catherine from time to time. She saw her lying on her back on the bed, arms at her sides, staring at the ceiling in the dark.

Catherine appeared in the morning wearing yesterday's dress, now wrinkled, and house slippers. She had not washed or brushed her teeth. "Aach," I said to Livia Spano, one of the nurses, "are we going to have to bathe her and brush her teeth for her?"

She gently told Catherine, "Dear, you'll have to shower and brush your teeth." Catherine left, then came back looking exactly the same. Livia returned to the bathroom with her and watched while she brushed her teeth and showered.

Catherine did everything in slow motion. At lunch, she sat for over an hour—she would take one distinct chew, then stop and take another. She walked in the same manner; first she slid one foot forward, then, slowly, she brought the other along.

Later that afternoon, Ruth discovered Catherine sitting alone in her room. She was grinding her teeth so loudly that other patients heard it in the hallway.

Florence arrived at my office at precisely one o'clock.

"Hello," I said. "Come on in."

Office assignments were based on seniority. As a first-year resident, I had to make do with an eight-foot by eight-foot space—just enough room for a black-linoleum-topped gray-metal desk, a matching gray-metal desk chair, and my "thinking chair," which, when reclined, offered up a small footrest. I had to step back to allow Florence in.

"Thanks for coming. I'd like to know as much as you can tell me about Catherine's background, and about you, too."

"I don't know what to say. You'll have to ask me questions."

"Okay. Let's start with you. Tell me about your childhood—your upbringing."

"Well, I was the youngest and I was spoiled."

"You were spoiled?"

"Yeah, I think so. I don't remember."

"What do you mean?"

"Well, my mom let me do pretty much what I wanted to do, and I didn't really have a lot of—I don't know, I guess she never said too much to me or anything like that. I don't know if she did to my sister or not, except that it seems to me that my dad and mom, not mom, my dad, was a little harder on my sister—like not wanting her to go to a dance or do this or that. I don't remember him ever saying anything except that he didn't want me to get a car, which I wouldn't have gotten anyway. But, I really think more or less they catered more to me than my sister."

"They catered to you?"

"Um-hum, they did."

"You were the favorite?"

"It seemed that way to my sister."

"Well, perhaps it was true," I replied.

"It was. It really was. Of course, my sister got married when she was eighteen and moved out. She wasn't home as long as I was. I worked and lived at home until I got married at twenty-three. My parents never wanted room and board. They never asked for it. In fact, if I didn't make my bed, my mom would do it. She never said a word. You know, if my kids don't make their beds, I won't make them. I close the door. When they get tired of seeing the mess, they make it. But my mom wouldn't do that. Of course, she was a better housekeeper than I am. She couldn't stand anything out of order, so she did things for me other parents expect their children to do."

"Like what else?"

"Oh, I never had to do housework or anything, really. She never made me do anything I didn't want to do. Like, I never had to finish eating anything. But I was always very obedient at home. I never gave them any problems."

I felt a peculiar unease talking with Florence—a sense that she was fragile, or that she might slip away at any moment. It seemed that she told me just the facts of her life, with little feeling.

"What about your relationship with your mother?"

"There's not much else to say. I was very close to my mother. Her friends in her age group were the mothers of my friends in my age group, and we all did things together, like go to the beach. Now, my mom didn't swim a stroke or play cards, but I did, and she would join us to talk and visit. Everybody liked her, and we had a lot of fun together. I enjoyed being with my mother. This was through adolescence and after marriage, too. I can remember I enjoyed being with my mother all the time. My girlfriend and I liked to swim, so we'd go swimming and Mom would go with us a lot of times—there wasn't any barrier between my age group and hers. Things on that order."

"Go ahead. I'd like to know more."

"My mom always worked when I was younger—she worked six days a week in a drugstore at the soda fountain. She had arthritis and thought she should keep her hands out of water, so she quit. That was when I finished high school and we started doing more things together because she was home more."

"And your father?"

"I loved my dad, too, except that he wasn't there all the time. He had to go to bed early and he got up early. He worked at a produce company where they brought in fruit. Years later he went to work as a maintenance man at a college gym. I was proud of him because even though he went through only the fourth grade, he could talk about any subject; he read sets of encyclopedias like I read a novel. I saw him read two sets at home. He would say 'ate' in wrong English, but when you sat down with him he knew about any subject."

"Did you date in high school?"

"I've told Catherine I didn't enjoy my teens. I didn't enjoy that time at all until I got out of high school. Then I started dating and doing things. I never felt I was that attractive and—I participated in things but I didn't date. I really don't remember all that much about that time."

"You participated in what?"

"I was a majorette and I started ice skating, and I'd go to school dances and I was in the drama club, but I didn't date. I had lots of friends on both sides but they weren't personal relationships. They were acquaintances. I started dating, I think, right when I graduated. I went with a boy for three years and then I met Chester again—because, you know, we already knew each other. He had been overseas—this was wartime. It was when this boy and I broke up that Chester came back. I saw him up at Yosemite, and four months later we got married. So I really didn't date that many people. I dated one boy and I might have gone out one or two times with other boys at school. I know I went to a dance with one. I didn't like him and I could hardly wait to get home. Things like that, but that's about all. I never did much dating."

"So, in essence, just one—Chester."

"Two, really. Chester and the boy Bill or whatever his name was. He was gone a lot, too. I remember when the war was on I was engaged and I didn't date anybody. I was always—true blue."

"Wait a second; let me make sure I understand. You were engaged?"

"Yeah, we got engaged."

"You and Chester? Or Bill?"

"Yeah, we got engaged. Bill. Got engaged and he went in the navy."

"You and Bill were engaged?"

"Uh-huh. I was eighteen."

"Oh, I got confused."

"Yes, we got engaged and he was in the navy, and he came back and forth. It wasn't like he was gone all the time—we dated for about three years."

"So that means you didn't see much of him or anyone else?"

"No, not too much. There was another thing too. We grew up at school together."

"And you did not date him, Bill, in high school?"

"No, we didn't start dating until we got out of high school, until I met—then that just went, you know."

"You were engaged, and what happened to that?"

"We just—when he came back he was interested in somebody else. It just didn't work out. I hadn't gone with anybody else."

"I guess you *were* true blue."

"Dumb. That's the way to put it now. I look back on it, and it is so silly. I tell my kids that I don't know why they want to go steady at eighteen. I told them that by the time they're married they might have dated so many different people—and there they are, just sitting there. I guess through experience . . . It didn't seem so bad for me, though. I never felt I missed out on too much. I told Catherine I sure was never any gadabout or popular at school. She always felt like she wasn't popular and that it was important to be popular. A lot of people aren't . . ."

"Shortly after the engagement broke off, you met Chester?"

"Yes."

"So, there is another fellow you knew all the way through high school but never dated?"

"Joseph is the first one I dated that much—for two years, but that was because he was afraid to get married. He was a bachelor until he was thirty-five."

"Let's see, you married Chester Penney when you were . . ."

"Twenty-three. We moved to the El Toro Marine base and lived there for—a year. The Korean War broke out and he was called up. He was only there two months when he got killed. Cathy was just a baby—nine months old. And I was pregnant."

Florence lowered her head slightly.

"I'm sorry. We can talk—"

"No, it's all right."

"Well, tell me a little more about . . . when he died."

"I was visiting with some friends in Burbank when the news came about Chester's death, and Catherine was with me. After that, I stayed in quite a bit; I didn't feel like going anywhere. I stayed home and watched television with my folks. I didn't do anything, didn't work or anything until the baby was born.

"Gee, I can't even remember part of that period. It must have been very uneventful. That's all I can remember is . . . just staying at home with my folks. Oh, I know! I got interested in the house. I had bought it before it was built, and my dad had me drive out and see how things were going. It gave me an interest. I was really more interested in the house than anything. When it was completed they got me moved, and picked out furniture and things like that. I think that's what occupied my time more than anything else. I just didn't go to movies or anything like that."

"What about the effect of his death on you, emotionally?"

"I think it might have bothered Catherine when Chester died. Everybody was so upset. I know a baby can feel that. After I found out he was killed, I was driving home and Catherine just hung on and wouldn't let loose. She was crying, too. She had nothing to cry about other than I was crying. After that . . . I can't think—she stayed real close to me and, oh, she felt left out, so we put milk in a bottle for her. That kept up until she was two years old. I started feeling more responsible for Catherine because I felt people were making so much over Cindy that it was hurting Catherine. I wanted to compensate. She did feel it, too. I know she did. She felt hurt. She started to do things she didn't do before to get attention, like dance around."

"Do you think you gave her more attention?"

"I can't remember if I did give her more attention—maybe I did. My mom did all the babysitting, and it seems to me that my folks would take the kids on weekends. They would go to the local amusement park or places like that. Maybe I did, but I can't remember how I did it. I probably did, though. Catherine was more or less close to my dad, and Cindy was close to my mother. It just sort of worked out that way. I think I was close to both of them. I can't remember feeling different about either of them, except I felt sorry that Catherine was being hurt. I didn't have any problems with Cindy in that way. She was a good baby. Catherine just didn't want to go to sleep, and I had a heck of a time. I would become irritated, which she would pick up. Then I'd feel bad the next day. She'd wake up in the middle of the night, and I'd get up and rock her to sleep. I didn't think she would ever get to sleep by herself."

"So there you were with two little girls—"

"After Cindy was born, I was there alone with my two little ones, but I went home every night and ate dinner with my folks. I had it pretty easy compared to a lot of girls, you know, because my folks lived so close. My house was only eight miles away. Also, Chester's folks lived real close too, and they helped a lot. I wanted to move away and be on my own, but like I say, I was there every day, so it was like being back. It's just that I had my own place and I could still go home.

"I had a lot of friends, and they came over. They were very good. A lot of nice people. That's about it. I think I just got interested in the house business. In fact, when I moved into the house my girlfriend stayed with me a couple of days because actually I'd never lived alone before.

"But I did it. We lived there for six years. I worked in a factory. My mother took care of the children during the day. We all ate our evening meals at my parents' house. Cathy slept with me for two years because she cried and clung to me all the time."

"Tell me a little more about your father."

"My dad was very sensitive. When Catherine's dad was killed and I moved home, my father put her crib in his bedroom. My father was very fond of Catherine. He wanted to be around Catherine more than Cindy. I heard my mother say he had had a nervous breakdown when he was a young man—that was when they turned to Christian Science, which was the way I was raised."

"He had a breakdown? Do you know anything about that?"

"All my mother told me was that he was depressed. They gave him shock treatments and he came out of it."

"Did anyone else in the family have a breakdown?"

"No, not that I know of."

"How about in Mr. Penney's family?"

"No."

"Let's see. Then you met Mr. Lindner."

"Joe. He's a good person, but he's an alcoholic. When he's around, he is very sensitive to it because he knows it. Deep down he knows it, but he won't talk about it. I mean, you don't mention it around him because he gets very upset, very mad. I think that's hard on the kids. It's hard on his kids, let alone Cindy and Catherine.

"He's been a good father, as far as that goes, but when he drinks he has a personality change and he's very difficult to live with. That's all. That's the whole point. If he didn't drink, there would be no problem. Outside of his military attitude. When he's at work, he doesn't drink. It's his way of relaxing when he's home. He relaxes, but we don't. And he won't drink in a bar. Like we'll go to dinner and we'll have a drink before dinner, and maybe after. He does not bar hop. He doesn't drink before he comes home. But he drinks plenty when he's home. I think he doesn't want people to know. He won't talk about it forthright, you know what I mean? Admit his problem or anything. He holds it in. He's very, very sensitive about it."

"Was it that way at the beginning of the marriage?"

"When he was in the Marine Corps, he was never home very much, and when he was home he drank. He just got a job at Lockheed Aircraft. He stays there all week and comes home on weekends. He's that way, drinking on the weekends, and we're glad to see him go back to work on Monday. I mean, you can't enjoy him. You can't go out or do anything. It's too embarrassing to walk into a place. It's so obvious when people are drunk. He doesn't get violent. He's not the type who breaks furniture or hits you. Mainly he just rambles on, and it seems like something is always upsetting him. We don't say too much because we know that after he eats dinner, he'll go to bed. If I sit there and pick at him about his drinking, it would be just one battle after another, and he still wouldn't quit. I used to do that. I tried that and everything else. I finally just shut up.

"I think his drinking has a lot to do with Catherine's problem. Catherine always tries to please him, to do what he wants. You can't please people when they're drinking. I mean, they don't want to be pleased, anyway. Cindy handles it differently. Cindy gets mad, bangs the door, and goes in her bedroom. That's it. She won't come out. I think Catherine gets frustrated because there's no way she can please him. *I* can't. I keep my mouth shut because I know it's useless to argue, but you get so mad you finally erupt, you know? Then that makes it worse for the kids. I try not to argue or say anything to him. Usually he'll eat dinner and go right to bed. When he's home, he's in bed by five o'clock every evening.

"On the weekends he gets up early, about six, and sometimes he eats breakfast. Then he reads the paper, and a little later he starts fixing himself a gin or vodka and grapefruit juice. He starts in about ten-thirty in the morning, and by two o'clock in the afternoon he's so stupid. That's the only way I can describe him. Stupid. His eyes are—you know. As soon as he eats supper, he goes to bed, so we only have to listen to the bad part between ten-thirty and suppertime. He might not like it if he finds out I'm saying anything."

Joe and Cindy arrived promptly at eight o'clock the next morning. I introduced myself, and Joe said, "How ya doin', Doc? This is my daughter, Cindy."

"How do you do?" Cindy said.

Joe had an engaging, direct smile. Cindy looked like Florence; at least she had her mother's clear-blue eyes. But there was something different—

maybe it was her tightly set jaw. There was something different about her greeting, too. More like Joe, direct, and with emotion.

"Thanks for coming up. I'm glad to have the chance to talk with you both. Perhaps I'll talk with you first, Mr. Lindner?"

"Lead the way, Doc."

Upon entering my office, Joe said, "My oh my, Doc. You sure you have enough room here? You must have drawn the short straw."

"Ha. There aren't any long straws. Take the only seat."

"What do you want to know, Doctor?"

"I'd just like to know anything you can tell me about yourself. Start with your childhood."

"Oh, just growing up. Not much to say."

"Just tell me whatever you think is important."

"I'll give you a for instance about myself. I was going to a Catholic school. I was forced into it. I should not have gone because they were pumping too much Latin and French and all that stuff into you. I didn't need it. I wasn't about to be a priest—I had no motivation to go that route. I still had my religion, but I should have been going to public school.

"It was a big class. The rest of the guys had to quit because of their parents. Like, the father would die, and they had to go to work. The only reason I kept going was so that my father and mother wouldn't go nuts. The community just didn't have the background for a school like that. Everybody had to work hard, and there might have been a half-dozen people there with enough money to run their kids through medical or law school. I notice that all the lawyers from there are ex-judges' sons. I would have been better off not continuing there. I should have gotten into economics and business.

"The athletic program was nothing either, and I mostly ran that myself. The Mother Superior gave me the upper hand and I took advantage of it. I nominated this gal who was my classmate to take over the girls, and between us we put the school into shape. We went to this field and wiped 'em out. The only reason the Mother Superior gave me the upper hand was because I could take these guys and work 'em out and do just what I wanted to with 'em. I didn't even go to class. I sat in her office. That Latin and French was getting to me. You get Cicero and all those guys. That's real great, you know?

"I was never a good boy, you can say that. I mean I was into anything I could get my hands on. I chased the gals as hard as I could. Every night. I was driving a truck during that time, and when my father would go on vacation he turned the wheels over to me. I had to do the whole administration, the whole scoop. In those days you had to be pretty well up on your toes."

"So you were always the in-charge guy?"

"You bet. Once my dad got pyorrhea and damn near died, because they had to wipe out all his teeth in one throw. He was down for six weeks, and I ran the whole thing. I was getting paid twenty dollars a week, which was good money."

"So you worked as a teenager?"

"Yeah. I drove a gasoline truck for my dad, who was an independent jobber. After high school I worked as a bulldozer operator, then I joined the Marine Corps as an enlisted man in pilot training. I was commissioned as an officer. I got to fly larger planes with sophisticated gunnery. When I was thirty-five years old, I was stationed in Hawaii."

"That's when you met your wife?"

"I had been chasing Maggie for about two years. I was in Hawaii and I called her up and said, 'Do you want to come out here?' and she said, 'Let me talk to my mother.' She called me back, and out she came. It was just the routine military for me until I met the old slew, or whatever you want to call her. I had no previous marriage or anything. Just a running-hard bachelor. Real hard, you know?"

"Tell me about Catherine."

"After I retired I took a job flying recovery aircraft for the military, picking up missiles shot into the Pacific from Vandenberg Air Force Base. Now I have a job at Lockheed, in Burbank. I'm gone from home maybe four or five days at a time. I started getting these letters from Cathy. She always wrote—the rest of them didn't. Too much trouble. At the end of one letter she said, 'I'm getting tired,' and I thought jeesh, this can't be right; she's not the type to get tired. So when my contract was up, I came home."

"What did you find?"

"It didn't take me any time at all to see what was going on. She was hiding food and all that stuff. It was all such a multitude of Mickey Mouse, the way the doctors went around taking care of Catherine and trying to diagnose her. And I could see that everyone at home was getting all this service from the in-laws and what not, you know: Do this and do that. Nana, for one. I broke up bad and let them have it."

"What did you do?"

"I told Maggie she should have done something. Cathy was dirty and smelly, and she hardly ate."

"Why do you think your wife wasn't able to do anything?"

"The thing with Catherine was about to drive Maggie crazy," he said. "I could see that Maggie was in pretty bad shape and was about to go berserk—really. She had enough on her hands with the twins. She was doing everything possible that she knew how to do. She is just that type of woman. She will just bend right in half."

"What did you do?"

"I took Cathy to the bathroom, put her in the tub and peeled the dirt off her body. I told Maggie we had to find a new psychiatrist."

"Well . . ."

"Doc, tell me what you think."

"She suffers from schizophrenia. And she is in danger of starving herself to death."

"To *treat* her, how long do you think it will take?"

"Years."

"Good. You give me the scoop right away. That's the words I want to hear. I can see the handwriting on the wall. I just have to go about what I have to do and what not—mainly try to keep the insurance policies going. Doc, it's a pleasure meeting you. I like getting the scoop from you without any words."

"It's my pleasure. You've been most helpful. I'll accompany you out to the waiting room."

"I do appreciate your coming all the way up here," I told Cindy, as we walked to my office. She seated herself, and waited.

"Maybe you can tell me about growing up. What was home life like?"

"Okay. I remember that up to the time my mother remarried it was blissful. I felt all kinds of love and attention from both sets of grandparents;

more from my mother's parents. We spent most of the time at my grandparents' house. I don't recall much about my mother's house.

"After my mother remarried and we moved to Hawaii, it was downhill all the way. I was shaken out of my equilibrium when we moved there. Catherine had an asthma attack on the night my mother went to the hospital to have Mary Beth. I remember it all vividly. My stepfather had been drinking, and he didn't know how to handle it. He doesn't remain cool in a situation like that. After Hawaii we moved around a lot, and all the while my father was drinking. He would be in terrible shape; my mother would get frantic and they would fight."

"Tell me a little about your mother."

"My mother has a way of not coping with any situation. She just snaps completely off the handle. She does it with us kids at home, too. Just completely raving. There were times when we did just what kids do—behave badly or whatever—and she would react in that way that was really scary— raving and screaming. How do you handle that? Mother is an extremely passive person. She hardly stands up to anybody, and when she does, it's so illogical.

"There was something about her passivity—you couldn't depend on her. She just ignored all feelings. She just didn't think there was a problem to be handled. You had to deal with it on your own. I think both my parents weren't able to think that anything mattered. Like, when Catherine was really getting sick, they probably thought it didn't upset her too much, so they just let it slide. Mother thought it was 'just a thing—she'll get over it.' She certainly didn't take it seriously in the beginning. When Catherine was over the brink, then she got concerned about it."

"Now that's helpful to know."

"Mother's lack of concern with things is strange because she *does* get concerned—but always about the wrong things, like 'Where are you going?' and 'Who are you going with?' When it came to larger things, like feelings, piano lessons, or Catherine's feeling ugly, she just ignored it. It was like going through adolescence with a few obscure comments, such as 'Don't get into trouble with boys.' She never explained what the 'trouble' was.

"It's not that she isn't a good mother. She is, and I love her to pieces, but I never felt very secure with her. I still don't. Couldn't rely on her at all. If

I had a question, she would say, 'I don't want to talk about it.' Especially sex—she was embarrassed and just wanted to avoid the subject, so we never had any way to find out about social relationships, no way to see how she would react. How do you react to men? How do you get comfortable? It was out of the question to talk with my stepfather."

"Tell me how you felt about yourself growing up."

"The feeling I had growing up was one of constant oppression. I have had dreams of being in a room with an exit door that's out of reach, and surrounded by blackness. I never could see the walls. I just felt the blackness in a claustrophobic kind of way. The oppression was never being known. I have a certain personality and certain beliefs I've developed over the years, and a way of thinking that's different from theirs and that I wanted to express—but I never could. I *still* can't when I'm with them; it's as if I'm a small child when I go over there. I always wanted to get away from that old small-child-trapped-in-a-room feeling, but I feel it every time I see them. I want to get out of here, to go thousands of miles away, or I'll always be a small child.

"Feeling myself diminished or shrunken is to not have a self or an ego. All that derision from my dad; he never could say anything nice. And mother didn't understand me, or understand anybody else for that matter. She just had this fixed conception of what the children were about, and it has never changed. If I tried to assert myself, I was just 'going through a phase,' which 'would pass,' and I was back at the start. There was no way to make an impact on her. The only way was to be passive, which is the way I feel when I'm with her. Passive and placating. Being that passive is like having a nonidentity. It's like having stunted growth.

"That placating, nonidentity feeling gets into other relationships, too. I go right back to the old 'Gosh, please don't think I'm a rotten person' kind of thing. When I do that, it just encourages the other person to take a dominant position."

"You know yourself, and you know what's going on at home. What happened to Catherine?"

"I was wondering why Catherine reacted differently to what went on. I think Catherine never got the idea that there was anything wrong. As little kids, you know, you see your parents as perfect. Grandmother knows best.

Adults can do no wrong. As I grew up, I found out that grandmother didn't know shit. Catherine never understood that these people are no more perfect than you or me or anybody else in the world. Catherine always turned inward. She was very passive, like my mother. She would agree with everything.

"We have this aunt who goes on and on telling everybody what their problems are, and Catherine would say, 'She means well, you've got to be nice.' It was the same thing with my grandmother, Nana, who is a real domineering woman. I am known as Miss Bitch because I didn't want any of it. I had no sympathy for any of them. Catherine would sit and listen. She'd try and be helpful. They just loved Catherine. Catherine never wanted to come into disfavor; she always wanted their acclaim and affection. I don't give a damn whether I get it or not. Wonderful and sweet—my grandmother and Catherine."

"Sounds depressing. Have you ever been depressed?"

"I used to get depressed as a girl because of the feeling of being trapped. At first I'd get irritable, then I'd get very depressed. I'd withdraw to wait for it to subside. I used to think of ways to get out of it, like just going to the airport and getting on a plane, or just sailing off somewhere.

"I have dreams now about raging at my parents. I had a dream where I was screaming at them, saying what they did. How blind, how lousy they were. It was so real. It would be a terrible thing to do, you know, because obviously I love them. They're still so stupid, though. I have one dream that has repeated itself several times, where I'm raving at my stepfather. I guess as long as it stays down there in my unconscious, it's fine.

"There were times, though, that I felt I was on the edge. Sometimes I still do. Wouldn't insanity be a luxury? A luxury I couldn't afford. Just to check in somewhere and get out of it all. I guess the thing I couldn't stand would be to lose control. I couldn't bear to have the thing controlling me."

"Do you still have a tendency to become enraged?"

"I do have a tendency to get violent. I still have a terrible temper, and I'm afraid I will do something one of these times. I get so angry I want to rip things apart. Normally, I hate violence. I hate to see people lose their tempers. But sometimes I just want to throw things. I'm known as the incredible bitch. What I am is the Incredible Hulk.

"I find myself displacing a lot of my hostility onto my husband. I over-react because of my rage, and I feel terrible because he doesn't understand. It bothers me, so I've been trying to realize why I do that, and so far I've managed to keep a rein on myself. It's such a vicious cycle. I was abused—not physically—and then I take it out on others. Will I take it out on my children? Aren't I a perfect case out of one of those books on child abuse?"

"What are you doing now? Going to school?"

"I wanted to go to college back east. But I met someone on my vacation to Europe this last summer, right after graduation. We just got married. I'm going to Cal State Fullerton."

"Cindy, this is all very helpful. Might I call you if I need any more information?"

"Sure. I hope you can help Cathy."

"I'm certainly going to try. Bye."

Three

BE MY GUIDE

Beyond this present ill
and worse to dread, lead me to Peter's gate
and be my guide through the sad halls of Hell.

Dante, The Inferno

I DIDN'T DISCOVER MY interest in psychiatry until I took my first course in the subject in medical school, taught by lecture in a large amphitheater to 200 first-year medical students at Indiana University School of Medicine. I liked it because I wanted to understand the mind—all those mysterious forces.

After graduating from medical school at age twenty-four, I took an internship at the District of Columbia General Hospital. I chose that particular internship because it was part of Georgetown University, which meant high-quality teaching. Also, an urban general hospital afforded lots of opportunity for interns to take responsibility for a variety of medical problems. The indigent of Washington, D.C. came there for treatment. Some of the hospital buildings dated from the Civil War. The interns' sleeping quarters was such a place—a dark, cold, brick barn of a building. Phones rang all night among rows of beds. We worked thirty-six hours, then were off for twelve to twenty-four hours on some shifts. I loved the serious responsibility.

After my one-year internship, I took an eighteen-month postdoctoral fellowship in neurophysiology at Albert Einstein College of Medicine in New York City. Neurophysiology is the study of how neurons and neuronal networks function within the brain. I thought I wanted an academic and research life, but I was bored after just a few months. I needed contact with people, a clinical setting.

Since I had to support myself through medical school by working and obtaining student loans, a residency—specialty training—was out of the question. I had to earn a decent income to repay my debt, so I entered the general practice of medicine. I wanted to come to Southern California because the population was rapidly expanding and I could establish a solo practice. I settled into Huntington Beach, a rapidly growing suburb sixty miles from Los Angeles. I rented an office and hung out a shingle in a mini-mall medical-office building, and signed on at the local hospital to handle the emergency room so I could refer patients to myself. Then I waited.

As a family doctor, I was privy to the kinds of psychological problems a psychiatrist is not. Through treating people, I became a quasi–family member, a confidant. I was only twenty-eight years old. I looked much younger, yet patients would call to make appointments "to talk" or to seek advice, such as the Mormon father who wanted to know what I thought about his newly married eighteen-year-old daughter who could not "make it" with her husband. He then brought both of them in. They told me that they had tried and tried but he could not enter her. I asked if I might examine him. He was normal, but she was not. She had an intact, fenestrated hymen, very thick and rubbery, which required my incising it to create an opening. Her father was happy to know of proof of her virginity. I was interested in the family dynamics. I could see how she deferred to her father. Later, I helped her understand that as a grown woman, she did not have to go to her father with her problems. I delivered a lot of babies, too, allowing me to get as close as a man can to that female experience. Sometimes I was up to my elbows in blood, and death stalked nearby. These real-life experiences gave me a better grounding for understanding mental problems than speculations about ids and egos could.

My interest in psychiatry never left me. I wanted to specialize, to know as much about psychiatry and the mind as there was to know. I found I wanted to explore my own mind, so I began seeing a psychoanalyst in Los Angeles. I drove the ninety miles round-trip four mornings a week for three years. Then I found a partner to take over my general practice, and I began training to become a psychiatrist with a residency at UCLA. At thirty-three years of age, I was older than the other resident physicians, most of whom were twenty-six or twenty-seven and had entered residency training directly after an internship.

The training program at UCLA, three years in duration, was designed to expose the resident to a variety of psychiatric patients and treatments, such as family and group therapy and electroshock therapy, which I thought was barbaric. It was generally understood, although there was no written rule, that patients would not stay longer than three months. This reflected the general pessimism about successful treatment of psychotic patients like Catherine. These kinds of patients were usually hospitalized primarily so the residents could gain exposure to or learn what a schizophrenic or manic-depressive person was. They would then be referred to other mental health agencies: community-care clinics, residential centers for the mentally disabled, or hospitals for the chronically insane. "Disposition" is what it was called. The best social workers were those who knew the intricacies of where to find community resources and whom to call to gain access.

A ward psychiatrist, a full-time faculty member of the medical school, was responsible for each ward. His duties included administration of the ward and coordination of medical students, student nurses, social workers, psychologists, and resident physicians.

Patients admitted to the ward were the direct responsibility of the residents, all of whom were in their first year at UCLA. When I met Catherine, I had been a resident for just three months. Second- and third-year residents spent most of their time in the outpatient and child clinics. We, in turn, were expected to seek consultation from senior members of the medical staff.

According to my teachers, schizophrenia was an incurable disease of the mind. The best one could do was to control it. Control meant the sufferer might live in a restricted way, perhaps holding down a low-level job and residing in a "protected environment"—a euphemism for another euphemism, a halfway house or board-and-care home. This really meant living in a kind of foster-care group home for the "emotionally disadvantaged."

Psychiatry was proud of its system of classification of mental states into syndromes. Schizophrenia was first known as dementia praecox, or premature dementia. Emil Kraepelin, a German psychiatrist, called it that because the syndrome typically first manifested itself in young adulthood and progressed to mental deterioration. In 1911 a Swiss psychiatrist, Eugen Bleuler, called the syndrome schizophrenia, the name that has persisted to the present. The term does not mean two personalities. It's what Bleuler saw as a splitting of psychic functions: paranoid thinking or auditory hallucinations occurring in the presence of an unimpaired intelligence.

The classification system made no sense to me. For example, some people are called "crazy" because their mental functioning is disturbed, but they are not crazy enough to warrant an official diagnosis of schizophrenia. Is the woman who haunts Hollywood Boulevard wearing a black derby and an excess of bright-red lipstick and rouge, but who manages her needs with her welfare money, a schizophrenic? If a psychiatrist were to examine her mental processes, this woman might, at times, meet the criteria for schizophrenia. And what about the hobos, hermits, skid-row bums, or drug addicts? We have no difficulty identifying such people as disturbed, even mad, but they might not fit the definition of schizophrenia. Some people seem to function well overall, yet their thinking seems odd, fragmented, or otherwise hard for other people to understand— similar to that of the schizophrenic. Any one of us might have come across the professor whose discourses are so abstract that one wonders whether even he understands them. Or a patient who conducts what appears to be a normal life, but admits, in the privacy of the consultation room, that he is beset by demons and monsters. It is not a radical jump to consider that the patient, the obtuse professor, the Hollywood Boulevard woman, and the hospitalized schizophrenic share the same problem, except in terms of degree.

The treatment of schizophrenia has also rested on the assumption that "they" are different from "us." Galen, a Greek physician and philosopher who lived during the second century A.D., practiced fumigation of the vagina, believing that mental symptoms were caused by malposition of the uterus. Bleeding, burning, hypnosis, shocking by electrical or other means, lobotomizing, and now drugs have all been used to excise, obliterate, crush, or modify the offending neurons.

But more modern physicians have sometimes seen things differently. For example, before entering residency, I had read some histories of psychiatry and accounts by psychiatrists and analysts who had worked with schizophrenics—Frieda Fromm-Reichmann, the psychoanalyst in *I Never Promised You a Rose Garden*; Harry Stack Sullivan; Lewis B. Hill; Harold Searles; and others. They emphasized that one could not really know the human condition without trying to understand these people, and that we all had madness within us at some level. These writers seemed to understand the mind of the psychotic. Madness, in their view, was not another world.

I was intrigued by this viewpoint. The more I thought about it, the more I felt that drugs might modify Catherine's strange behavior, but they wouldn't help her self, her soul. The problem is not the use of drugs; rather it's what the use of drugs *means*. Declaring that someone has a disease of the mind that requires treatment with drugs is to tell her she has a permanent and profound flaw, that she will never join humanity. If Catherine was one of "us," simply human, then she should respond to a human touch. I had to find out.

After I interviewed Joe and Cindy, I went up to the ward and found Catherine sitting alone on a couch in the day room. I sat down next to her. "Hi," I said. "I'd like to make arrangements to talk with you. I have an office here on the ward—it's a converted patient room located near the entrance to the men's ward, just over there. Could I see you there at two o'clock today?"

"Okay."

I answered Catherine's knock for our first session that afternoon and said, "Hello, how are you?"

"Okay."

Catherine sat down, rested her chin on her chest, and clasped her hands together in her lap. Her knees touched, and her legs extended straight in front of her. She began a slight, steady rocking of her head and shoulders, back and forth, back and forth.

"Can I have a pill?" Her voice came out in a high-pitched squeak.

"Why?"

"I can't stand it."

She lapsed into silence, sitting and rocking.

"What can't you stand?"

No answer.

I sat in silence, too. After three or four minutes, I said, "I think using medication is not a good idea. What I'd like to do, for us to do, is to get at what your problems are, not cover them up with tranquilizers. I think drugs would be a way of distorting your problems. Our ward social worker, Barbara Jensen, met with your mother yesterday to get more details of what has happened to you over the past couple of years. I understand you were on tranquilizers, antipsychotics they're called, for about eight months. Your mother told Barbara that you said they did no good."

"That's true," Catherine said. She sat silently, head down and eyes unblinking. "The pressure in my head," she said finally.

"Oh, how's that?"

"I can't stand the pressure. I want a pill."

"Well, like I said, I think it best not to use medication."

She fell silent again. About twenty minutes crawled by.

She interrupted the silence. "Do I have to go to the activity deck?," referring to a large, open game area adjacent to the swimming pool.

"Perhaps a little exercise would be helpful."

"I don't like it."

"Oh, why is that?"

No answer. She remained silent for the rest of the session—about forty minutes in our fifty-minute appointment.

At the end of the hour I thought about Franz Kafka's short story "The Burrow," about a mole who spends all his waking moments making sure his hole is safe. He digs deeper and deeper, finally creating an inaccessible castle keep. He is cut off from the world and even from the rest of his underground labyrinth—the ultimate in safety. But even within his lair, the mole hears creatures burrowing through the ground. He must be ever watchful that they do not invade his passageways. And when he must exit his burrow from time to time to obtain food, he dashes frantically about, fearful that a large creature will step on him before he can regain the safety of his hole. It seemed to me that Catherine had tried to dig a safe hole by shutting herself down to avoid her voices, and her feelings. Like the mole, she remained fearful anyway.

What does odd or strange behavior really mean? Is it just the product of an insane mind, or is there a method behind the madness? It seemed to me that my job was to try to understand what the person was saying, even though his or her language or behavior was unusual. Did the person who left feces and urine in the elevator mean to say, "Piss on you"? Did he want attention? Was it an act of rage? Or was he saying, "This whole place is a joke"?

I remember two examples of strange behavior that had commonsense meaning. We residents were required to spend the night at the hospital in case of emergency. Before I met Catherine, on my first night on call, the phone rang at ten o'clock in the evening.

"Dr. Dorman, this is Ruth Sargent on Three West. I think you had better come to the ward."

I raced over to the ward. A group had gathered in a circle in front of the nurses' station—two sizable fellows, two nurses, and three aides, all in white uniforms. In their center stood a young man, about twenty, motionless, his arms stretched straight out in front of him.

Ruth nodded at me, then looked at the young man. "Dr. Dorman, this patient is Roy Ferrar. He was admitted just last night, so we don't have a doctor's order for an injection of Thorazine. He's pretty agitated, as you can see."

I stepped into the circle. Roy was sweating profusely, slowly repeating, "Kill, kill—kill, kill."

"I'd prefer to talk with him," I said to Ruth.

"Well, I don't know," she said. "We should just bring him down with an injection. We have help here who can do that."

Here I was, my first night on call. These nurses were experienced. Ruth Sargent was trying to show me the way. "I'd still prefer to talk with him."

"If you must, but not alone. I insist on leaving the door open."

I turned to the young man, "Mr. Ferrar, might I talk with you?"

He followed me into a consultation room. I sat down and leaned back slightly in a tilt-back grammar-school-teacher's oak chair. He slowly approached me, arms still outstretched. "Kill, kill." The door was open about a foot or two. Faces looked in at us. Roy placed his hands on either side of my neck. I did not resist.

"Where did you get the idea to do this?" I asked. "This is just like a scene from a movie about an insane asylum."

He blinked, removed his hands from my neck, and collapsed in a heap on the floor in front of me. The door opened.

"Perhaps you can just take him to his room," I said.

The orderly, a burly man used to "restraining" patients, looked right at me. "I'll be damned, Doc. You've got—well, I'll be damned. Come on, Roy, let's go to bed." Roy allowed himself to be helped up.

And there was Sheryl Roth, twenty years old, who deliberately broke her arms, right on the ward. She calmly walked up to a corner where two walls met and threw her right forearm against it, thump. Then just as calmly, she turned around and did it again with the other arm. She was the talk of the ward, walking around with both arms in casts, certifiably crazy. I had inherited her from a resident who was leaving. At our first meeting, she said, "Aren't I the craziest person you've ever seen?"

"Why do you want the blue ribbon?" I asked. She had no answer.

Over the next several days, Catherine sat mute in the dayroom, hour after hour locked in a rigid position, or slowly rocking back and forth. She walked with an odd, halting manner, not even lifting her feet from the floor. And her head would suddenly jerk to one side, then the other. She contorted her mouth back and forth with an incessant grinding of her teeth.

A particularly able nurse noted the following in Catherine's hospital chart:

> Very low in early afternoon. She asked if your doctor had to discharge you or if your parents could take you out of the hospital. Feels she wants to go home because she had been happier in her little world there. Here she sees how other people are and it frightens her and makes her more depressed. She feels that several weeks ago she was capable of loving, but now even that is gone. She refers to the "voices" and compares herself to Richard Speck, the Chicago mass murderer. She was tearful during most of this conversation and she often appears to be swallowing rapidly

as though to keep back tears. She referred to starving herself but went on a walk outside the hospital and got an ice cream cone. She seemed pleased when I offered to manicure her nails and she allowed me to do so, though with limp hands.

In the evenings the nurses frequently found her kneeling in her room with her head on the bed, or lying face down on the floor. When roused, she complained that the only way she knew to control the murderous voices and her mind was to remove herself from all stimuli, to retreat to a dark room and remain rigid.

Catherine timidly knocked at my office door at the exact time of our next appointment. Then, with her head down, and leaning against the hallway wall, she waited for me to open the door. She sat in a chair and remained silent for three or four minutes. Then she said, "Can I have a pill?" After that, she lapsed into a long silence, perhaps fifteen or twenty minutes.

"What are you thinking?" I finally asked.

Silence. I watched the top of her head move slowly back and forth like a pendulum. She kept her hands in her lap, but her bony fingers were in constant, slow motion, curling, uncurling, interlocking, and twisting one upon the others. Twenty-five more minutes passed before she said, without raising her head, "I talked to my mother on the phone today. She's going to bring me some pie when she comes on Sunday. Can I put it in the refrigerator?"

"I don't see why not, but you should probably ask one of the nurses." Catherine made no reply.

"I know you're in a great deal of pain," I said. "What I'd like to do— that is, the two of us—is to get to know you. If you can see how and why you got into this state . . ."

"I can't get out," she interjected.

At the beginning of our next appointment, Catherine sat down and said, "I don't want to go to occupational therapy."

"Why not?"

"I don't like it."

"Tell me why."

No answer.

"I wouldn't argue with you if you think making clay pots is silly, or if it's just not an interest of yours," I said. "But occupational therapy is a reality of ward life. It might even benefit you. After all, what's the alternative? The nurses tell me you would prefer to stay in your room all day."

Still no answer.

"I don't mean to say it's wrong or bad to stay in your room . . ."

"I don't want to go. There are too many people."

"Oh, I see. What is there about people that bothers you?"

No answer.

"Well, our hour is over for today. But I'd like to know more about your difficulty being around people. Or perhaps I might say that differently: Being around people just *is* difficult for you, so you'd prefer to stay away from them. Perhaps I can help you get at what the difficulty is, which might make it easier for you. Well, I'll see you tomorrow."

"Okay," she replied.

On Monday of her second week in the hospital, Catherine opened our session with, "Do I have to have a roommate?"

"Well, I think there are too many patients in the hospital for you to have a room alone. But feel free to ask the nurses. It's really their domain."

"Can I have a pill? Other patients get pills."

"A pill for what?"

"I have headaches and I can't sleep."

"Where are your headaches?"

"In my neck."

"You know, I would guess that your neck ache comes from holding your head down. I'll write an order for some Darvon, a mild analgesic, which might give you some relief. But there's really nothing that will take the pain away completely."

Every week, nurses, aides, social workers, residents, and Robert Rubin, our ward psychiatrist, met to discuss each patient. Ruth Sargent expressed concern about Catherine's weight, now eighty-four pounds. I shared her concern. When I was doing research in neurophysiology in New York, I worked some evenings at a general hospital in Staten Island. An anorexic girl, nineteen years old and weighing only seventy-nine pounds, was admitted to the hospital and died a few hours later. I thought, and Ruth and the others agreed, that since Catherine's weight had dropped below eighty-five pounds, she would be required to drink Sustagen, a protein and vitamin supplement each day. We would force-feed her if necessary. I informed Catherine of the decision.

The next day she asked me, "Do I have to drink the Sustagen? I don't like it."

"Catherine, your weight is too low; you could die."

"I don't care. I should be dead."

"Well, I can see your point, living the way you're living. You have no hope of getting out of this, do you?"

"I'm hopeless. I'm finished."

"You know that I can't just sit by and watch you kill yourself. But I'm not big on arm-twisting you into anything. Did you develop your diet as a kind of ritual, to shore yourself up, to survive? I know you need it. And I believe you feel hopeless . . ."

"I don't *feel* hopeless. I *am* hopeless."

"Just the same, you can't weigh less than eighty-five pounds or we'll have to feed you through a stomach tube."

Silence can have many meanings. For example, there is contemplative silence, terrified silence, silence meant to intimidate, and stubborn silence. I thought most of Catherine's silences were of the terrified sort. I could feel it. But for the remaining thirty minutes of this hour, it was a stubborn silence.

"Well, we'll have to go for today. I can sense you're unhappy about this decision. But I can't let you starve yourself. I'll see you tomorrow."

Treatment of patients on a mental ward is a cooperative venture. The residents, social workers, and full-time nursing staff met frequently to discuss patient progress and difficulties. At one such meeting, just before Thanksgiving, Ruth Sargent voiced a concern of many nurses—that Catherine should not be allowed off the ward without a staff member. "What do you think might happen if she left the ward on her own?" I asked.

"She's been in the hospital nearly a month now," Ruth replied. "We, the nursing staff, have had to make sure she dresses herself in the mornings; we watch her every bite of food lest she starve herself; we actually have to bathe her. Once, after a great deal of pleading from us, she agreed to take a bath herself. Then she sat down in the tub and didn't move. Eventually Alicia looked in and there she was, just sitting in the cold water. Alicia had to insist that Catherine get out, which she did, but then she just stood there, shivering. Alicia had to help her dry off."

"I think she's trying to fix herself in the position of an infant," I said. "I gather from my interviews with her family members that she's always behaved like a shy baby. If she succeeds in getting us to treat her as a baby—she *is* succeeding to a degree—we'll end up helping her not grow up. I'd suggest relating to her as a grown-up, at least as a nineteen-year-old young woman, as best we can. I understand she doesn't want to participate in ward activities, like walks in the village, or movies. I think she should be held responsible for meeting the standards of ward life. I would prefer she be allowed off the ward alone, too, but I'll wait until you all are more comfortable with that."

"What about Sunday visits with her mother off the ward?" Ruth asked.

"Feels normal to me," I said.

As usual, Catherine was waiting for me before our next appointment, leaning against the wall, her head down. "Hi," I said.

She didn't answer.

Was I just now getting the whole picture? Here stands this waif-like child-person, as still as a goose shot in the wing by a hunter. Splat! The goose falls to the ground. After a few moments of flopping around with its one good wing, it spots the black Labrador retriever bounding over clods of dirt in the rice field toward it. The goose freezes in terror, and waits. The dog grasps the bird loosely in its mouth and proudly returns to his master, who takes his prize—and snaps its neck.

"Everything is out of control," Catherine said just before our hour was up. "All my thoughts are out of control. I don't know where dreams stop and reality begins. I'm living as though I'm in a dream. I feel dead, like when I was at school. I make up thoughts because there aren't any, like seeing my mother dead because I don't have any thoughts about her. Then I develop pins in my head, which drives me deeper. If the pins were not there, I'd be running around with a knife."

Christmas time in Southern California has none of the sparkle of an East Coast Christmas. The same sunny days roll by. Front lawns shimmer with winter rye grass that glows yellow-green, like spring. "Happy Holiday" banners float from street-light standards. In our hospital, the thin pretense of celebration in the wards—mistletoe and pine branches strung in arcs from the ceiling around the nurses' station—only emphasized the dreariness of the place.

On Christmas day, Florence and Nana brought Catherine some presents: a pink, long-sleeved button-down-the-front sweater; an ankle-length flannel nightgown; and a jumbo bean-and-cheese burrito, Catherine's Christmas dinner. Other than saying, "Thank you for the presents," Catherine sat mute in a corner of the day room. Florence talked of household doings, and reported about the younger children.

Two weeks later, on January 14, Catherine opened the session with, "Can I go home? What are the legal requirements for keeping me here?"

"You are a voluntary patient. You cannot be committed to the hospital against your will. But I think your question refers to your futility . . ."

"What you say is true, but I can't do anything with it."

A long silence. Then: "Can insanity be treated? You are not insane, so how would you know?"

"Perhaps you don't know how to utilize me?" I offered. Catherine was silent, but she looked about my office for the first time, at the Van Gogh print on one wall, and at the opposite wall. Then she stared at my shoe.

"Anything good gets destroyed," she said at the end of the hour.

"That has been pretty much the truth for you. So you are hopeless about ever expecting something good. That's really what futility is. Perhaps you have no basis to feel other than futile. I can imagine you have no basis, no internal reference point, to feel that anyone might help you. Maybe it's not that anyone might help you; rather that anyone *could* help you. Even more so, it looks like you've organized your life around futility. Hole up and wait it out."

In early February, Catherine told me of a dream she had had the previous night: "A black snake was getting me. I know what that was. I'm evil. I have bad thoughts and I do bad things, like I'm angry at the nurses. I have to go deeper inside myself now to get away from the voices." After a silence she asked, "How long can I stay here?"

I wondered whether she might be afraid of getting kicked out of the hospital. If so, perhaps she was making some investment in treatment. After all, she could have remained silent, not revealed her dream, or refused to come to her sessions. She could have obstructed treatment in any number of other ways.

"Are you making some investment in me and the staff?" I asked her. Catherine nodded once, in agreement.

During the rest of the month, our sessions focused on Catherine's concern that she was wasting everyone's time and effort. "I can't do what they want me to do," she told me.

"Well, that's probably a reflection of your belief that you're worthless—a waste of people's time."

"If I don't measure up, everyone will leave."

"Look what you've learned about yourself and other people. It's your job to measure up. You have to take care of the other person's expectations. But is no one supposed to take care of *you*? To know you?"

During another session, Catherine told me, after about a twenty-minute silence, "I hear voices to kill my mother. I'm evil."

"You've been talking lately about feeling worthless. That's reason enough to feel rage."

She burst out, "I can't get out! I don't know how to think any other way! I'm crazy and I know it. The food thing is getting worse, and I'm getting worse through knowing myself!"

In March, she told me, "Until therapy, I used to feel content because I thought I was normal and that I loved people. Now I know that's not true."

Catherine began to speak in a much more fragmented way and to fall into longer and longer silences. During one meeting, the only thing she said was, "Do I bore you?" However, in other sessions she began to describe to me how she did think. "I have no comprehension," she told me. "My perceptions are all off. Everything has ceased to be as I once knew it. Someone else has stepped into my body. The voices are weird. They're not mine. But I know they're mine because my whole body is reacting. I have murdered myself. I've done something unnatural. I am a black, evil person. I don't feel death. I *am* death."

On the ward, she now sat for hours, transfixed. She didn't even bother to swallow. She sat with her head bent forward, and her mouth open, drooling saliva all over the front of her dress. She began to resist going to any of the ward activities. When she did go—for example, to the occupational therapy, which offered drawing and sculpting—she simply sat and stared at the table. She did nothing unless the therapists prodded her.

One nurse found Catherine sitting alone in her room, silently crying. She wrote the following note in Catherine's chart:

> After supper she was begging the staff for medication for anxiety. I went with her to her room and allowed, but did not encourage her, to talk. She poured out her depression and deep discouragement with her condition. She feels her voices are becoming unbearable and says that she thinks about food as a crutch, to focus her attention, so that she can shut out the voices. When it became apparent that talking was upsetting her even more—she became hysterical as if the voices were closing in—I pulled the conversation up short and made her focus on washing her face and hands and combing her hair.

Catherine had spent many years fending off the truth about her life, and now she could no longer deny her condition. I knew that she had to be apprised of the truth, so that she would know what she was up against. There is no way to fight what is undefined. But her reaction was to further withdraw. She told some nurses and patients that she felt totally hopeless about her condition, and that she would be better off dead.

During a session in late April, Catherine's first words were, "I want to go to Camarillo. I belong there—in the state mental hospital. I can be crazy there and be left alone and given pills. Food isn't working anymore. I hear voices to kill everyone in my family now. Why? Is it possible to love with all these feelings?"

Her question was legitimate. "I know it doesn't feel like it will ever be possible to love. You are becoming aware of how much hate you have, which makes you feel more and more evil—so much so that you can see no way to ever be rid of it."

By this time, Catherine had been at UCLA six months. She repeatedly told the nurses that she felt she was deteriorating. She harangued any passing nurse or staff member to send her to Camarillo so that she could sit in a corner with other people like her. She told one nurse, "God damn it, let me die. I want to go home and die. Don't you see it would be a mercy killing?"

The nurses grew even more worried. At our weekly staff meetings, they told me that Catherine had scratched her wrists with pins and then with a razor blade. One nurse had found scissors hidden behind some clothes in her closet. When confronted, Catherine admitted they were for killing herself. The nurses decided to initiate a search for dangerous objects, a formal procedure used for potentially suicidal patients. This meant that Catherine was subjected to a room and body search several times a day. I knew that Catherine might kill herself. I thought that if she did, it would be by accident. We were taking reasonable precautions.

Suicide seemed to have three meanings for Catherine. As the nurses' alarm intensified, she received more attention—she found another way to gain a sense of aliveness by worrying the nurses. She also admitted to me that cutting herself with razor blades took her mind off her anguish. The third meaning was more serious: Catherine had reached the depths of despair and suicide offered a way out. At some point, however, she would have to choose between the possibility of my helping her and the certainty of death.

"I'm close to death" was the only sentence she spoke during one session. She told several nurses the same thing. One day, when the nurses went to check on her in her room, they discovered that she had poured some leather dye into her cocoa and was drinking it down. She told the nurse, "Killing myself is better than killing someone else. I'm awake all night seeing skulls and hearing voices. I can't stand it anymore."

The nurse called an attendant, who put Catherine in a wheelchair and rushed her to the emergency room. She protested, "I have a right to die! I have a right to die!" as attendants lifted her onto an examining table.

"Just lie still," ordered Fran Tartino, the evening charge nurse who accompanied Catherine to the emergency room. "You're going to be examined, whether you like it or not."

The doctor did not believe that she had drunk only "a little bit." He threaded a narrow hollow rubber tube through her nose and down into her stomach so he could flush out its contents. Catherine lay perfectly still.

The doctor extracted a small amount of dark liquid, determined that she was not in danger, and sent her back to the ward.

A few days later, Catherine was walking with Kitty Tate, another nurse, along a fifth-floor hospital corridor that had a ceiling-to-floor plate-glass window on one side. Kitty kept her hand on Catherine's shoulder to push her along, since Catherine walked so slowly. Suddenly, Catherine wrenched herself free and threw herself against the window, which only swayed back and forth under the impact. "Cathy! What do you think you're doing?" Kitty cried. "That was very bad! You could have hurt a lot of people!"

Some of the staff members complained about my refusal to transfer Catherine to the suicide-observation ward, where patients were never out of sight of a nurse. They instituted a rigid, more frequent search procedure.

When someone is determined to commit suicide, it is difficult, probably impossible, to stop him or her. Shortly before I arrived at UCLA, a patient on suicide watch put a hanger wire around her neck, tied one end to the head of the bed, and slid down under the covers until the wire was tightened. When the nurses looked in, all they saw was the young woman on her back, seemingly asleep with the covers up to her nose. In the morning they discovered that she was dead. Another man, while on the suicide-observation ward, managed to finagle a visit, accompanied by a staff member, to the ninth-floor roof lounging deck, from which he promptly jumped. A fellow psychiatry resident drove to the Anza Borrego Desert, 120 miles from Los Angeles, parked his car, and walked several miles into the rocky, lunar landscape. He sat down behind a pile of boulders to write a suicide note, then swallowed a handful of Quaaludes, a popular sedative used as "downers." A search-and-rescue team found his body several days later. Catherine was permitted day visits on Sundays out of the hospital with her mother, and if she really wanted to kill herself, she could have done it then.

It was difficult trying to convince the nursing staff that Catherine was becoming more invested in the treatment process, which spoke against her committing suicide. Being invested or engaged meant that she nursed some hope. But the nurses remained convinced that she would prevail, probably when I took my two-week vacation.

"She's not engaged in anything," said Alicia Robinson, a senior nurse at our staff meeting. "I think she's getting worse. She hasn't killed herself— yet. There's plenty of evidence that psychotherapy is not appropriate with schizophrenics."

"You, and others, sit with her for hours in the evenings, talking. There is nothing beneficial in being with her, talking with her?" I retorted.

"You know what I mean," Alicia said.

"I'm afraid I don't," I replied.

"There are papers showing that psychotherapy makes schizophrenics worse. She *is* worse than when she was admitted. Everyone can see it."

"I've read all those same papers," I said. "Nothing but theory. Schizo- phrenics can't tolerate relationships, they say. You're probably referring to the Philip May paper, too, where he compared drug treatment with psycho- therapy. Psychotherapy? Two thirty-minute sessions a week for a month or two, done by residents. That's proof of what?"

I did have to justify my stubbornness about not admitting Catherine to the suicide-watch unit to the ward psychiatrist, Bob Rubin. A man my age, he was more interested in brain chemistry than people. He asked, "Are you comfortable leaving her on the ward while you're away? She has told Ruth that she's going to kill herself."

"Bob, she comes to treatment every day right on time. She is beginning, just now, to tell me about herself. It's pretty horrific, what she has to say, but she's *there*. She's not just complaining any more about every damn ward activity. She's still silent for most of the sessions, but I do think all this speaks against suicide."

"Okay," he said. "I'll go along. I hope you're right."

As my vacation approached, the nurses watched her every move. Catherine accommodated them by giving them something to watch. Three days after I left on vacation, a nurse found her in her room standing near her dresser with a long tie belt in her hand. When the nurse asked what she was doing, Catherine dryly replied, "I've been trying out how it feels to have this around my neck." She had a few bruises on her neck, and since I wasn't around to veto the decision, she was transferred to the suicide-observation unit.

On my first day back, I moved her back to our ward. At our session that afternoon, she said, "Thanks for getting me off that ward. It was awful. Someone watched me all the time, even at night. How can you sleep with someone sitting there?"

Thirty minutes of silence.

"Why is it that when nice people go away I have killing thoughts about them?"

"You are hearing voices to kill me, aren't you?"

"Yes."

"I think that you don't know what separation is. Ordinarily, as a child grows, he experiences more separation from his mother, a greater separate identity. Throughout your entire childhood, you were too closely intertwined with your mother. Being 'nice' means securing a symbiotic tie. Symbiotic means that two people exist as one. Then, when the other person proves that there *is* no such symbiosis by leaving, like my leaving on vacation, you become furious. Hearing voices to kill me is kind of natural, I think, in that you don't know how we—you and me—can be a good thing, if the two of us are separate beings."

Catherine sat utterly motionless. Her eyes were filled. At the end of the hour, she said, "I need to be left alone."

Over the next few weeks, Catherine openly told the nurses she had "killing thoughts" toward all members of her family, the nurses she especially liked, and me.

"I hear voices all the time to kill my mother," she told me. "I hear voices to kill my sister. I hear voices to kill you."

"You know, we've been talking about your murderous rage as natural. Look at what you've told me. You live in a black, death-like hole. You feel there's no way out. Perhaps as a child you felt helpless, with no one to depend upon—not even your mother. She is a pretty insecure person."

"I *could* be violent. I could do it. I have to keep still or think of my diet or pretend the voices aren't there, because I could do it. It's better to kill *me*."

"Talking with you makes me afraid," she later told me. "I have electricity in my head; I see coffins floating around; I can smell the graveyard. The voices are shouting at me day and night to kill myself. I can't sleep. There is no escape."

"It feels like . . ."

"It's not about feeling anything. I don't *have* feelings. I have voices. The graveyard is there. So is the smell. I know people can't see or hear these things, but *I* can. I'm crazy."

It was just a few blocks' walk from the hospital to the local shopping area. Groups of ten to twelve patients, accompanied by one or two staff members, often went shopping, to buy ice cream, or go to a movie. When Catherine joined them, usually objecting that she wanted to be left alone, she shuffled along behind the group, mumbling under her breath. On one occasion when the group was going to a movie, the nurses had to keep prodding Catherine to keep up. Once inside and seated, she lowered her chin to her chest and drooled so much that she soaked her clothes and the seat. One nurse got up, took her hand, and brought her back to the hospital. Catherine told the nurse that she didn't see any point in going anywhere or doing anything; she might as well behave as if she were dead.

It was July. Eight months had passed since Catherine had arrived at UCLA. She said that her "system" was failing her, and again began to talk of suicide. She asked a nurse, "Can people burn themselves up with gasoline?" One day she informed the nurses that the following Wednesday she was going to have a "farewell dinner" with her parents. Before, she had asked that only her mother visit her; this time she asked her stepfather to come too. She told Ruth Sargent: "Yes, I know exactly what I'm going to do, and you know that no one can stop me." Ruth asked her if she planned to tell me, and she replied, "No."

"Cathy, you know I will tell Dr. Dorman, whether or not you tell him. You will be on close observation, within eyesight of the staff while on the unit, and within arm's length of staff while off the unit."

"It's my right to decide if I want to live or die. I'm tired of everyone making decisions for me."

Ruth called me at home and insisted that I see Catherine that evening, which I did.

"The nurses tell me you are going to kill yourself," I said.

"I have to decide," she told me. "Bill Sorenson was in the hospital almost a year and they wouldn't let him stay any longer. He was always sweet to me, and he said, 'Well, they're never going to get me to Camarillo. I'll shoot myself first.' He did, too. There were two other patients who committed suicide. One was a blond fellow who wore cowboy boots all the time. He shot himself, and there was another guy who hanged himself. *They* escaped. I need to escape."

I chose to rely on my gut, which told me she wouldn't kill herself. I told Ruth I didn't feel anything had changed greatly; I didn't feel she should be transferred to suicide watch. Ruth then decided to go over my head. She called her supervisor, who gave her permission to continue to watch Catherine closely and to post a staff nurse in her room for the night. In the morning, she brought the matter to the attention of Bob Rubin and the chief physician of the inpatient service.

Even though I had to discuss the situation with the psychiatrists in charge of the ward and the hospital, I knew it would be difficult administratively to transfer Catherine to the suicide ward against my wishes. Again I told Bob that I thought there was a suicide risk, but that it was no greater now than it ever was. In listening, he wanted to satisfy himself that I was acting reasonably, which was his chief responsibility.

The nurses, nevertheless, still felt worried that Catherine would kill herself the following Wednesday, as she had warned. Catherine was correct that she held the decision to live or to die, but what was she doing broadcasting that decision around? I thought she was using the threat of suicide to force me and the nursing staff to watch her every move and to think about her twenty-four hours a day, much like a worried mother stays awake listening for her ill baby's every breath.

She told another nurse that the next time she attempted suicide she would do a good job; the nurse underlined this in her daily notes. Catherine then phoned her parents and asked them to come up a day early for her farewell party. She told a nurse that next Tuesday, not Wednesday, would be her last day on earth.

Tuesday came and went—and nothing happened.

George Bell, the psychiatrist in charge of inpatient services, wanted to meet with me. He reminded me that UCLA was not a chronic-care hospital, and that he wanted Catherine discharged to Camarillo Hospital for the chronically insane. I replied that UCLA was also a teaching hospital, and that I was learning how to do psychotherapy with schizophrenics. He did not relent. Neither did I.

About a week later, when we met again, I repeated that I would not discharge Catherine. I gambled that he would not discharge her over my head, although he certainly had the power to do so. But that would have created too much of a stir. What happened? He gave the problem to Bob Rubin, who respected what I was doing. But even if he, too, had insisted, I would have taken the same position. My insistence on keeping Catherine would have forced him to take an unusual action: discharging a patient or otherwise formally stepping into clinical decisions. The usual approach was for senior staff members to discuss clinical problems with residents, and influence care that way. But still, I was worried that he might remove Catherine from my care, or discharge her anyway.

Catherine now often refused to dress herself in the mornings, showing up for breakfast in her rumpled night clothes. She started to walk in a peculiar, sideways fashion: While staring at the floor, she would slide one foot out to the side, then follow with the other. She hardly spoke to anyone, and when she did, it was mostly to wheedle some change in her diet. If anyone—even other patients—spoke to her, she just grunted in reply. She reminded me of a back-ward catatonic as she sat, drooling, on the dayroom couch, her body twisted sideways, head down. She refused to meet anyone's eyes, keeping her own eyes downcast when she was speaking. The nurses noted in her chart that, undressed, she looked like a skeleton. Since she ate only carbohydrates, I insisted on another protein-rich supplement and again threatened to force-feed her if she did not maintain eighty-five pounds.

The other patients frequently ignored Catherine by conversing among themselves as if she weren't there. Patients often went into the dining room to talk. If they sat down near Catherine, who sat motionless, with her hair hanging over her face, they felt they had complete privacy.

It is an ominous sign when a patient seems to be accepting her withdrawal. For centuries, this kind of settling in has had a poor prognosis. In the first century A.D., the Greek physician Aretaeus of Cappadocia wrote that such patients "fall into such a degree of degradation that, plunged into an absolute fatuousness, they forget themselves, pass the remainder of their lives as brute beasts, and the habits of their bodies lose all human dignity." Catherine seemed to have resigned herself to this fate.

Four

My Blood Ran Cold

. . . my blood ran cold
and my voice choked up with fear. I cannot write it:
this is a terror that cannot be told.
I did not die, and yet I lost life's breath:
imagine for yourself what I became,
deprived at once of both my life and death.

Dante, The Inferno

I WAS THE LAST to recognize my obsession with treating psychotic patients. Something about psychotic patients attracted me deeply. I had realistic reasons to be doing what I was doing—for example, my interest in psychosis as a way to understand the troubled human mind. But there was something else. While I was treating Catherine, I had taken on the treatment of another psychotic patient, Brian Leffler. This young man suffered from hebephrenic schizophrenia, which is characterized by unintelligible speech and bizarre posturing. He was nineteen years of age and began speaking in a strange tongue during his first year at Reed College. Rarely coherent, he often talked in a singsong, private language, all the while twitching and grimacing. In high school, his IQ had been measured as a formidable 180, yet now he would wander off in a confused state if left alone. Still, his behavior and appearance did not deter me from treating him.

I could barely understand him. One day, he came to my office and began, "L—A—C—C; C—C—; L—A—C—Sun."

I had previously figured out by sheer guesswork that this was his shorthand for Los Angeles Community College and California State College at Northridge. "Are you thinking about college?" I asked.

He twitched one shoulder, then the other. "Par, par, tic, u—do—do—d—do you nn—n—know wha—what I mean?"

"No, Brian, I don't understand at all."

"Humph, neither do I," he replied.

Underneath his odd exterior, he *was* an aware person, someone I might reach.

I saw Brian five days a week. I tried to decipher his stammering, most of the time without success. I knew I was getting somewhere, though. He often wandered around the hospital, twitching and mumbling aloud, and had to be brought back to the ward. But he knew the times of our appointments and rarely missed them. Once, he failed to show up for an appointment, so I went to the ward. He was in bed in the dorm room, under the sheets, naked. I pulled up a chair.

"Brian, it's time for our appointment. Is anything wrong?"

Silence. The mass moved.

"I was wondering why you didn't show up."

No answer.

I waited in silence for ten minutes. "I guess you're not going to say anything." I sat quietly for another twenty minutes.

"Well, Brian, I guess I'll be going." I scraped the chair on the floor as I replaced it in the corner and started to walk out.

"Thanks," from under the sheet.

"Okay, see you tomorrow."

I allowed myself to drop into my patients' worlds. What were Catherine and Brian really doing in those depths into which they had descended? What prevented them from leaving their mental prisons? To find out, I had to know everything about them. If I could understand how they slid into madness, I might help them find a way out.

When someone reacts strongly to external events, he or she may well be reacting to an internal event or situation. For example, by focusing so intently on psychotics, was I trying to cure myself? The person in jail, struggling against the world—was it Catherine or me? Or both?

I did have a version of Catherine in me. My mother wasn't too happy with my birth. The family story is that my maternal grandmother tried to abort my mother. So she was unwanted as well. My mother ended up a rather infantile woman, bonded in a childlike, needy way to her two daughters, and emotionally distant from her two sons. I do not remember her ever touching me. Nor do I remember much emotionality between my parents. My father was more emotionally present for me than my mother. However, he was immersed in his excessive religiosity, which he practiced daily and insisted his family follow suit. Under these conditions, I had no way to come to know myself, particularly my emotions. It was no wonder I recognized Catherine's emotional underdevelopment.

I surely was not as underdeveloped as Catherine, but I had faced a similar struggle. Through trying to encourage or nurture her development, I was probably also mothering myself.

I think all empathy is based on this principle of projection. It is present to a degree in love. Perhaps the key is the extent. If I treat you as a projection of *me*, I am not relating to *you*. If I understand you because I have had a similar experience, but I recognize our separateness, and therefore your uniqueness, I *can* relate to you. But the you–me separation can still break down. I think it did to a degree between Catherine and me.

I had earned a reputation on the wards of being able to talk to psychotics, to understand them. Some thought I had a gift. "He's got a gift, all right," Steve Sonneberg, a pills-cure-everything resident told his fellow-traveler, Dave Sheffield. "He's as crazy as his patients. Talking to schizophrenics. Right. He thinks he understands what they're saying. That makes *him* delusional, too." It seemed to me that I could just hear the person underneath—which I thought was what psychiatrists did.

With Catherine some hope had stirred. She was talking about herself for the first time in her life. Verbalization, or the admission of a thought, is important. Through it, an idea assumes a form. It becomes a realistic entity, as opposed to the vagueness of an unspoken thought or fantasy. The person can then take the next step: testing the idea in the world. This process gives the idea a needed dimension or structure upon which further thought and action can build. Articulation and testing also help destroy dread. For example, I did not become angry or frightened when Catherine told me that she heard voices to kill me or to kill herself. And nothing terrible happened to her.

In treatment, every statement made by the patient is important. This is different from a social situation, where a person can more easily disguise, or not follow up on, a spoken thought. I listened carefully to everything Catherine said, and both interpreted and expanded on what she shared with me. Our entire relationship centered on my efforts to help her make sense of what she experienced. And it was not just a verbal exchange. For example, Catherine's sense of omnipotence, her feeling that she exerted a profound effect on everyone and everything, was tested by my calm tolerance of her prolonged silences. She once blurted out, "Why don't you just get up and leave?"

I further explored her omnipotence by interpreting her thinking. Over several months, Catherine had repeatedly brought up her feeling that she was a "dangerous person." She told me that her "bad thoughts" had caused the death of her grandfather and a boy in school who had died mysteriously. She said that she "ruined everything," even a flower that had promptly wilted after a fellow patient had given it to her.

"I don't think you caused the death of your grandfather or the boy at school," I said. "You tend to think that you cause everything to happen. It's really not true. You don't have the power to cause flowers to wilt. You are not that central to the goings-on in the world. It might be a relief to you to find out that other people's actions and thoughts are relatively independent, not so influenced by what you say or do." Catherine was speechless for the rest of the hour. She sat and rocked back and forth.

Her behavior was a curious mixture of obstreperous withdrawal and some enjoyment of ward life. Even though the nurses had to prod her to attend ward functions, she did go. One such function was the Thursday-night party. Patients from three wards got together in the day room of one ward. Attendants moved the furniture out along the wall to create a space for dancing. An old record player cranked out some lively music. Catherine usually sat quietly, with her chin on her chest and her eyes downcast. One August evening, Tim Boswell, a tall, blond young man who was hospitalized because he had repeatedly threatened to kill himself, sat down next to her and asked her how she was doing.

"Okay," she replied.

"How long have you been here," he asked.

"Ten months."

"Whew. You going to get to go home soon?"

"No."

"Hey, it's 'Blue Suede Shoes.' Would you like to dance?"

Catherine rose and followed Tim. As they began dancing, she was suddenly transformed. She danced with abandon, twisting and turning. The others stopped dancing. No one spoke. All eyes stayed riveted on the two. After the music stopped, Catherine lowered her chin back down upon her chest, and shuffled back to her seat, to general applause. "Boy, Catherine, you're good," remarked an aide who had accompanied the patients from our ward to the dance. "You can really swing."

Over the next weeks, she danced several dances at each Thursday-evening party with the same young man, and in the same animated way. Catherine told me she thought it was "peculiar" that a boy would want to dance with her. She omitted telling me that she had won admiration for her dancing.

"I don't think dancing is a small thing," I told her. "Your mother told our social worker that you took flamenco dance lessons. You have a healthy side . . ."

"I'm not me when I dance. It's stage acting. I'm someone else."

"It gives you a way to pretend?"

"Yes."

Tim came to visit Catherine every few days. "Are you glad to see me?" he'd ask, the two of them sitting together on the day-room couch.

"Yes."

"How are you feeling?"

"Fine."

"What are you doing?"

Catherine would not answer.

Tim told her that he missed their dancing between Thursdays, but Catherine again did not reply. Whenever he visited, they mostly sat in silence. After two months in the hospital, Tim was discharged. But every few weeks for several months, he came to visit. He would ask her the same questions, and Catherine would reply with the same one-word answers, or would not answer him at all. Finally, he stopped coming.

During this time, Catherine told me that she had a visitor, but she never mentioned any feeling about it other than, "He was nice."

She also attended Tuesday-night group meetings with the ward psychologist. Usually she sat silently while the others competed for time to talk about themselves. On one occasion, the psychologist asked Catherine what might be bothering her. With the group raptly attentive, she said, "I hear voices to kill everyone. Bunches of voices all at the same time. I see mouths talking, then I hear a voice going off in a mouth or just coming from somewhere. My mind is like a tape recorder playing voices. At night I lay down and wait for the screaming voices to lessen so I might get some rest. I don't sleep. I hear birds outside and wonder if they are voices."

"When did you first start hearing them?" asked a young woman, newly admitted to the ward.

Catherine retreated into silence.

These were positive developments, but most of the time Catherine remained withdrawn. The nurses noticed that for several weeks she had rarely looked directly at anyone. On September 16, eleven months after I started treating her, Catherine began stumbling over tables and chairs. One nurse realized that Catherine was walking about with her eyes closed. The nurse asked Catherine what she was doing, but received no reply. Instead, Catherine stood still, like a child being criticized.

Catherine steadfastly refused to open her eyes. I had had to leave my office on the ward to make room for a new crop of first-year residents, so I now met with her in an office on another floor. Since she was not allowed to leave the ward alone, I would go to the ward each day to get her. I would find her sitting alone in the day room. I'd tell her it was time for our appointment; she'd get up and follow slightly behind me, peering at my heels through slitted eyes. She would follow me straight into the crowd in the elevator, bumping and jostling the other passengers. Once, when we reached my floor, she could not get out of the elevator fast enough—and was hit by the closing door. "Shit," I heard her say through her compressed lips. She still refused to open her eyes.

"Why have you closed your eyes?" I asked.

"I don't want to see anything. It makes me worse. There's too much going on. I'm confused. And I don't want to see colors."

"Colors?"

"Colors are what the world is. I don't belong in the world. I am a vampire. I belong in the dark."

During most of our sessions that autumn, one year after treatment began, Catherine was still talking about how evil and mean she was: "Voices, all voices, both inside my head and outside, including yours, make my head split. You can't understand how bad it is. You don't believe how crazy I am. Bad people should be put away. All I hear are voices to kill all the time. You consider me rational, but I should be certified crazy. The only way I know how to live is with my badness." It was true that she was certifiably crazy. It was also true that I spoke to her healthy side, which was the only handle I had.

In November, Catherine told me of a dream she had had several times: "There was a bad cat at home. It once was good. In the dream, mother picked it up and it bit her, so she threw it down. I am that cat."

In another meeting, she told me, "I am one-half wolf, like Dr. Jekyll, a monster ready to rip everything apart. I don't *feel* like the wolf-man; I *am* the wolf-man."

"All your badness is an unchangeable fact?"

"It is real. You should know that, and leave me to rot."

Just before Christmas, Catherine told me, "I am ugly. You will be made ugly. I have the kiss of death. You'll be sorry. You should stay away from me."

"I can see why you want to avoid people, including me. It's out of concern, isn't it? You really don't want to harm anybody, and you're afraid you will?"

Catherine clenched her fists. Did I see a tear? It would be too intrusive to ask. I thought of a short story by Nathaniel Hawthorne, "Rappachini's Daughter." In the story, Professor Rappachini, a botanist, raised poisonous plants. His daughter was the only person who could tend to the plants, because her touch was also poisonous. A young man, observing her from an adjoining building, was captured by her beauty and called to her. Might he talk with her? She agreed, but on the condition he not even brush her skin. She knew she could not restrain herself, so, to protect him, she drank a vial of poison and killed herself.

The next time we met, Catherine was silent for the entire hour. I finally asked, "Are you silent because of what we talked about yesterday?"

"Yes. I am full of hate."

I did not want to hear such a negative self-evaluation day after day, month after month, so I said, "You have nothing good?"

"No."

Well, I thought to myself, *maybe she has a point*. She knew herself: she was infantile, bitter, recalcitrant, given to manipulating others for the sake of her precious rituals, intolerant of the slightest frustration, and filled with rage.

Then, suddenly, Catherine began speaking about how "nice" various nurses were. She said that she occasionally talked with Marion Rogers, a nurse whom she liked. The two would speak in Catherine's room. In these moments, Catherine would tell Marion about how sad she felt about all that had happened to her, and how she liked Marion and me. "It makes me uncomfortable," Catherine told her, "that he is so nice. I'd like it better if he got angry at me."

"Do you look forward to your hours with Dr. Dorman?" Marion asked.

"Yes. I have no good feeling, though. I hear voices to kill him. Here is somebody who is trying to do a good thing, to help me, and I'm nailing him to the cross."

During one session, Catherine told me of another dream: "A snake was slithering around, and there was a voodoo man directing things. The snake turned on the voodoo man, who was surprised and threw the snake off. The snake then slithered off to its owner." She told me she was the snake, and I was the voodoo man. She then lapsed into silence.

After a few minutes, Catherine told me that my office was chilly and that her hands were cold. It was a dark, rainy day.

"Are your hands cold?" she asked.

I started to reply, but she continued: "Can I see if yours are cold?"

"Sure."

She reached out and briefly touched the backs of my hands with the tips of her fingers. "I was walking in the hall with Kitty Tate," she said, "and I took hold of her hand, but she pulled it away."

To say anything would have taken away her moment and made it mine. We both sat in silence. *Tender feeling*, I thought to myself. *What in the world will she do with that? Perhaps it will drive her away.*

In another meeting, Catherine warned me that she was "out of control." She didn't say it, but I knew she was wondering how she could feel affection without rage. To her, affection meant a symbiotic knot that obliterated any vestige of an independent identity. It was not possible to feel one without evoking the other, and she had no idea how to separate them or discern their boundaries. In another dream, she "called for mother, the Virgin Mary, and you, while faced with ghosts, and it was frightening. But there was a mistiness and no one was there anyway."

"Perhaps your experience in the dream of no one there refers to no one upon whom you can depend?" I asked her.

"I want my mother, but I can't have her. When she comes to visit, a third dimension separates us. I've tried reaching out to her, but I can't. She once gave me her sweater, and I hold onto it because I can smell her odor. She's dead. I was safe as long as she was alive. I can't have anyone.

"I told you, I'm out of control. I don't know anything any more. The talking mouths are only part of it. At night I wake up and the bed is going across the room and the walls are caving in. My grandmother's two dead dogs were in my bed. I could hear them breathe! I hear Michael and Theresa crying. They were right there in my room."

One day Catherine asked a nurse, "Does Dr. Dorman care for me?" The nurse replied that she thought so, but why didn't she discuss that with Dr. Dorman? Catherine told me that Marion Rogers had suggested she bring up her feelings about me. She described a dream in which I was Jesus. "That has to be confusing," I told her. "Love and worship are inextricable." Catherine turned away with a sad expression, then told me, "I don't want to be near people. I'm so crazy. There is no way I can ever have any fun."

Catherine now sat in silence throughout our sessions. I was often silent, too. The winter passed that way, and on into April. I could occasionally pinpoint the source of her silence by her physical expression—by the tightness of her facial muscles or by the loudness with which she ground her teeth. During one of these totally silent hours, I knew she had just returned from an outing with Marion. I commented on her inability to make contact with a person for whom she felt some affection. I received a raging, teeth-grinding response. A few minutes after the hour ended and she had returned to her room, I heard a mournful wail coming from her room. I did not try to decipher her thoughts from nonverbal clues only. Now and then, I guessed them correctly, but these were still just guesses. Also, guessing her thoughts would have been tantamount to my thinking for her, a duplication of her symbiotic tie to her mother.

The nurses often noted that Catherine sat in her room with her hands up to her face, quietly crying. Moreover, she would walk about slowly, with her lower lip slightly protruded, eyes shut, her mouth turned down sharply in a grimace, and her neck muscles taut. It was an expression of silent, tortured agony.

In the spring, one and a half years after she entered UCLA, the nurses described some changes in Catherine's behavior. She began to horse around a bit. One of the nurses noted in her chart: "She said she was going to spend some of her money to buy a bottle of wine. She left and came back smoking a cigarette, and put on a seductive act saying, 'Why don't you come up and see me sometime?' Lenore Pinia, another nurse, visited with her, and Catherine was warm in her greeting." Was she beginning to feel some internal permission to fool around, to play with sexual innuendo and humor?

A different nurse wrote, "She has been talking about ways to kill herself by putting a bag over her head or drowning herself in the tub. She said if she used a tub, she would be dressed, because it would be embarrassing otherwise."

Another nurse wrote the following note:

> She was interacting with other patients and staff today, but mostly about food. At seven in the evening she acted like running off the unit. I took her arm and brought her to her room, where I sat and talked with her. She said that she is hearing voices telling her to kill people. She was feeling sad and cried, but this was over in about ten minutes. I was with her

most of the time, and she told me to be sure and tell Dr. Dorman about this. She also said, "I like Dr. Dorman." She went out to the day room and talked to Sandra Peters, another patient, and asked her for some whipped cream. Sandra said she would get her some and Catherine seemed happy. When Sandra came back she asked Catherine for a kiss, and Catherine went to the bathroom, washed out her mouth, put on some lipstick and kissed Mrs. Peters on the lips. She then smiled and asked, "Where is Dr. Dorman?" Then she went over to William R. and asked him if he wanted a kiss. William didn't even reply. Catherine had her bath and went to bed at nine.

There was little question in my mind that something had started to shift. Catherine began to ask me for "naturalistic" explanations of her experiences, as opposed to her own religious, mystical, or childlike explanations. After my sessions with her, I usually spent fifteen or twenty minutes writing, sometimes my impressions, sometimes what Catherine had said. My notes for May 19 read as follows:

In the last week she has been questioning her religious explanations of the world. Yesterday she "dared" me to say that St. Joan's visions were not real. Today she told me the story of St. Bernadette, whose well water was curative of various illnesses, even polio. She asked me, "What kind of naturalistic explanation is there for these things?" She also told me of a vision she had of Barry, a patient who hanged himself, coming out of a closet. How did I explain that? I tried to show her that her visions and voices were actually a statement from another part of herself. Her voices were saying her own disavowed angry thoughts, and her vision of Barry probably had something to do with her own feeling of being dead; perhaps she was alive—coming out of the closet.

In early June, we talked again about how bad and evil she felt. My notes read: "I talked with her about how she regarded her badness as the devil. I pointed out that it looked like she was getting the devil to do her dirty work for her, rather than taking the responsibility herself."

Much of my effort with her centered on translating her childlike thinking into adult thought and feeling. For instance, one day she asked me, "What does food mean?"

"You treat food as a replacement for people. It is sweet; you can hoard it; you can have something to look forward to; it can be produced at will; it satisfies a sensual longing; and it can be managed in a consistent manner."

"I *have* to talk to people about food," she replied. "I try to make myself into a nice little girl talking about food so I won't have to admit I really feel like an ax murderer."

It seemed to me that Catherine was asking for my help in understanding herself in a more consistent way. She talked about her rage, and one day nodded in agreement when I said, "Perhaps your rage is also about your experience that humankind is a curse, yet you have no replacement."

But it was difficult to be too optimistic. Catherine still looked like a living corpse, slowly shuffling about with her eyes closed. Her personal hygiene habits had once again deteriorated. She rarely bathed, and she wore the same clothes day after day. She ate with her hands and was a mess after meals. The nurses correctly surmised that she merely spread the food around on her plate to avoid eating. Most of Catherine's conversations with them consisted of whining complaints, in her high-pitched babyish voice, about food. If the nurses threw away some of the old pie or cookies she had stored in the community refrigerator, they would later find her picking through the trash. She sat in the hospital arts-and-crafts room with her head down, wads of toilet tissue poked in her ears, refusing to take part. When the group went out to the recreation deck or the swimming pool, Catherine retired to a lounge chair.

Many patients treated Catherine as if she were a tiny child, offering to bring back sweets from vending machines located elsewhere in the hospital, or otherwise asking if she needed anything. But others found her unlikable.

"Get away from me," one young woman frequently said to Catherine. "You're disgusting. Why do you slink around all day expecting everyone to wait on you?"

Barbara Sovodny, her roommate, once growled at Catherine: "Can't you stop grinding your teeth? Look at you. The only reason you do it is because you're so hungry you have to grind something. Why don't you eat? And why don't you get out of here once in a while so I can be alone?"

On another occasion, Barbara tried to engage Catherine in conversation: "What do you think of Dr. Dorman?"

Catherine sat on her bed and rocked back and forth.

Receiving no answer, Barbara stomped out of the room and told another girl, "She's weird. I might as well talk to a rock."

One day, a nurse badgered Catherine about her body odor and prodded her into taking a bath. Catherine locked herself in the bathroom, lay down on the floor, and screamed, "Let me alone! I just want to die!"

Usually Catherine wore a loose cotton dress, but she would dress up for Sunday breakfast with her mother. One such morning, she appeared on the ward in a bright pink-and-red dress with her shoes on the wrong feet. Her hair hung in tangled skeins.

I felt sure that Catherine could hardly become more infantile that summer, nineteen months after I started seeing her. But I was wrong. She threw herself down on her bed and screamed, "I hate you!" and "I want to get out of this place!" at anyone who came in. She told one psychiatric aide that she was driving her crazy, ran off the ward about ten or fifteen yards, then stopped dead still, head down, and eyes closed. When the aide approached her, Catherine began hitting at her, and ran another ten yards away. Finally she agreed to return.

Because Catherine tried to hide in her room as much as she could, the nurses and other staff members thought it best to restrict the amount of time she spent there in the daytime. So, instead of sitting in the day room with the other patients, Catherine often sat in the ward dining room while Veronica Anderson, the cook, and Arlene Washington, a food handler, cleaned up and chatted.

"She always stays behind," Arlene said. "Poor child. Just sits there and rocks. Reminds me of an old rocking chair, except no one's in it."

Veronica inspected a pot. "Pay her no mind."

"Veronica," said Arlene, "let me ask you something."

"Yeah?"

"Does your man ever satisfy you? Nothing ever happens to *me*."

"What do you mean, nothing ever happens?"

"Nothing happens. I always expect something will happen. I mean I get excited, sometimes, but . . ."

Catherine stopped rocking back and forth.

Arlene nodded toward Catherine. "You think she's listening to us?"

"Nah. They say all she hears are voices inside her head. Poor child." Veronica turned her back to Catherine. "Men don't know anything. You have to teach them . . ."

"Hush up, Veronica. We shouldn't be talking with her sitting there."

Later, Catherine told me, "Everyone thinks I don't hear what's going on because I sit without moving. I have big ears."

That winter Catherine developed an eye infection and I made an appointment for her with an ophthalmologist. At the eye clinic, she clenched her eyes shut and refused to open them when the nurse asked to examine her. She then settled in for an hour's wait for the doctor. When it came time to see him, she jumped up from her seat and ran out the door to the hospital parking lot, with the nurse from our ward in hot pursuit.

"Save me, save me, they're keeping me here!" she screamed to a policeman. The nurse caught up, scuffled with her a bit, and told her she was acting like a baby, while the policeman knowingly looked on. The nurse brought her back to the eye clinic, where she still refused to let the doctor examine her. Back on the ward, she sat rigidly and ground her teeth so loudly that everyone in the dayroom could hear it.

On a group trip out of the hospital the next day, she walked behind the group with her eyes still closed, holding a nurse's hand and complaining about the long walk. Suddenly she broke her grip and ran off the sidewalk into the street, but stopped short of running into traffic.

California state law requires that anyone confined to a mental hospital must be granted due process if he or she is involuntarily hospitalized. If, however, like Catherine, she is a voluntary patient, she has the right to leave whenever she wishes. Catherine badgered the nurses with requests for an "Against Medical Advice" form, which patients signed when leaving the hospital without a formal discharge by the physician. At first the nurses had to bother me at home in the evenings about this, but eventually they learned to do nothing, since Catherine never followed her threats with action. In fact, she told me in one of our sessions, "I know I'll never leave the hospital. I can't even make it in here." Nevertheless, each time she pressed the nurses about leaving, they were legally obliged to at least call the nursing supervisor. She would arrive on the ward to see Catherine screaming at the nurses. They were inhumane, she'd yell. Then she would stagger around, bumping into walls and crying, holding a wet cloth to her face.

Once, the nurse accompanying Catherine exited an elevator, leaving her, eyes closed, standing in the back. The nurses tried not to do everything for her, like telling her to get off the elevator. Catherine rode up and down a few times, mumbling under her breath, until someone else finally got off at the correct floor, where the nurse was waiting.

A kind of compromise emerged between the nurses and Catherine. They required her to maintain her weight, make her bed, and generally to participate in patient activities. And although she continued to complain and tried to negotiate, she met their demands.

Catherine did complain bitterly of her confusion and depression to some trusted nurses and staff personnel. She told one nurse that people from outer space had control of her mind. Often, mental health professionals dismiss such statements. Harry Stack Sullivan, a psychiatrist at St. Elizabeth's Hospital in Washington, D.C., in the 1940s, told the story of how he was discussing the treatment of schizophrenia with his resident physicians. A young doctor asked him about the origin of the delusion, which many schizophrenics have, that alien beings are controlling their minds. Dr. Sullivan replied, "If you think the schizophrenic does not feel his mind is controlled by sources other than himself, then that is *your* delusion, Doctor."

If one were to judge Catherine's progress by her behavior, she certainly had not changed. Most of the staff, and my fellow residents, even thought she was getting worse. I thought I detected some internal change, however. She seemed to speak to me in a more abstract way. She now looked sad at times, whereas before she had looked grim. Maybe it was the little droop at the outer corners of her eyes. I couldn't be sure. On the other hand, maybe it was my own sadness I was feeling.

"I'm digging my own grave by talking with you," she told me one day. "I can't protect myself any more. Tears come into my eyes. I can't ever have anything good again. I've tried to hide—I know it's from me. I can't stand to look at the world. That's why I keep my eyes shut. Everything has to be dark. I'm like a vampire bat. I don't want to see any light, or any color. When my mom takes me to the pancake restaurant on Sundays, the first thing I do is turn over the place mats because they are colorful. I keep my eyes closed except for squinting around to see if there is anything that has color.

"And I have to keep everything away from me. If my mother sits too close to me, I tell her to move away. I always sit in the same place, on the outside, by the window. When I get my waffle, which is the only thing I ever order, I always give half of it away. No way will I eat the whole thing and feel full.

"I can hear me talking to you and I know how crazy I am. All I can do is dig a deeper hole."

Catherine's sadness also signaled that her "system" was breaking down, a necessary step in the change process. The more narrow the base of operations, the greater the dislocation a person feels with change. Catherine had little margin of safety on her tiny base, and her realization that her system of protection was illusory frightened and saddened her.

Catherine's increasing investment in me, and good feeling about a number of patients and staff members, only intensified her confusion. An investment in someone demands a great deal of emotion, and Catherine was trying to feel as little as possible. So to feel something meant that the boundaries that determined her existence had started crumbling. All this dissolution caused Catherine to cling more tightly to her "system": eating specific foods at specific times, keeping her eyes closed, and withdrawing from contact with others. She was looking for familiar territory, retreating, as it were, back behind the lines. No longer able to count on her own perceptions and inner resources, she fought change.

I had now been treating Catherine for nearly two years. Many of the doctors and nurses regarded her as a hospital curiosity—Dr. Dorman's experiment. One resident dubbed her "the question mark," which was apt. She looked like one when she stood still, as she often did, with her chin down and her upper back bowed out.

It was traditional that the residents discussed their patients at periodic case conferences with invited senior psychiatrists. Often patients were also interviewed at these meetings. On one occasion, it was my turn to discuss Catherine. The invited psychiatrist that day was Andrew J. Adams, who held an honorary chair. This silver-haired, straight-backed man had chaired the psychiatry department at UCLA for nearly two decades, finally succumbing to pressure from other members of the department to step down in favor of a younger, nationally known psychiatrist. Eleven of us were seated around a rectangular conference table. Slowly, Adams settled into his chair at the head of the table.

"I understand we are going to hear from our resident analyst today. Dr. Dorman, tell us about this young schizophrenic woman."

I told the group what I knew about Catherine's early years, her rituals concerning food, and her deteriorating mental life from ages seventeen to nineteen. Some of the nurses and social workers described her ward behavior.

Catherine was waiting outside. Ruth Sargent brought her in, and she noiselessly sat down and bent her head down, a position she held for the entire time she was there.

Dr. Adams introduced himself and said, "I'd like to ask you a few questions."

"Okay," she replied.

"What are these peculiar habits you have about food?"

Catherine sat transfixed.

"You like your mother to bring you pie every Sunday?"

"Yes."

"What does pie mean?"

Her jaw twitched.

"Perhaps control of food is your way to control your sexual impulses."

Catherine rocked her head slowly back and forth.

"Perhaps your silence means that your sexual feelings are out of control. Did your father ever make advances?"

Her rocking stopped. She sat motionless, with a stony expression on her face.

"You told Mrs. Sargent that you liked Dr. Dorman. Are you having any sexual fantasies about him?"

"No."

Several staff members were by now shifting around in their chairs. I was enraged. How dare he? Sexual fantasies? I couldn't believe his smugness.

"Does anyone have any questions to ask of Catherine?" he asked.

Glances darted around the circle.

"No. Well, thank you, Miss Penney, for coming."

"You're welcome."

Ruth took her from the room. Adams informed us that Catherine was suffering from sexual trauma that I had not yet discovered. He was sure I would get to it all, and dismissed the group.

I apologized to Catherine later that afternoon. I told her I should not have allowed such a meeting. She just stood silently while I spoke. I told some friends and staff members that I planned to make an appointment and tell Adams what I thought. They suggested that I might only provoke even more of a battle or get kicked out of the program.

I didn't care about provoking one more battle. I made an appointment to see Adams the next day. I said, "I want to tell you that I think your interview style is accusatory. If you are again the attending psychiatrist at a conference, I will not allow my patient to be interviewed by you." His response? "Thank you for coming in, Dr. Dorman."

It was also common teaching practice for an experienced analyst to interview patients alone in a room with a one-way mirror so the residents could observe interview technique. I did not allow my patients to be interviewed that way. I considered it demeaning and a farce. The analyst was not alone with the patient, and both analyst and patient knew it. So why the charade?

At one weekly staff meeting, David Sheffield, my fellow resident, declared my treatment of Catherine "unethical" because I did not prescribe antipsychotic medication. I knew he spoke for other residents who also criticized my approach. He then said, "The physician's obligation is to relieve suffering, and here she is, in all this obvious agony." He saw his patients only twice a week, so I asked him, "Do you think seeing your patients less than five days a week is also unethical?" He glared at me. David was headed for a career in medicolegal psychiatry, which meant evaluating criminals or working on the defense or plaintiff side of civil cases. Such evaluations are defined strictly by the law—perfect for a psychiatrist who could not imagine someone's soul.

I do think that psychotropic drugs have a place in psychiatric treatment. If a patient is in physical danger, say in a manic psychosis or really about to commit suicide, it makes sense to use drugs to save him. A manic psychosis can be a truly frightening thing. Afflicted patients often don't sleep for weeks on end in a whirlwind of ceaseless activity that sometimes ends in exhaustion and death. I once treated Mark Lefkowicz, a promising third-year medical student who had begun to talk too much in class and then began missing his clinic assignments. His roommate telephoned his parents when Mark missed an exam and had not been seen for a week. The police found him at three o'clock in the morning in a bean field near Bakersfield, California, eighty miles from Los Angeles, howling at the moon.

"I am a wolf," he told me, "in human clothing."

He was probably telling me some version of his truth. However, I couldn't talk with him about why he felt so inhuman if he died, so I explained to him why I needed to place him on antipsychotic medication. He decamped from the hospital one month later, after he had calmed down somewhat. Then he stopped his medication and was brought back to the hospital after he called his parents from Los Angeles's skid row. He didn't like the psychic numbness that the medication produced, he told me.

Most of my sessions with Catherine still passed in near-complete silence. At times Catherine insisted, albeit half-heartedly, on my dropping her treatment. "Let me rot in Camarillo," she said. "That's where I belong." She also continued to press for tranquilizing medication. During many, but not all, of our meetings, she complained about something having to do with food, or with some detail of ward routine, usually the ward rules.

On September 28, I wrote: "She was silent for forty-five minutes. Just before the session was over, she said that she was just like another patient who was sent to a chronic-care facility because of an organic brain syndrome, and that she should be sent away because she is 'like a horse put out to pasture—useless. All I do is sleep and dream.' Catherine sees herself as the misfit she is, and she asked me, again, to just let her die as a 'hopeless case.'"

On November 8, Catherine again said nothing the entire hour, except at the end: "I am Humpty Dumpty, in pieces, and there is no way to put broken eggshells back together again. I am cracked up. Who says it's good to cry? Once you start, you can't stop."

On November 15, she spoke only at the beginning of the hour: "I feel no comfort from people. I might as well kill myself because it is too hard to come up or go down. When I come up, talking to you, I get confused and I have unhappy memories, like I think of my mother as a hand cutting a pie, so I don't want to feel anything at all." One week later, Catherine sat down at our session and began grinding her teeth. About halfway through the hour she said, "I am upset leaving mother on Sundays. I have to straighten out my feelings. I don't know whether I am sad, mad, or happy. I hear voices all the time. What I really want is to be inside my mommy's tummy."

I made mistakes, too. For example, I sometimes assumed that her anger was directed at her mother, since her auditory hallucinations kept saying, "Kill your mother." She did not correct me. In late November, she again spent most of one session grinding her teeth. Toward the end of the hour, I once more began talking about her rage as a response to her relationship with her mother. She interrupted me by shaking her head in disagreement.

"I'm worthless. I have destructive thoughts about everyone."

"Perhaps you are afraid your thoughts can destroy . . ."

"Who are you to be telling me? All right," she said with her voice raised. "I'm mad because no one is alive. I'm mad because I see myself doing it. I love my mother, but a ghost tells me to do you-know-what to her. She becomes a monster." After a few minutes of silence, she continued: "I can't change what I am. It is like waiting for the buzzards to finish me off. It has got to come."

I was surprised at her outburst. "Ah. You're enraged at *yourself*. I've not been hearing you correctly."

If I tried to be perfect, make no mistakes, Catherine would, correctly, detect insecurity in me. This would call into question my reliability. I had to learn to be changed by her experiences and her world. If I held tightly to theories, it would denigrate her existence. She would feel that and stop relating or exploring her experiences.

Catherine began telling me that she was afraid she was going even more berserk. On January 4, early in her third year at UCLA, she told me she was "slipping down a cliff with nothing to hang on to. The rocks are being ripped as I slip down." I thought she was experiencing both the dismantling of her psychotic identity and an increasing awareness that she never had much to hang onto in the first place. A few days later, she said, "I can't tell the difference any more between the voices and myself." A hallmark of Catherine's early years was her need to deny reality, external and internal, by separating or splitting off what she needed to deny. Acknowledging these previously split-off portions of herself was tantamount to losing the ability to deny what was indeed her own being. Thus she sensed that her psychotic identity wasn't working anymore.

On March 10 she reported a dream in which her voices said, "Who are you?" and answered, "I don't know." The dream gave her a sense of existing in many pieces. To me, this suggested that her attempt to exclude her emotions was beginning to fail, and because her sense of herself was based on denial of feeling, she experienced herself as fragmented. The fragmentation also reflected her lack of a cohesive identity; without her adopted identity of the good, quiet, self-abnegating child, she felt in pieces.

During another session, she asked me if I told her mother anything that she told me. I said that I did not. She then told me that she liked me "better than a bean-and-cheese burrito, my sister, uncle, and mother."

Catherine's sense of futility now tended to dominate the sessions. She had dreams of "walking into quicksand." She also told me that when she could no longer continue her food rituals and withdrawal, she would kill herself. I made a note to myself that I had failed to take notes for three weeks. Catherine's futility had infected me. I feared that Catherine's soul would remain imprisoned by her madness. Perhaps my teachers were right: I should just relieve her pain. I should let her exist just the other side of sanity, a cripple forever, held together only by drugs and a protected environment. For the first time, I began to imagine defeat. Catherine's defeat would be my defeat.

"I am only partly alive," Catherine told me. "My body is a blob, suspended in time. Nothing is real. The clock doesn't move. There is no night or day. A minute is an hour, a day a month, and months are like years. Do you know how you have a sense of things moving, a rhythm? I am at a standstill. Everything has stopped. During the day, I sit and recite the names of foods over and over to myself. That's the way I get a rhythm going, to make me feel a little bit alive. Sometimes the only way I know I am alive is that I feel my teeth grinding together, or by rocking back and forth. You're right, Dr. Dorman. Futility is always there. I just hang onto my diet."

In July, three months away, my residency would end and I would leave UCLA. In most training centers, some patients of graduating residents are transferred to incoming residents, others are referred to community mental health centers or chronic-care hospitals. Occasionally a patient will continue to see his or her physician in a new setting.

I planned to enter private practice in Beverly Hills, a short distance from UCLA. I had been appointed to the clinical faculty, which meant that I would devote two hours a week to teaching residents. However, I could not treat Catherine there. UCLA did not have a private psychiatric ward where faculty members could hospitalize their patients. Moreover, most patients' UCLA bills were paid by public funds, making it difficult, often impossible, to transfer someone like Catherine to a private facility. The state's public social services agencies usually directed such patients to a state institution. Fortunately, Joe's retired officer's insurance covered eighty percent of Catherine's expenses, and I was able to make arrangements to continue as her psychiatrist. She would become a patient at Westwood Hospital, a small, private mental hospital not far away.

At first, Catherine joked with some of the nurses about leaving UCLA. "I'm going to be transferred instead to the Burbank cemetery," she said. But after a few weeks, she tried to isolate herself even more, and she stepped up her childlike behavior. In June she walked out of a patient talent show, locked herself in the bathroom, got down on her knees, and beat her hands on the floor, yelling, "Mommy, Mommy, why don't you take me out of here?"

The next day, a nurse wrote the following note in her chart:

> She was in her room most of the day today, and talking to me about her fear of getting a [new] noisy roommate. She also told me how she had an increase in "killing thoughts" towards people about whom she cares. She was resistant about going to occupational therapy, but went after much encouragement. Once there she began yelling, "Get me out of here,

I'm going to hurt someone!" She started kicking the door and pulling at her clothes. I had to command her firmly and she stopped. She sat in the corner for a short period, then she ran out but returned shortly, yelling again.

A week before I was due to leave, another nurse wrote: "She was isolated most of the day. Refused to go on ward outing to the zoo. Whined all afternoon to various staff members, saying how destructive she felt. She said she is having bad dreams; last night she dreamed she turned into 'a voice without a body, floating in the air and asking who am I?' Then she said she was afraid of losing the security of the ward routine when Dr. Dorman leaves."

Catherine told me that there would be no place for her pie in the new hospital.

I imagined myself, years later, visiting Catherine in Camarillo Hospital, having failed to help her. She would be sitting in a corner with her head down, eyes still closed, and would not even return my greeting. I am not, by nature, a quitter, but I had treated Catherine for three months shy of three years in an unsuccessful effort so far.

I met with Brian Leffler's parents about also continuing with his treatment. They could afford private care.

"We looked at the living arrangements the social worker told us about," Mrs. Leffler told me, "and the place is, well . . . to be frank, dirty. We know you have been dedicated, but we have been investigating other approaches. We've decided on vitamin-immersion therapy. We've found a place where vitamins A, B, and C are given along with other drugs."

Abandon Brian? "You know," I said, trying to stop my voice from shaking, "there have been changes. I can talk with him, despite it appearing otherwise. I am a connection for him to the world outside his psychosis."

"No, we've made up our minds. We've decided not to continue with you treating Brian. We'll pick him up tomorrow."

"Can you give me a week? I can't just disappear on him. I need to explain to him what's happening."

"We'll give you tomorrow, and we'll pick him up the day after, on Wednesday morning."

That afternoon, I asked Brian if I might talk with him. I told him that his parents no longer approved of my care and explained what they planned to do. I also told him how helpless I felt. He sat in silence, blinking his eyes.

"I'll see you tomorrow. That will be our last session, unless I can find a way . . ."

He got up and walked out. The next day, he refused to leave his room or talk with me.

Five

MOUNTING A LIGHTLESS ROAD

My Guide and I crossed over and began
to mount that little known and lightless road
to ascend into the shining world again.

Dante, The Inferno

July 3, 1972: moving day. Catherine was sitting in the day room with Ruth Sargent when Florence and Cindy arrived to take her to Westwood Hospital. Ruth tried to reassure her that she would be all right at the new hospital, but Catherine was not consoled. She sat quietly, her face pale and rigid. A few patients gathered around and wished her good luck. Lenore Pinia even put her large arms around Catherine and gave her a long hug, which Catherine received passively.

I had talked with Susan Glass, the nursing administrator at Westwood, about Catherine. Upon hearing the details of Catherine's condition, Susan worried about her safety. She did not want to admit her to an open, or unlocked, ward where she could easily walk off the hospital grounds. So she insisted on a locked ward. With its cavernous dimensions, high ceilings, sparse furniture, and bare terrazzo floors, the locked ward contrasted with its counterparts at UCLA. Those wards had had a more friendly atmosphere: an abundance of furniture, rugs on the floor, and smaller, cozier dimensions. Moreover, nearly all the patients housed on UCLA's locked wards were young and acutely psychotic or suicidal. Many at Westwood were older and chronically psychotic.

At the new hospital, Susan escorted Catherine, her mother, and Cindy to the ward. Just after the door was locked behind them, a middle-aged woman with unkempt hair approached Catherine. With her arms open wide, she shouted, "My daughter! Oh, you're my daughter! Come to me, sweetheart!"

Catherine backed up a few steps and stood behind her mother. "I'm not staying here," she told Florence.

Florence looked at Susan. "Catherine can't live in this place," she said. She grabbed Catherine's arm and turned to leave. Susan reassured Florence that Catherine would get used to it—but Florence insisted. Susan unlocked the door and Florence kept on walking, with Cindy behind her and Catherine bringing up the rear.

I had just finished with a patient at my office, when I heard a knock on my door. In my waiting room were Catherine, her mother, and Cindy. I had a free hour, so I invited them in. Catherine sat on the edge of a chair and told me through grinding teeth, "It's a free country. You can't make me go there. I'm a voluntary patient, and I want to go home." Florence added, in her usual monotone, "All Catherine needs anyway is love, which I'll supply at home." Cindy glared at me.

My irritation showed in my voice. Ignoring Florence and Cindy, I turned to Catherine: "You know you'll never last at home," I said. "At the worst, you will murder your mother and at best, you'll sit in your room rocking back and forth. Anyway, I *can* hospitalize you against your will because you fit all three categories for involuntary hospitalization, and only one is necessary. You're a danger to yourself, a danger to others, and unable to care for yourself."

Catherine replied, "I won't go to the locked ward."

I picked up the phone, called Susan, and told her that I thought Catherine would not run away from the hospital if she were on the open ward. I would take responsibility. She agreed to admit her to an open ward on the condition that I transfer her to the locked ward if, after a few days, Catherine appeared to need close supervision. I relayed this information to Florence and told her to take Catherine back to the hospital and then to go home.

After they left, I realized how angry I was—mostly at myself, for not meeting them at the hospital. There, I might have been able to deflect their repugnance at the sight of the locked ward. But still, there was something maddening about both Catherine's and Florence's cavalier denial of Catherine's condition.

When I arrived at the hospital about an hour and a half later, an attendant met me and said that he had never seen anyone as "sick" as Catherine in that hospital; he thought she wouldn't make it on an open ward. Still upset by the encounter at my office, I brusquely replied, "Want to bet?" and proceeded to set up an interview with Catherine.

When we were alone, Catherine sat as usual with her chin down on her chest and her eyes closed. The first thing she said to me in her squeaky voice was, "Thank you, Dr. Dorman, for not letting me go home." During the rest of the interview, she plaintively concerned herself with my arranging things so she could store her pies, eat alone, and avoid taking part in hospital activities.

The nurse in charge of Catherine wrote the following note that first day:

> Catherine appears to be catatonic in her mannerisms. Her eyes are kept closed most of the time, and she squints them open to see her way around. Ate only her butterscotch pie for supper. She asked to sit alone at dinner because people made her nervous. She ate slowly with her head down and almost to the plate, using a napkin to partially cover her face. After dinner she called her mother, talked about ten minutes, and spent the remainder of the evening in her room. She was nervous, afraid, and crying. She said, "I am a weirdo and insane. My only grasp with reality is food; it's the only meaningful thing in my life and all that I have." She also said she is afraid she will hurt others and hears voices.

The hospital required that all new patients have a physical examination within a few days of admission. The internist who examined Catherine wrote the following report:

> This is a 22-year-old, single, Caucasian girl who is quite uncommunicative. She sits with her eyes closed and sways back and forth on the examining table. She shows substantial evidence of weight loss and neglected personal hygiene, and when asked about this she says she is

on a special diet that she has followed for three years, which consists of proteins and vitamins and very nourishing foods. She states her general physical health has never been better since the onset of the use of this special diet and that all she has to do is meet with the agreement she has made with her doctor that she not let her weight fall below 85 pounds. To accomplish this she is permitted to have an occasional alcoholic drink before meals to stimulate her appetite. However, she claims the appetite is excellent and, as noted above, she insists her physical health has never been better. She states that when she was heavier prior to the age of 18 she had a number of different maladies, including what she refers to as asthma and colds. This patient, as noted, has no specific complaints and seems somewhat delusional in a general sort of way and not entirely able to respond in an intelligent manner to the questions asked.

The doctor went on to note the results of his physical examination:

The examination shows a thin, pale-appearing girl. At one point, when I asked her about her general health, she blurted out, "I'd like to be dead." She has an unpleasant body odor. When I asked her to open her eyes for examination, she shut them more tightly. She has numerous excoriations of her back, chest, and face that appear to be self-induced. Medical diagnosis: (1) Moderately severe undernutrition; (2) Moderately severely neglected personal hygiene, with evidence of need for bathing and attention to her general appearance.

Her teeth were caked, and after the exam the nurses asked her to brush them and to bathe. She told the nurse assigned to her, "The towels might need burning after I bathe."

During the next three weeks, Catherine sat alone during meals in the community dining room, where patients and staff were served on a cafeteria line. She had five roommates, and she complained about the noise they made at night. She asked me to change her room so she could be alone. The hospital was nearly full, and I saw no reason to help her bypass the reality of ward life. She talked about the same old things with me, mostly about her sense of badness, and worried constantly about where she was going to store her pie.

In the first of our once-a-week meetings, I asked the nurses to let her go her own way, which meant to not unduly force her to attend occupational therapy or ward outings if she preferred not to. I wanted to see if she would participate on her own. The hospital was small and well staffed, making it difficult for patients to hide. As it turned out, Catherine did attend all hospital activities, including patient–staff meetings, but she rarely said anything during them.

Toward the end of Catherine's first month at Westwood, things took an interesting turn. The occupational therapist wrote the following note:

> She said she felt good, and that she was going to use the color blue on her next drawing as it was her favorite color. All of Catherine's drawings at UCLA were in black and white. She seems to need reassurance, but wants to do things by herself, without someone standing over her. She said this applies when she goes into the pantry for a piece of pie, too. She drew a picture for her mother "with blue eyes so that my mother won't have to wait until I open my eyes."

Catherine said nothing of this to me.

Change was in the air. Catherine talked more freely with the nurses and other patients, and she began to speak up at group therapy meetings. Her face looked less frightened, more relaxed. Perhaps our long years of work were paying off.

On August 16, a month and a half after her admission to Westwood, she came in, sat down, and was silent as usual for quite a while. She told me that something strange had been happening to her over the past several days: "My eyelids are fluttering in a way I can't control."

A few minutes later she suddenly opened her eyelids. She stared wide-eyed at me, and then at the room, slowly looking up and down.

"How do things look?" I asked.

"I don't know."

My underreaction surprised me. Rather than being thrilled by this sign of progress, I was just keenly interested. It was strange to watch her fluttering her eyelids for a few minutes, then see them—pop!—open up like two snap-up window shades.

After a few minutes Catherine said, "Everything looks very strange. The table and chairs are floating. It's eerie. My face feels . . . not together. I don't know where my face is. I'm seeing through my mouth." Catherine probed her face, touching her nose and mouth with her fingertips.

At the end of our session, Catherine retreated to her room for an hour, then walked into the dayroom. A chorus of voices greeted her: "Catherine!"

"Wow, Cathy," exclaimed Anne Levey, one of Catherine's roommates. "Your eyes, they're open!"

"Yes."

"What do you see?"

"Everybody looks upside down."

"Like we're standing on our heads?"

"I don't know if I'm upside down or you are."

That afternoon Catherine sat for three hours on the patio and stared at the grass and the solitary fig tree planted in the middle of the lawn. Tears welled up in her eyes. One of the nurses quietly sat down beside her, and Catherine said, "I can't believe it. For years I've had eyes inside my head, not looking out. I can see reality. Outside reality."

I could hardly contain my excitement the next day. "What do you think happened?"

"About a week ago I started seeing colors inside my head," she answered. "What I mean is a *feeling* of a color. I didn't actually see red or blue. Colors are feeling tones. I was aware there was a patio here at the hospital, and grass. That brought back childhood feelings of going camping. I wanted to pursue feeling, in spite of the voices."

The next day a nurse wrote the following note:

She is very, very personable, talking openly about her feelings and able
to carry on interesting sociable conversations. Expressed how spooky
and frightening it was to see things again. She did appear to be enjoying

herself in that she was receiving a great deal of positive feedback from other patients and staff. She asked some nurses to eat lunch with her and she was tremendously talkative (for Catherine), cracking jokes and talking about her past. She said, "I still like my pie, but it's not what it used to be." Very anxious to go home on pass to "see" her family. She said she doesn't want to go back to where she was, down inside herself: "I'd rather do myself in." On the whole she seemed quite pleased with herself, but also quite anxious with her new life.

That same day, the nurse on the evening shift noted the following:

> Her eyes were open all evening. Catherine washed her hair and asked me about current hair styles. She said she is too impatient to sit and get her hair done, but she might try to do her own. She is also asking what clothes are in style because she will be going shopping with her mother tomorrow. She ate alone, but approached other patients in the dining room, and she allowed some staff members to sit with her after she finished eating. Later she was sitting on the patio and asked other patients about clothes and styles. She attended the group meeting for a short while, but said nothing. Overall, a good evening.

The night nurse wrote: "Wearing mascara and eyeliner. Her eyes are open more often, and she flutters them open and closed. Then she slept without pulling the covers completely over herself, as she usually did."

The following day, I opened the session: "Everyone is pretty excited, including me."

"Changing hospitals scared me to death. I thought I would no longer have a place for my pie or they would not let me eat what I wanted to. I thought I would have to kill myself. At UCLA I fought the nurses, and they fought me. They even chased me when I sneaked food into my room.

"Here no one pushes me. If I feel like wandering around, it's okay. All the staff are nice to me. The nurses have never searched my room for food; they just come in and say that it is against the rules to have food in your room. At first I thought, 'I'll show you,' and I hid food. But they never did search, so I wondered what was the use of hiding it. It wasn't important any more. The lack of pressure here has taken away my whole system of negativity.

"When I first came here, I was paralyzed. I had my own corner in the cafeteria where I sat. And of course no one wanted to eat with me because I looked so strange. I just sat there and it was going good, too good in fact. I was getting bored. One day I was sitting there and a nurse was fixing my hair, and for some reason I was able to comprehend more what people were saying. Before, my voices were so consuming that what people were saying was not too comprehensible. Little by little I was beginning to understand what they were saying. Then I began feeling colors, like I told you."

Catherine's changes seemed sudden and dramatic. But behavior—action—is the last step in the process of change, most of which takes place within a person's internal world, slowly, over much time. For example, talking with me, and others, created a small change within Catherine—she discovered that she would not be annihilated by this sharing. So, she was emboldened to reveal, and to try to understand, her deeper terrors. As her fears lessened, a process that took years, she began to feel the need to expand her world. Each tiny step along the way created a base from which she climbed to the next.

Catherine had fought the nurses at UCLA not because they were more restrictive than the nurses at Westwood, but because she experienced a sense of power, an identity, by resisting their demands. Perhaps that resistance was equivalent to an adolescent's rebellion. But human beings, by nature, strive to grow and develop. After a time, Catherine's unchanging identity became tiresome. After she had been at Westwood for a while, she was ready to open her eyes, both figuratively and literally.

Catherine wanted to spend a night at home. I quickly approved. I wanted to encourage her to make contact with the world outside the hospital. That way, she could learn about normal living. She immediately called home. Her sister Theresa, now thirteen years old, answered the phone.

"Hi, Theresa? This is Cathy. My eyes are open! Go tell Mother my eyes are open!"

"Wow!" Theresa dropped the phone and ran to tell Florence. "Mom! It's Cathy! Her eyes are open!"

"Where is she?"

"She's on the phone. From the hospital!"

"Cathy?" Florence said, picking up the phone, "It's true?"

"Yes, mother. My eyes are open. I can come home for an overnight visit this Friday."

"You can?"

"Yes, Mother. I know you're shocked."

"I can hardly believe it."

"Can you come to pick me up Friday, around noon?"

"We'll be there."

Florence arrived at the hospital that Friday, with Theresa. When Catherine walked into the day room, Theresa jumped straight up—her feet literally left the floor. After she landed, she ran and grabbed Catherine around the waist. Florence got up slowly, and hugged Catherine carefully, as if either she or Catherine might crack. "Do I have my daughter back?"

"I'm right here, Mother."

On the drive home, Florence was mostly silent, while Theresa kept up a nonstop chatter. "Wow, you've been in the mental hospital a long time. What was it like in there? Are you out for good now? You have to go back? Nana's waiting at home for you."

It was Nana's eighty-second birthday that day. As soon as Catherine walked in the front door, she reached out and cupped Catherine's face in her hands, tears running down her cheeks. "You are my birthday present, Cathy, my granddaughter coming home."

Bunny, now fifteen, was with her boyfriend, Mickey. "Hi, Cathy," she said as she embraced Catherine. "It's good to see you here."

"I'm really glad to be here."

Joe walked up and put his arm around Catherine's shoulder, pulling her sideways to him. "How's it going, kiddo?"

"Fine, Dad."

Michael was at a motorcycle-racing track. Cindy and her husband came over for dinner. Cindy wanted to know how Catherine saw things now. "What's different?"

"I'm back, but I'm not. I'm changed. I don't know exactly how. I'm having a hard time keeping my thoughts straight. My thinking is slowed, so I'm having a hard time answering your questions."

Florence rose. "Well, let's not worry about it. Let's just have dinner."

"I'm still not eating too much," Catherine said. "I think all I want is some salad and dessert."

"That's all right," Florence quickly replied. "That's all right."

That evening Catherine seemed to sniff every corner of the house. She burrowed into her bedroom closet, and pored over the 1968 Tustin High yearbook. That night, as she lay in bed, she could hear Bunny's radio. *Are they voices?* she asked herself. "Kill Theresa," several voices said in unison. Catherine got up and knocked on Bunny's door.

"Cathy. Do you want to talk?" Bunny asked.

"No. If it won't make you mad at me, I just wanted to know if . . . you could turn down your radio?"

"Oh sure. I didn't even think. There you are in the next room. Sure."

Back in bed the voices retreated.

The next morning, Florence and Catherine went to the market. Catherine found herself rolling cans over and over to see how many calories were in each.

"Cathy, are you still on your diet?"

"At the hospital I'm able to forget about it sometimes. But here, I keep thinking about calories."

The next day, as Catherine was about to leave with Florence for the hospital, Joe, his eyes red, asked her, "Will you be coming back soon?"

"I'll talk with Dr. Dorman, but I think he'll let me. Yes. I'll be back, maybe for a whole weekend."

On Monday morning, I asked her, "How did it go?"

"They were glad to see me. I was glad to see them too, but . . . the voices got louder."

"Tell me what was going on."

"It was at night. Bunny was playing her radio. I wanted to ask her to turn it down, but at first I thought she'd get really mad at me. Finally I got up and knocked on her door. She didn't mind at all. Then the voices were softer."

"I'll bet you were getting angry thinking she would be angry at you. Maybe more to the point, you thought you didn't have a right to ask. That's what made you angry."

"I think you're right. There was something else. I felt like I was in the twilight zone being there. Not only did the voices get louder, I felt I should be on my strict diet. The old me was there and so was a different me."

"Well, there are two of you, so to speak. I don't mean literally there are two of you—just an old identity and a newer one. It doesn't surprise me that the old one returned. You felt insecure at home. You had no way to ask for anything for yourself. You were left with rage and voices. You had returned to the scene of the old you."

"I did. But I'd like to visit again, maybe for a weekend?"

"I think that would be a good idea. We all have old and new identities. Part of the complexity of building a new identity is to know that the old one is part of you. I'll arrange for a weekend pass."

"Thank you."

Catherine began listening to music, played cards with patients, danced, and wore some new, better-fitting clothes instead of her shapeless dresses. She gave playing cards depicting a round, yellow smiling face on one side to everyone. She gave me one of these cards, the king of spades. She had chosen it for me, she said, because, "You call a spade a spade." She also began to use an exercise machine. At the end of August, two months after her admission to Westwood, she announced that she was going to have "no more pie."

But Catherine also told the nurses that she felt precarious about her new self. She was still hearing voices, and she was afraid she might slip back "down" again. During her sessions with me, she focused largely on how strange she felt. Her entire perceptual apparatus was turned on its side. People seemed to be moving in slow motion. Objects were distorted—elongated, moving, insubstantial, and floating. She grew hypersensitive to light.

Her experience reminded me of a study done in 1932, by M. von Senden. This physician examined sixty-three people between the ages of three and forty-three who had been born blind and then had their sight restored through surgery for congenital cataracts. None of these people experienced sight wholly as a blessing. It turned out that though they now had vision, what they saw looked distorted to them. Learning to see became a laborious and painful process that took years and that caused profound mental anguish and confusion. Some of the patients actually expressed the wish to be blind again. Dr. von Senden reported that "the newly operated patients do not localize their visual impressions. They do not relate them to any point, either to the eye or to any surface. . . . They see colors as we smell an odor of paint or varnish, which enfolds us or intrudes upon us, but without occupying any specific form . . . in a more definable way." One woman could not be certain that her new visual sensations were coming through her eyes until she closed her lids.

Catherine had not been blind and then suddenly supplied with vision. Nonetheless, she had tried to shut down her feelings as a child, and to stop her entire perceptual apparatus from functioning when she reached age seventeen. Now, as she became flooded with new sensations, she experienced distorted perceptions and confusion.

One day, in a group-therapy meeting, a young man told Catherine, "You look like you've just come back from the dead, the way you stare at everything."

"I have. Nothing makes sense. I've been thinking of jumping through that plate-glass window. I'll do it. Then I'll know what I'm feeling."

John White, an artist who worked as an aide, was the group leader. The patients adored him. He always seemed to put his finger on what was going on, in a gentle, direct way. Some of the patients had talked about how looking directly at Catherine was "creepy," since she rarely blinked. John looked directly at her and said, "Cathy, I want you to know that I'm not going to let you run through the window. You are safe here. And I should say to the group that Cathy's feeling of wanting to jump out of her skin is normal, given how withdrawn she has been. Perhaps as she becomes more familiar with the healthy side of her that is emerging, she will feel better."

Several weeks passed. Catherine retreated somewhat to her earlier seclusion. In her meetings with me, she described how frightening it was to experience perceptual disorientation. She told me how "weird" she felt, "not human," looking at objects that seemed to freeze in motion, or at people moving in stop-start-stop fashion.

I thought that Catherine would put her perceptions back in order if she continued using them. The danger was the temptation to retreat back behind her wall. Patients who make gains, however, are loath to give them up; they know how devastating it is to go back to their imprisonment.

After several months, some of the distortion Catherine experienced began to fade, but she was still perplexed. She often twisted her jaws and lips, trying to produce sensation there so as to locate her mouth—similar to the blind woman who shut her eyes to register the source of light sensations. Catherine told me, "I have damaged my brain. I can't think like normal people. There is no flow. I think like a broken movie reel." Her conviction that her brain had been damaged was understandable. Her brain indeed was not working well. She had great difficulty reading. Only one word would register at a time, making it hard for her to comprehend sentences.

During one session she said, "I am bombarded with feelings. It is both wonderful and horrible. I can feel one me trying to get back down, and the new me saying, 'No, don't go back.' Other patients and the staff are very kind and helpful. Their kindness makes me feel human. But I am so overwhelmed that most of the time all I can do is to sit and rock back and forth."

The next day I began the session with: "You look sad."

She softly cried. "Yes, I am. I have to learn how to use my brain again. I don't know if I can. I don't even know the basics—how to smile, how to talk about normal things. All I know is to talk about food or complain. You are not right when you say I'm just like a little child. I am not *like* a little child; I *am* a little child. My growing-up years are over. I can't go back and do it again. I'll never catch up with other people. I'm finished."

Catherine's sadness seemed different from what I had seen before. At UCLA she had cried, and she was withdrawn, but more in the fashion of a frightened child. Now she looked despairing. Her movements slowed, and she sat still and quiet. She began reading her Bible, and the nurses frequently observed her on her knees, her elbows resting on her bed and her hands clasped in prayer. Her extreme religiosity had been her last line of defense before she became overtly psychotic at seventeen, and she returned to this familiar protection.

Catherine told the nurses she did not know what she was feeling. She tried to express herself, but found it difficult. Not being able to verbalize her feelings frightened her. She walked about grimacing and twisting her mouth into all sorts of shapes. She told me that this was an effort to "find a way to connect which feeling went with an appropriate facial expression, and with what word." She also started walking about the hospital with an odd, fixed smile. It appeared to me that she was genuinely attempting to be friendly, so she plastered on a smile.

Many of the patients, from nineteen-year-olds admitted for their first psychotic break to sixty-year-olds suffering from depression, rallied to help Catherine. On a group outing to the Los Angeles County Museum of Art, these patients explained what the paintings meant to them and pulled Catherine into the discussions. A grandmotherly patient, on a trip to the Los Angeles Zoo, treated Catherine as if she were three years old, naming the animals. Catherine did not mind this. She told me that she felt as if she "belonged."

Four months after her admission to Westwood, Catherine began to venture out of the hospital without a staff member along. She went out for breakfast, and for walks, with other patients. I arranged for a social worker, Sandy Trout, to come twice a week to the hospital to take Catherine out shopping. Sandy also took her on buses, to restaurants, and helped her to get familiar with being out in the city.

Catherine began to spend entire weekends at home. During these weekends, her family treated her as if she were made of porcelain. Florence and Joe showed no excitement; they only told Catherine that it was "nice" to have her home. When Theresa, on Catherine's first weekend visit home shouted, "Hey! All right!" her parents quickly hushed her. Cindy came over, and the family members all talked about their home lives, as if to update Catherine on events she had missed. And, before Florence took Catherine back to the hospital on Sundays, she and Catherine went to brunch, as had been their custom for the past three years.

In the midst of this general atmosphere of change, Catherine still heard voices telling her to kill her mother, me, and others whom she liked. Her speech was still very slow and precise. She often sat slowly rocking back and forth, and she continued her wide-eyed stare. Although she began to ask some staff members how she might gain some weight, she still counted calories and insisted on a ready availability of sweets.

A student nurse's note read: "Participated in volleyball and slimnastics. Seems to be upset throughout the day, hiding her face in her hands. She says she is hearing voices and has 'so many feelings mixed up, I can't sort them.' Her speech varies; it slows, then increases, as she talks."

It was November 29, 1972, nearly five months after Catherine had left UCLA. In her session with me that day, I watched her twist her mouth and purse her lips. "What's wrong?" I asked.

"I don't know what's wrong. Everyone is always asking. When I am feeling things, whatever that is, I make faces. I don't know what it is. It's confusing. A million things are going on all at once. I don't even recognize my family or me."

"What are you thinking about your family?'

"What are you talking about? It's hard enough for me to just keep straight what I'm telling you, let alone answering you!" Catherine put her chin down upon her chest and looked at the floor. "I only know a nothingness when my voices speak. It is just empty. But I won't go back. I feel like I did when I was getting sick." Tears began to trickle down her cheeks. "I don't know what's next or where it will go. I was at home and my hand just grabbed a knife and I put it to my stomach. I wish I could just feel something. I would rather have stakes through my hands than this. What I have inside are pinpricks instead of feeling. Maybe that's what is meant by Jesus' crown of thorns. People who cry and have normal feeling don't know how lucky they are. I put them away and have gone to a dead, no-feeling place."

During the next session, she sat in silence, but for two sentences: "I want to know how the world works, and how I'm supposed to work. I have no idea."

In mid-December, just after sitting down for a session, Catherine said, "I don't know anything about sex. Maybe I should go to a topless bar or see a pornographic movie."

"Well, that's an idea. You've been trying . . ."

"I watched a couple kiss in the hallway. I always thought that just occurred in movies. Now I am seeing it up close for real. When they use their tongues, ugh." She sat and thought. "The only thing I ever wanted was pie and food."

"I guess you've used your tongue to taste food instead of people."

Catherine smiled.

In another session later that week, Catherine said, "Angry words like 'shut up' and 'damn it' just escape my mouth. My roommates were talking all night long last night, and I couldn't help saying 'shut up' over and over. I can't seem to stop talking, either." A few moments of silence passed. "My voices—something is happening. They are not as loud. They have been in the background yesterday and today, just like the background whispering before I was hospitalized at St. Joseph's. Do you think they will ever go away?"

"Catherine, I think you are undergoing real change, not just behavioral change. What I mean is that you're talking more to everyone. You told me that you are feeling more feeling, if I can say it that way. As you speak and feel more, there is less need for the voices."

I detected a faint smile. "I hope so," she said

A few days later, Catherine said, "I only have a few normal feelings, mostly good ones toward members of my family. How do I convert my private thought-world into reality? What is a feeling anyway? Everything still is so bizarre and strange. I saw a fellow on the ward 'eye' a girl and I knew he was giving her the eye. I went up and asked him if that was true, and he said it was."

"That's an example of understanding a real thing or feeling in someone else—that is, to correlate what is going on *in* you with what is going on *outside* of you."

Catherine's comment about the fellow who gave a girl the eye illustrates the great difficulty she had understanding reality. One must know oneself in order to understand others, and she was only just beginning to clarify her sense of self.

Just before Christmas, Catherine asked me why she was having "visions."

"What visions?"

"I see all sorts of things. I see an empty shell, floating in space. I see a shadow of myself. I see a bleeding heart. I see ghosts—my grandmother and my grandfather—at night. I see death."

"They're projections. I think your visions are the same kind of phenomenon as your voices. They represent your feelings. You never really developed, so you feel empty. An empty shell. Or you have a shadow, but no substance. You are sad—your heart is bleeding. But instead of feeling those things, you see them. Seeing seems to be a step toward feeling."

"I'll never catch up."

There was a small kitchen just off the ward, and Catherine asked Ann Lefkandi, one of the nurses, to help her learn to cook. "Sure," Ann said. "What do you want to cook?"

"I don't know."

"Want to start with salad?"

"That's fine."

"Grab your jacket and we'll drive over to the market." Once at the supermarket, Ann steered Catherine to the produce section. "There are lots of different kinds of lettuce. Iceberg lettuce has no taste, but it's crunchy. Romaine has a slightly bitter taste. Boston lettuce is good and so is this red-topped lettuce. Let's get some of that. You can mix in anything you want. Do you like onions?"

"No."

"How about radishes? They're just a little tangy. And we need some tomatoes."

"Okay."

"Great. Now, we need dressing. Look at all this: honey-mustard, garlic. Want me to pick?"

"Yep."

"Fine. Personally, I like oil and balsamic vinegar. Now I think Greek olive oil is the very best, but that makes the Italians mad. Most of the olive oil for sale here is Italian. Ah-hah: There's a bottle with Greek letters. Let's try it. Balsamic vinegar is an Italian specialty. The longer it ages, the better it is. Whew. Here's some that's six years old—too high priced for me. Okay if we start with one for the common folks?"

Back at the hospital, Ann and Catherine tore up the lettuce and sliced radishes and tomatoes. "Everyone has a different formula. For my taste, I like just a splash of balsamic vinegar. Gives a salad a delicate touch."

"This is awful nice of you."

"Think nothing of it. We've all been talking about how much progress you've made and how you'll want your own place soon. You have to know how to cook. We'll do this again, okay? I'll show you how to prepare some simple meals. You'll catch on."

"Thanks."

Catherine spent Christmas week with her family. In our first session afterward, she said, "I talked with my mother, and she said a bond was bought for me when my dad was killed. It could be cashed to help me with rent if I leave the hospital. Do you think I'm ready to leave?"

"Catherine, I do. I think the only way to learn about the world is to be *in* the world. I actually think it would be wonderful for you."

Each day, Tamako Uyema and Judy Petrosian, both nurses, went through the apartments-for-rent classified advertisements with Catherine. Then Catherine walked through the area or drove to look at apartments with her mother. Catherine wanted to live close to the hospital, so she could walk there to attend the day-treatment program for patients two or three evenings a week. The program consisted of group therapy, talks with staff members, and some recreational activities, like volleyball and table tennis. All of this offered Catherine a way to preserve some familiarity as well as a place to talk with others about her new experiences.

Catherine located a furnished, second-floor, one-room studio apartment that rented for $130 a month and that overlooked a small, courtyard pool. The sofa converted into a bed, and Florence bought her an electric hot plate. "It's a castle," Catherine told me. She applied for Social Security Supplemental Income disability insurance, which would pay $198 a month. Florence offered to contribute $100 a month for the first four months and $50 a month thereafter. Catherine secured the apartment to begin February 1.

On Catherine's last day, Tamako told the other patients that Catherine was an example to all. John White told her the hardest part was yet to come, but "you can do it. Look at what you've already done." Many of the patients hugged Catherine goodbye. A newly admitted patient, a woman about thirty, told Catherine, "Good luck. It's a jungle out there. Don't give those motherfuckers any reason to send you back here." On the way to the car, Catherine looked back to see some of the staff members wiping away tears. She waved.

Six

Escape from the Prison of the Dead

Who are you two who climb by the dark stream
to escape the eternal prison of the dead?
Who led you? Or what served you as a light
in your dark flight from the eternal valley,
which lies forever blind in darkest night?
Are the laws of the pit so broken? Or is new counsel
published in Heaven that the damned may wander
onto my rocks from the abyss of Hell?

Dante, The Purgatorio

ONCE CATHERINE HAD MOVED to her new apartment, Florence, often accompanied by Cindy, visited on weekends and took care of what was needed. The three women went shopping for kitchen utensils and cleaning supplies and then, just as in the old days, stopped for a late breakfast or lunch at the International House of Pancakes. On that first Sunday, as they were driving home, Catherine asked Florence and Cindy, "What does motherfucker mean?" Cindy opened her mouth, but Florence replied, "It's a nasty word. The nastiest word I've ever heard!" Florence then switched the conversation to Nana's health.

Catherine explored her new neighborhood, which included a market three blocks away. She spent a lot of time in the bakery department, walking back and forth past the desserts and pastries, "just to feel something familiar," she told me. She walked up to Santa Monica Boulevard, about a mile away, and investigated the mostly small neighborhood shops: the hardware store, tile store, a motorcycle shop, and clothing boutiques and restaurants. Twice a week, she ate breakfast at one family-style restaurant, frequented mostly by seniors, loading her usual Belgian waffle with butter and maple-flavored syrup. "I can pig out," she told me, "since I burn off the calories walking." From time to time, her landlords, an English couple, invited Catherine to have a jigger of Scotch. She told them about her hospitalization of over three years and how this was the first time she had ever lived on her own. They repeated, over and over, "Oh, you poor dear," and "My, you've come a long way, haven't you?"

Every weekday, by bus, Catherine came to see me. Halfway between my office and her apartment was a commercial center, not far from UCLA. The center was often thronged with students. Catherine sometimes got off the bus there after she saw me, ate dinner, and strolled around. Nearby was a nightclub, called Earth and Fire, where a rock band played on Friday and Saturday nights. The habitués were a mix of college students and biker types. The club looked like a barn, with a dance floor in the middle, a raised stage for the band at one end, and a wooden bar with neon signs advertising beer brands all around. A faint haze of marijuana hung in the air. Catherine occasionally went in, ordered Perrier water with a twist of lemon, watched people dance, and then walked home.

"Being on my own is the greatest thing ever," Catherine told me. "At night, about eight-thirty, I go for a walk in the neighborhood. I have nowhere to go in particular. I am aware of things other than the voices—the smell at night, the darkness, and the apartments and houses with lights on. I go to bed feeling good."

"That's so good."

"But I can feel the pull to cloister myself in the apartment, or to run to the hospital. I'm scared. Sometimes I feel like just running away—to where I don't know."

"What are you scared of?"

"I feel like I'm in outer space. Nothing is familiar. I expect all sorts of negative things—I was so negative growing up. Like I think I'll meet someone on the street and he, or she, will call me ugly."

A week later, Catherine was contemplative. "I don't know how to place what I feel about you. There is father love, mother love, and husband love. I do depend on you. And it is like . . . love."

"Our relationship, it's pretty close. I've been your ally for a long time now. Affection—love—seems pretty natural given something good happening in a relationship."

Catherine stared at me for a few moments. "I depend on you more now than before."

On another day, she told me she still had trouble matching up her facial movements and expressions with what she thought her feelings should be. "I'm always asking other people what they are feeling and I watch their faces. I watch television and try to imitate their faces, and I watch the faces of people on the bus." One Sunday, while driving near where Catherine lived, I spotted her walking along. She looked odd: she swung her arms, but also held them stiffly. She appeared to be forcing herself to swing her arms. She had a kind of forced grin, too. To avoid embarrassing her, I said nothing of my seeing her.

Two evenings a week, Catherine participated in the day-treatment program. Nurses, aides, and other patients seemed concerned that she did not look "normal" enough for the world. Her baggy dresses, unkempt hair, and gawky appearance were no big deal in the hospital. Tamako Uyema accompanied her to a hair stylist. Tamako and Judy Petrosian were the nurses who had helped Catherine look for an apartment. "Cut it just like hers," Catherine told the stylist. Tamako showed Catherine how to blow-dry her hair and to use "just enough" hair spray. Judy bought Catherine a book about the female body. "You are very childlike," Judy told Catherine. "Tamako and I want to talk with you about sex and how to avoid getting pregnant."

"I'm just having a few sensations. I'm not ready . . ."

"You will be soon enough. We're worried you'll get into trouble."

In one of the group-therapy sessions held on Wednesday evenings, a young man said, "Catherine, you smile too much. Guys will get the wrong message."

"I don't know how to stop it," Catherine retorted.

After the group meeting, John White, the aide much adored by patients, took Catherine aside. "Cathy, I know your smile is not intended to be some kind of message to anybody. You're just struggling with figuring out how to feel. The problem is that out there in the world, facial expression conveys meaning to other people. I think some members of the group are responding to what happens when you smile at men. Some men may read your smile as an invitation to approach you."

"Thanks, John. You understand a lot."

At another group meeting, Mary McGinnis, a patient, suggested taking Catherine to Charlie Brown's, a pick-up bar in Marina Del Rey, "for experience." Everybody thought it was a good idea.

At the bar, Mary said, "Let's order some wine. I'll have some Chardonnay. What do you want?"

"I've never ordered wine before."

"Hey, try Chardonnay."

"This is exciting. There are so many people here. Why are they all standing packed together around the bar?"

"The meat rack. Guys and girls come here to meet. Standing makes it easier to go from one to the next."

After dinner, as the two walked toward Mary's car, two young men stepped out and blocked their way. "Get lost," Mary immediately said.

"Just looking for a little action," slurred one.

Mary rose to her full height of five foot two. "Get it in the bathroom."

"Fuck you, bitch."

On the way back, Mary told Catherine how she had suffered incest at the hands of her uncle when she was ten to fourteen. "You have to be firm with men, or they'll charge right at you. Don't get me wrong. Sex is fine. But men think with their pricks."

Every morning Catherine read from Psalm 121: "I will lift mine eyes towards the mountains, whence help will come to me. My help is from the Lord, who made heaven and earth. May He not suffer your foot to slip; He slumbers not who guards you. Indeed he neither slumbers nor sleeps, the guardian of Israel. The Lord is your guardian; the Lord is your shade; He is beside you at your life. The Lord will guard both your coming and your going, both now and forever." Each evening she repeated Psalm 23: "The Lord is my shepherd . . ." or Psalm 91, "You shall not fear the terror by night or the arrow that flies by day—not the pestilence that roams in darkness nor the devastating plague at noon." She told me that as she walked through the neighborhood at night, coming back from the hospital or just enjoying the city, she spoke aloud from one of the Psalms to avoid being "spooked." Alone in her apartment at night, to drown out the voices, she played songs by the Rolling Stones, the Kinks, or the Moody Blues on a small tabletop tape deck.

Sandy Trout wanted to teach Catherine about living alone. Sandy also operated an "enrichment center," a supervised gathering of old folks. Catherine spent two or three afternoons a week at the center.

"You received your Social Security Disability check yesterday, didn't you?" Sandy asked Catherine.

"Yes."

"Maybe today, then, I'll teach you about banking. Let's go open a checking account. You know what that is?"

"Sure. I had a life—once."

"Oh, I know. You told me the other day I treat you like you don't know anything. I'm sorry. But you *are* schizophrenic. I think you need some socialization skills."

"I do, but . . ."

"Off we go to the Bank of America."

Sandy also counseled Catherine about posture: "Catherine, you just have to get your head up. What's it doing down there? You're always hunched over. It's not feminine. Throw you chest out. That's it. We'll go to some restaurants. We can practice posture and table etiquette. I'm going to make a reservation at Lawry's. They have the best prime rib. Doesn't that sound good?"

"Well, I don't eat very much, you know."

At the restaurant Catherine said she wasn't hungry. "Just a salad, please."

"It's okay. Order what you want. We're here to learn about dining out. See how they place the silverware? I'll write it down for you." A tuxedoed waiter glided by and whisked Catherine's napkin into her lap. "You're supposed to do that, right when you sit down," Sandy instructed Catherine. The waiter returned, placing salads in front of them. "Try not to take big bites. And try not to let anything drop from your fork back onto the plate. It's not ladylike. Some women never order salad on a date because it's so awkward to eat. I think you're doing fine. Keep your head up."

Catherine, her eyes downcast, shook her head to her right. "There's a man at a table over there. He looks like Robert Redford, and he's looking at you."

"How do you know it's not you he's looking at?"

"Oh, I'm weird."

The gentleman, at that moment, got up and approached Sandy and Catherine. He looked first at Catherine, then addressed both: "Hello. I just wanted to wish you a great day. Have a great lunch."

"We are, thanks," Sandy replied as the man turned to leave.

While waiting for the car, Sandy asked Catherine, "Did my little pretty have a good time?"

"I've never been to fancy restaurants before. If you take a sip of water, someone comes by and fills the glass."

"That's proper service. Oops, here's the car. Let the valet open the door for you."

Sandy thought Catherine could learn some social skills at the old folks' center. Seven or eight ladies, all over seventy, showed up at the center, located on Fairfax Boulevard in a district of Los Angeles where many Orthodox Jews lived. Many of them spoke with a thick Yiddish accent. Catherine told me, "They treat me like their grandchildren. What does 'sweet punim' mean?"

"Ha. It means sweet face," I told her.

Sandy also took Catherine out shopping for food. There were a number of kosher markets near the center. Sandy, Catherine, and Angeline, a social-work intern who worked for Sandy, prepared lunch for all. "Hey pal, how are you doing?" Angeline asked Catherine.

"Fine," Catherine replied.

"You and I, we'll have to do some swinging one of these nights. Can't learn what you need to know playing cards with these folks. What do you think of that, pal?"

"I'd have to ask Sandy."

"Oh, no, don't do that. I know some dance clubs, whenever you're ready."

Sandy, Catherine, and sometimes Angeline went shopping to get Catherine "properly dressed." "Your clothes are a little too old for you," Angeline told her. "Actually, you're still in the 1950s—enough of those floppy skirts. You need something hip. Tight jeans and an open blouse. But you've got to gain some weight. You've got to have something to put into a blouse."

At the end of April, Catherine told me, "You know I'm going shopping and exploring the city with Sandy two days a week. It's been helpful, but she treats me like a child, a child who is liked, but still a child, which makes me angry. Don't get me wrong, I like her. She's helping me pick out some clothes—she told me I dress like an old lady. In the afternoons I meet her at the old people's group. I like all the people there. I play cards and talk with them. But I'm tiring of it. I think I've outgrown it. It was important at first, just after I got out of Westwood. Do you think I can stop going?"

"Why don't we follow your instincts? You've outgrown it, so stop. Do you want to tell her?"

"Okay, I will. I'll be altogether on my own. Well, I'm still going to group therapy two days a week. What do you think about that?"

"What do you think?" I asked.

"Maybe in a few weeks."

Catherine was becoming a regular at Earth and Fire. Customers, waiters, and the bartender always greeted her. She wore her usual: a long-sleeved white blouse with the top two buttons unbuttoned, blue jeans, brown leather camping-style boots and a red-and-white bandanna around her forehead, tied in back. She never initiated any contact, but always within fifteen minutes of her arrival, someone asked her to dance. She was pretty relaxed and animated out on the dance floor. She told me she liked to dance with black men because they were "not inhibited." One of these men once asked Catherine to go drinking with him afterward. When Catherine refused, he accused her of being a racist. Catherine felt she had hurt his feelings, so she spent the rest of that evening dancing just with him. On another evening, two young men asked her to dance at the same time. They began gesturing and nipping at each other like two bull sea lions, then went outside to settle it while Catherine sat at the bar, wordless.

Stanley Markovitz, a twenty-one-year-old film student at the University of Southern California, worked part-time as a waiter at the club. Tall, with soft blue eyes, he wore his blond-brown hair down to his shoulders. He always looked a degree out of plumb, though. Perhaps it was his too-short, wrinkled pants, or his shirt, which always hung half out. "Hey, Catherine, how's it going? The usual?" he'd ask, before she sat down.

"Yes, please," Catherine always replied.

One afternoon, she walked to the club at five-thirty. The place was deserted. Stanley brought her a Perrier with a twist, and sat down across from her. "Mind if I visit?"

"That would be okay."

"I was thinking. Maybe we could go to a movie sometime. There's a real good one at the Royal; you know they show art flicks there. Have you seen *Sounder*?"

"No."

"Whew. It's really, really good; it's about real people. I hope I can make a film like that someday. Could we go?"

"I'd like to."

"Hey, great. What do you think about this Friday? I'm off. I know it shows at seven o'clock. I've seen it once before, but I want to see it again, to get all the subtleties, you know. It's a tear-jerker."

"Friday would be good."

"I'll be by at six-thirty. Hey, where do you live?"

"Here, I'll write it down. I live on Barry Avenue, not far away."

"Great. I'll see you at six-thirty. Well, here they come. Back to work. You want another? On the house."

"Yes, thank you."

Stanley arrived at Catherine's apartment promptly at six-thirty in his dented 1958 Buick station wagon. After the movie, he asked, "Would you like to go somewhere to have a drink, and talk about the movie? Wasn't it great?"

"That would be fine."

"I know where there's a quiet bar."

Catherine had her Perrier and Stanley drank Heineken. "American beer tastes like water," he said, then launched into his analysis of the film. Catherine spoke not a word. An hour later, Stanley asked, "Would you like another Perrier?"

"No, thank you. It's getting late."

"Oh, well, sure. Let's go."

At the door to Catherine's apartment, Stanley held out his hand in a handshake. "Hey, I've had a real good time. Maybe we could do this again sometime?"

"That would be good."

"Great. Good night, then. I'll see you at Earth and Fire."

"Good night."

Stanley took Catherine to a Japanese restaurant on their second date. Again she was silent but for an occasional, "Thank you." Stanley talked about the health benefits of eating sushi. Catherine just nibbled. She announced, "It's getting late" as he was paying the bill, and he took her home. A week later, they went to an Ingmar Bergman movie. Catherine thought him a gentleman because he opened the car door for her. After Catherine opened her apartment door that evening, she turned to thank him, and he kissed her lightly on the lips. "Good night."

"I didn't know how to react," she told me. "I told him, 'God bless you.'"

Stanley still greeted Catherine as he always had at Earth and Fire, but he did not sit down to visit and did not ask her out again.

"What do you think?" I asked her.

"He was nice."

"I mean, these are your first dates."

"I don't know what to think. I can barely think. I'm not a man or a woman. I'm a neuter."

"*He* thought you were a woman. Going out with men will help confirm you are a woman."

"I was always fearful of men. Not that I was going to be hurt, but that they wouldn't like me. When I first started experimenting with eye makeup in the seventh and eighth grades, my parents talked about how cheap I looked. My father always used to say I looked like a whore, and he made fun of my hips when I was developing. I had the feeling only bad women wore mascara and makeup."

"That's certainly not true. It's confusing now, but you'll get it."

One day, on the bus coming to see me, Catherine met Rhonda Markham, a forty-three-year-old single woman who lived nearby in a studio apartment with no furniture except for a bed. Catherine thought she was "glamorous," with her black hair gathered tightly in a bun, her bright red lipstick, and false eyelashes. Rhonda chattered on and on. Catherine listened. The two women went shopping several times and occasionally went out to dinner. They went to a variety of bars, where Catherine danced and managed to avoid drinking much alcohol. She offered a timid smile and a pleasant, "No, thank you," to offers from men to have a drink with them at home.

Catherine and Rhonda also went to a discotheque club, which held dance contests on Thursday nights. There, a man in his late twenties approached Catherine, told her that she danced well, and asked her to enter the dance contest. They won, receiving two free breakfasts and dinners at local restaurants and $100 in cash.

One evening Rhonda suggested they go to the Whiskey Barrel, a nightclub just across the street from Earth and Fire. It was a workingman's bar and a little on the seedy side. After they had been there a while, Rhonda became interested in a dark-haired, muscular, thirty-six-year-old, six-foot-tall auto-parts salesman—who seemed more interested in Catherine.

"I'm outta here. You do what you like," Rhonda sniffed as she stalked out.

The man offered to buy Catherine dinner. She told him she just liked to dance—they could go across the street to Earth and Fire. They danced until one o'clock in the morning, then he offered her a ride home. He had had a few drinks, but Catherine had stuck to her usual Perrier.

"I have a yacht," he told Catherine as they drove.

Catherine made no reply.

"I need a secretary, too. Think you might be interested? It would be for a nursery school I'm starting."

"No, thank you."

As they pulled up to Catherine's apartment, he parked across the street and shut off the motor.

"Well, thank you for the ride."

"Don't go yet. I want to talk with you about being my secretary."

He leaned over and rolled up Catherine's window, locked her door, then did the same on his side of the car.

"Why don't you want to be my secretary?" he asked as he moved over to embrace Catherine.

"I think I'll go in now."

But he was not going to be put off. He pushed her down on the front seat and tore her dress while trying to pull off her underpants. Catherine struggled, but he pressed his forearm into her neck, nearly choking her.

"You're not a horrible man. You're just angry. God knows that you're hurting."

He ripped off her underpants and pulled at his belt, unbuckling it, all the while holding Catherine down with his forearm on her neck.

"Mary loves you, Jesus loves you," she whispered.

For a moment he stopped still.

"Keep on talking," he finally said.

"God understands, Mary understands. You feel you have to do this."

As he was about to enter her, he suddenly moaned, then ejaculated. There was a short silence. Neither moved.

"I don't know what happened to me. I'm sorry." He pulled on his pants, opened the doors, and walked Catherine to her apartment.

"I'm sorry. I'm sorry," he repeated as she opened her door.

"Whew," she said to herself as she locked the door behind her. "I'm okay."

She called me at two o'clock that morning. "I've had an awful experience."

"What happened?"

"I got raped."

"*What?*"

"This man . . . I was out with Rhonda. He said he'd take me home because she left. He ripped at my clothes in the car—he wouldn't let me out. Then, I had gunk all over me. I should burn the dress—just burn it . . ."

"Are you okay? Are you hurt?"

"He tried to choke me. I'm not hurt. I feel dirty. I'm going to throw the dress away. And I'm going to take a bath."

"Do you think you'll be okay until I see you tomorrow?"

"Yes."

"Okay. I'm glad you're not hurt. What an awful thing. I'll talk to you about it tomorrow."

"Okay. Bye."

The next day, I asked her, "How are you?"

"I guess I'm okay."

"Tell me the details."

"When I first met him, he was nice. When I was about to get out of the car, he did a hundred-and-eighty-degree turn. He pushed me down and put his arm up against my neck. I thought: 'Oh my God, I'm going to die.' I thought he had the same violence I have. I hear voices to kill, and I thought he must be going through the same thing. I can sympathize with the pain, so I started to pray for him. Then he just stopped. There was this gunk all over the car and on my dress. Is that semen?"

"It is."

"Well, I've never seen or smelled semen before. I was flabbergasted. After I called you, I took an hour-and-a-half bath. Then I took another bath this morning. I was in such a hurry to get up to my apartment I left my purse in his car."

"Cathy—"

"Can I say something about your reaction?"

"Sure, do."

"I'm mad at you, because I expected you to react more, like showing anger or some show of emotion. I thought you took it too calmly."

"You're right, I didn't get angry. I must tell you, I've thought about the danger of your getting raped. I know you've been hanging around with Rhonda, and it seemed to me, she's a bit on the hard side; she likes to go to some pretty rough bars. You know, I've been walking a fine line. I want to lend you my experience. I think I've been doing that in lots of ways, but I don't want to get in the way of *your* experience by crossing the line and overprotecting you. Because you're inexperienced, I anticipated that you might not read a sexual situation correctly and might get yourself into trouble. Maybe I should rethink all this, but I thought I should restrict myself to helping you with your internal experiences. Also, you've handled so much, I thought you would handle sex, too, when it came up. Like I said, though, maybe I'm not right about my role. So to answer you, I wasn't altogether surprised. I guess that showed in my not reacting strongly. But I want you to know I'm sorry it happened. Rape is such an invasion. I'm glad you weren't hurt."

That same day, after Catherine returned from her visit with me, she found her wallet and purse on her doorstep, under the doormat.

Catherine was flooded with negative thoughts. The rape meant she was "naive," would never catch up and would let me down. Her voices, which had diminished, at least in intensity, again spoke loudly to her: "Kill yourself; kill yourself; kill your mother; kill Dr. Dorman." She told me she would be better off not trying to get better—she was crazy and would always be crazy. "I don't have too many positive thoughts," she confessed.

Then she saw an ad for sermons that promised to help "reveal your positive energy." Dr. Joseph Kelly, at the Church of Religious Science, would lead the sermons, at the Wilshire Ebell Theatre in midtown Los Angeles, which also hosted concerts and plays. Florence, Nana, and Cindy came up to attend the first service with Catherine.

Outside the church, a sign said, "A nonorthodox spiritual experience." Dr. Kelly, in his eighties, five-feet, four-inches tall and dressed in a plain blue suit, observed his audience for a few moments. Then he began speaking in a direct and assured manner, "First of all, I would like to welcome the newcomers today. I am very happy to see all of you.

"In the words of our founder, Ernest Holmes, the Science of Mind reveals that every man is a potential Christ. Every man has inherent God-power within him. And how could this God-power be used other than through his thought? Since it would be impossible for a man to act as an intelligent being unless he could first think, the very idea of man supposes a center of consciousness, a center of thought activity. The Science of Mind reveals that this center of God activity within each person is a complete and a unique manifestation of the Parent Mind: that the power of God does actually exist in man.

"It is a basic proposition in our philosophy that we live in a mental or spiritual universe and that things can be resolved into thoughts. This is the foundation upon which all scientific practice must be established. And when you are able to establish this premise in your own thought, you at once find yourself equipped with an instrument through which you can change your environment.

"We must either conclude that there is an ultimate good and an ultimate evil in the universe, or we must conclude that there is but an Ultimate, which is good. This Ultimate, by Its very nature and by our very nature, is compelled to appear to each one of us in the form of our belief. If you can accept this proposition, it will be easy enough for you to see how it is that false belief blinds humanity.

"If that which binds is false belief and not the Truth, then you will see why Jesus told us that a knowledge of the Truth would produce freedom. He did not mean that knowledge of the Truth creates freedom, but that knowledge of the Truth makes us free by aligning us with that which was never bound.

"Perhaps one might at first have an aversion to the idea of using spiritual power for material purposes, but in the Science of Mind we discover that there are no final material purposes. Whether life exists in an objective or a subjective state, whether it is visible or invisible, all is Spiritual Intelligence. It constitutes the entire universe, including man."

Dr. Kelly continued, telling his audience that the principles contained in Science of Mind allowed one to become spiritual by converting thoughts into good. Good thoughts were a manifestation of the spiritual.

Catherine thought it important "to belong to a higher good, to counter all my negativity and evil." She made arrangements to attend services each week. Florence and Nana frequently joined her, and afterward they all went to the International House of Pancakes. Catherine ordered her usual waffle, which she still divided into fourths, eating only one piece.

Catherine had also started walking around the campus at Santa Monica College, a two-year junior college. "It's a real college, Dr. Dorman. The students are all younger, but I've got to start somewhere. I picked up a schedule of classes and an application for admission. I'm worried, though. I told you I'm having trouble just reading sentences in magazines or the newspaper. Words don't make sense."

"I think you'll have to push yourself some. What are you thinking of taking?"

"Philosophy and psychology. The summer session begins next month, in June."

Catherine did sign up for the two courses. After two weeks of classes, she told me, "I can't understand what I'm reading. I start at the top of the page but nothing clicks, just like someone who knows nothing about chemistry trying to understand chemical equations. The most common sentences just don't make sense. All I see are the individual words. I try to understand each word, but I can't string everything together. Maybe I starved my brain, damaged it, and it will never work. What was the point of getting out of the hospital? Just to get knocked back?"

Catherine received failing grades on every test. "Why should I live? To fight insanity the rest of my life? I'm thinking about suicide again. Only this time it's different. Dr. Dorman, when I first went into UCLA, I took the option for suicide with me. I knew no one could take that away from me. But a kind of dramatics got thrown in. I saw all the young girls my age go into anxiety attacks and scream, 'Oh, I want to die,' and the nurses would rush over to them. I wanted the same attention. I was partly serious about it, though. Suicide meant different things at different times, but basically I saw it as an escape. Remember those guys who killed themselves, when I was at UCLA? The strange thing is, I felt sad, but not because they had died. They had escaped, and I had a longing to join them. I didn't do it, though, because pain was familiar and death was unfamiliar. It would have meant taking an even greater risk."

"And now?"

"Now I see the reality. If I can't live a normal life, why should I live? I can't go back to being my mother's daughter. I'm just leaving that now. So I have nowhere to go. There's no forward and no backward."

"I know you can't believe it now, but I still think you will get your brain function back."

"I'm not giving up yet. I'll have to see. I'm going to stick with my classes, even though I know I'll fail. I'll take them again in the fall." Catherine went to class every day, but when grades were mailed in August, she received two F's. She signed up for the same two classes beginning in September.

Just before the new semester began, Catherine told me something "strange" was happening to her. "I'm saying out loud what the voices are saying. In the mornings, when I'm brushing my teeth or combing my hair, all of a sudden, 'Kill your mother, kill your mother' pops out of my mouth. I speak without being aware of what I'm going to say. I just start moving my mouth, and I say what I hear as voices. It's like someone is speaking through me, but I know it's me. It reminds me of how they say the apostles had spoken different tongues."

A week later, Catherine told me her voices had grown faint. "Do you know what I'm saying now?"

"What?"

"I sit in my apartment and 'Kill yourself' just comes out of my mouth, over and over. I hold myself and say 'Kill yourself.' I know it sounds weird.

It *is* weird, but I feel relieved. As I'm speaking, I can feel my whole body, mind, and soul acknowledging what is really there. It doesn't scare me that I'm saying 'Kill yourself,' or 'Kill your mother,' because for some reason I know it's a transformation. I just know it."

Through September, Catherine sat in her room in the quiet dark of night, straining to hear the softly whispering voices. On October 6, she announced, "They're gone!"

"They are?"

"Yes, gone!"

"Cathy, that's so . . ."

"They're gone!"

Other changes started happening, too. For instance, all through Catherine's stay at UCLA, and at Westwood Hospital, too, she had complained of constipation. When I first met her, I prescribed a mild, senna-based laxative. Many schizophrenics suffer constipation, often to the point of developing fecal impactions, rock-hard feces that sometimes lead to megacolon, an enlarged lower colon that does not evacuate properly. Without proper monitoring, this can progress to volvulus, where the bowel twists upon itself, or paralytic ileus, a completely unresponsive colon. These two latter conditions are medical emergencies, often requiring surgery. Catherine told me she had not taken her laxatives for about two weeks because she was defecating normally in the mornings. "I just never had any urge before," she told me. "But now . . . maybe it's because I'm feeling more. When everything comes out, everything comes out!"

The next day, she came in rubbing her arms. "I'm feeling changes in my skin. I think I'm feeling my skin. I remember, way back when I started hearing the voices, my skin began to feel numb. I didn't feel pain like normal people. Lately I can feel the wind on my skin. When I scratch myself, I feel pain. I know this all sounds strange, but I haven't felt pain for years." This phenomenon of decreased pain sensitivity is also well known. Some schizophrenics have suffered a ruptured appendix or myocardial infarction without saying a word. Several psychiatrists have written that this is due to the schizophrenic's inability to communicate his feelings to others. But it is my view that when the schizophrenic shuts down emotionally to protect himself, he also shuts down some of his bodily functions. Now that Catherine was loosening up, feeling her self, she began to feel her body, too.

"I'm eating more," Catherine informed me in November, a month after she stopped hearing her voices.

"Tell me what's been happening."

"I think it's about control. When I was, maybe seventeen, I felt that I was out of control. I *was* out of control. I didn't know what was happening to me. So I grabbed what I could. I got very religious. I still say a Psalm from the Bible every morning, and I started my diet. It wasn't to lose weight. Eating—not eating—was the only thing I had any control over. I needed something. At the time I didn't know I was going crazy. I just felt like I was falling down into a black hole. I had nothing to grab hold of."

"Perhaps being seventeen and seeing other girls developing into young women helped push you over? Your diet did erase your body."

"Look at how much trouble I'm having now. Before all I felt was terror. You're right. I didn't realize that until this moment. I got rid of my body. I made myself into an eight-year-old. You know what's happening now? I don't feel the need to control as much. I'm still scared. I can't grasp most of what I'm even thinking about, but I just don't feel the same need to control my fears."

"Trusting yourself more? I mean that you can better handle what comes up?"

"Yep."

Catherine still hoarded pie to "keep something special," but she often threw away old stale pieces she had squirreled away. In the next six weeks, she gained six pounds. Just before Christmas, she weighed ninety-eight pounds. She spent the week between Christmas and the New Year with her parents, and she and Florence visited Nana at her trailer near Palm Springs. Cindy told her she was glad to see that Catherine had "fattened up," but no one else said anything about her weight gain.

"How was your vacation?" I asked her when she returned.

"Palm Springs felt like it did before I got sick," she told me. "I walked in the desert and stayed out at night looking at the stars. I felt it all. Palm Springs is especially beautiful in December. It's so clear you can see every crevice on the mountains."

"Would you believe I've only been there once?"

"Palm Springs has special meaning for me. I used to visit with Nana there. But you should go."

After Christmas Catherine came in beaming. "I talked with my dad. He's going to give me a car."

"You don't say."

"Yes. He bought a 1966 Volkswagon Beetle for me when I was sixteen. It's pretty powder blue. I drove it until I was hospitalized at UCLA. He stored it all this time. But I'm not sure I still know how to drive. He said he would pay for a refresher course."

"That sounds like a good idea. You'll be liberated with wheels."

"Something else happened, just three days ago."

"What?"

"I'm bleeding. I haven't had a period since I was seventeen. It's been seven years."

"Well, Cathy, you really are becoming a woman. Congratulations!"

"Thank you, Dr. Dorman. I never thought it would happen. Now I think I need a boyfriend. I met a couple of girls at the college. We go to lunch in the cafeteria after psychology class. I've been watching them, how they flirt with boys. They do it with their eyes. I started looking around to see if any-body was looking—I never did that before. I never saw anything, except food, that is. I looked at that plenty! Anyway, once we were outside, I caught this boy looking at me, and I looked back. He smiled. So, that's how it's done?"

"It sure is. There are other ways, too. Pretty clothes. A cute hair cut. Smiling back."

"I got embarrassed, so I looked away. He was cute. Maybe if I go back at the same time?"

"Hey, you're catching on. What did he look like?"

"Ha! Tall, dark, and handsome; that's my type."

"Well, give it a go."

The next day Catherine saw the same young man ride away on his bicycle. The day after that, she planted herself at the same spot. Sure enough, he returned. She smiled when she saw him, and he smiled back as he dismounted his bicycle and chained it to a bicycle rack. He approached Catherine. "Hi. You usually eat with two other girls about this time."

"Yes, I do."

"I'm Paul Morse."

"I'm Cathy Penney."

"What are you taking?"

"Philosophy and psychology."

"Philosophy, that's a waste. I'll bet you didn't read Karl Marx?"

"No, we didn't."

"Marx is real philosophy—practical philosophy. He knew about the oppressed workingman. All those Greeks, going on about democracy, while only the noble classes had any power. Did you know that?"

"No."

"Yes, indeed. The Greeks talked about a self-governing polis—that's a city, but it really wasn't close to a democracy."

"What's your major?"

"History. Political history. They have a really good department here. Mrs. Smythe teaches history of Russia. I'll bet she's a Communist. It's not easy being a Communist in this country. The U-S of A. Freedom of speech and thought. Unless you're a Communist."

"Are you a Communist?"

"Not yet. But it's the way of the world. The capitalist system will end up with power in the hands of a few giant corporations. That will spark the rebellion. I better get on to class. What do you say we continue our discussion? How about having coffee tomorrow afternoon?"

"That sounds fine."

"How about meeting here? I don't have any transportation, other than my trusty steed, here."

"Okay, what time?"

"Four-thirty?"

"Okay. See you tomorrow."

"All he talks about is politics," Catherine told me. "But I like him. He wears little, round wire-rimmed glasses. It makes him look . . . intellectual. And he does know a lot. I like his spirit, too. We've been on two coffee dates. He told me he doesn't have much money, so we're going dutch for hamburgers next Friday night. I'm going to pick him up. Oh! I didn't tell you. There are two things. First, I passed my driver's license exam. They gave me this paper that says I can drive! They'll mail me my license in a few weeks. Second, I got my grades. I got a B in psychology and a C in philosophy. I'd like to talk with you about what courses to take next semester. I have to sign up next week."

"Good for you! That would be fine. Let me know what courses you're thinking about."

The week after their hamburger date, Paul told Catherine he wanted to fix dinner for her at his apartment. He bought a bottle of red wine and pan-fried T-bone steaks. "Let's toast our relationship." He filled Catherine's glass, and they clinked their glasses together. Around nine-thirty, Paul said. "Catherine, I'd like to talk to you about something. I believe in being straightforward. Some people say I'm blunt. I'd like to have sex with you."

"Sex?"

"Yes. I think our relationship is progressing. Sex is the next step. What do you think?"

"I've never had sex."

"You're a virgin?"

"Yes, I am."

"Well, I like that."

"What do we do?"

"I'll show you. Get undressed and get under the covers." Catherine went into the bedroom, took off her clothes, and slid into bed. Paul followed in the dark. He climbed on top of her, entered, and started thrusting. In less than a minute, he rolled off. "How was it?"

"It hurt."

"Did it feel good?"

"Not really."

"Well, it will next time."

Later, during her next meeting with me, Catherine told me, "He just got on top of me and went up and down. It was dirty, and it hurt. I don't think I can be normal. I know he'll want sex when we're together. If I say no, he won't see me any more."

"We'll talk some more about that. But did he use a condom?"

"I don't know."

"You'll need to use some sort of contraceptive. Perhaps I'll give you the name of a gynecologist. She'll talk with you about the various types of contraceptives. Would that be all right?"

"Yes. Thanks."

Over the next month, Catherine and Paul had sex every time they saw each other. "It still feels like I'm being immersed in shit," she told me. "I don't feel anything else. I think the problem is more than sex. He says sex is sharing. I get angry if he takes a bite off my plate. Mother told me not to give anyone anything. The 'anything' was sex. It means obligation."

"I don't doubt that you are wary."

"I do like sleeping with him. It gives me a safe, warm feeling. But it also makes me angry to watch him sleep. The same thing happened when I was a child. I used to stay up and listen to my sisters breathe when they slept. There was a kind of genital tingling when I did that. But I also wanted to hit them."

"I think it was, and is, all about not having a separate identity within a relationship. To watch your sisters sleep, or now to watch Paul sleep, stirs the intense, merged closeness you never really left. I think that's why it's exciting. Excitement, particularly about another person, spills over into sexual feeling. But closeness means loss of identity to you, the loss of your self. So you get angry."

"My sexual feeling was all messed up. Sex was distorted for me even as a child. I never knew what was real and what was not real. I always thought that there was something wrong with me, that I was weird or even queer. As a child, whenever I saw a woman faint in a movie or on television, I'd get excited, the same kind of genital tingling. My thought was that holding someone, taking care of someone, was sexual. I thought that meant I might be homosexual.

"One of my problems was that I had too much mothering in me. It was safer to be Mary. As a child I wanted to be a nun. The sexual part felt too vulnerable. I was the one who was taken care of, the fainting person, or the one who did the caretaking, the mothering person. I worried about who was in the dependent position."

"I think you are right on. The vulnerable person, the helpless person, is you. You worry about who is in the dependent position because that is such a completely helpless position. But we're talking about carrying over your childhood experiences into adulthood. It's not necessary that you be help-less in depending on someone. You have power with Paul. You don't have to go along with everything he wants or says. You don't have to take care of him. He's grown. He shouldn't need you to be the mothering person, as you say. It is *you* who feels the need to be the mothering person. Perhaps having sex is like giving in and taking care of him, so you tighten up and it hurts. Maybe we can talk next time about taking care of *yourself*."

"I'll vote for that."

Catherine received B's in both of her courses and signed up for biology, health science, modern dance, history, and an acting course—all to begin in February 1974. "I don't know if I'm taking too many courses," she told me. "I still can't get words to come out right. Words still don't string to-gether. And in biology they use some math. I don't understand how sym-bols represent numbers."

There were long periods of silence now in her sessions with me.

"You look sad," I said one day.

"I am."

"How come?"

"I want out. I appreciate your sticking with me, but I'm not going to make it. I can't get what I should get in class, and a relationship makes me feel bad instead of good. I should be left alone."

"What's going on with Paul?"

"It isn't just with Paul. If I feel good about someone, it's like crawling in the mire. That's what happened with Cindy. I actually crawled in the dirt to be with her. She never wanted me around. I'm always watching out be-cause I make other people feel bad. Paul gets angry sometimes, and he says it's my fault. I'm always worried about hurting his feelings."

"This is likely to be one of the toughest problems you'll have to get through. Relationships are always harder to come to grips with than school or work. Even though you're having trouble in school, the boundaries, or rules are pretty clear. You know exactly what has to be done. In relation-ships the boundaries are muddy. Paul, for instance, is a bit of a complainer. You, on the other hand, feel overly responsible for him. So the two of you enter into a collusion. What I mean is that he complains like a child; that is his way of behaving like a child. You try to fix him, but if he is fixed he won't be a child, so he keeps on complaining. You are stuck in childhood, too: fixing, taking care of the other person's every hurt feeling is what you did as a child. In the end, both of you are, psychologically speaking, children. The more adult thing to do is to not take care of his hurt feelings. Let him take care of himself."

"I can't do it."

"Why not?'

"I feel like I'm a bad person if I don't take care of him."

"You'll never get rid of your supposed badness by trying to be the good mother. I think you will feel better about yourself by being good to *you*."

Paul wanted Catherine to move in with him. "Think of it," he told her. "A man and a woman living together without a capitalist marriage document. Marriage is all about business. Capitalist economics masquerading as a religious union. I wrote a paper with that title for *The Guardian*. Religion oppresses man. It oppresses woman, too. Why do you go to that church? Do you need someone telling you what to do?"

"Dr. Kelly doesn't tell people what to do."

"Then why go? Religion is the opiate of the masses, belief that someone— God—is going to take care of you. We take care of each other. No one above anyone else. The Communist ideal is actually very practical."

"I go because I feel I belong to something larger than myself."

"That's the problem. There is nothing larger than us. We are it. But let us do our experiment. We can have a nice life together. Two can live more cheaply than one."

Catherine did move in with Paul in September. She also signed up for creative writing, history of the theater, and, over Paul's objections, sociology. "Capitalist propaganda," he proclaimed.

"I have to drive him everywhere," Catherine told me. "He doesn't have a car. I'm afraid to say no."

"Why?"

"I'm afraid he won't like me. He always tells me sharing is what a relationship is about."

"Doesn't sound like sharing to me. He doesn't have a car to share. If you just protest, you're in the position of a child trying to persuade him to change his mind. The problem is more about you than Paul. You have such a hard time making a declaration about yourself, like saying no."

"I can't say no. It would hurt his feelings. I don't know how."

One day, Catherine saw an ad posted on the Santa Monica College bulletin board: "Volunteers needed. Young women, age twenty-one to thirty, for socialization with hospitalized veterans on Wednesday evenings from 7:30 to 10:00. Must be personable. Good dancers a plus. Call the Veterans Administration volunteer services office." Catherine did call. The woman on the other end of the phone told her, "We have a social night with refreshments and dancing once a week. Most of the veterans have severe mental and physical disabilities and have spent a long time in the hospital. Many have no visitors. This is not for picking up men. Dating any of the patients is strictly off limits. Does it sound interesting?"

"Yes, it does."

Social night brought together twenty to thirty veterans of the Vietnam conflict, mostly in their mid-twenties. Many came on crutches or in wheelchairs and were missing arms and legs. Some came in groups. *The psychiatric patients*, Catherine thought, as some of them shyly sat down in chairs ringing an open area. The majority of the volunteers were young women from the Job Corps. Most of them picked out the healthier looking patients, talking and dancing to music from an old record player run by one of the volunteers.

On her first night there, Catherine approached a group of men who were laughing and joking and had gathered around a veteran named Michael. Michael's face was a mass of twisting and pulling scars. "Hi, I'm Catherine," she said. The group separated.

"Hello, I'm Michael. This is Bill here and Isaac, and that's Tim. I'm a mess, aren't I? Got caught at the wrong end of a hand grenade." The others drifted away.

"Have you had a lot of surgery?" Catherine asked.

"Surgery? Those docs have been shaving my . . . excuse me, taking skin from everywhere to patch up my face. My body looks like a patchwork quilt. I've been in and out of here every few months since 1968. The scars contract, so they have to do releases."

"Did you get depressed?"

"Oh yeah. A couple of years ago, I was going to cash it in. But I got to figuring; I'm lucky. I'm here. A lot of my friends aren't. My wife—we were married just before I left for 'Nam—couldn't even look at me when I came back. Once I asked her if I was disgusting, and she actually said, 'Yes, you are.' Can you beat that?"

"I thought you might feel that everybody would avoid you or think you are strange," Catherine said.

"Nope, never felt that. What are you about? What's your journey?"

"Well, I'm a former mental patient. I was in a mental hospital for over three years. I got out ten months ago."

"What put you in there?"

"Schizophrenia."

"How did you end up that way?"

"I was pretty shy, except for dancing and acting. I was always self-conscious. That's why I thought you might have felt bad about yourself."

"Nope. Once I decided I would just have to accept starting over, I figured that there was no use wallowing in misery. What good does that do? What good is resentment? Tackle things head-on. Get a goal. Help others. I'm going to school part-time. I'm going to get my Ph.D. in psychology."

"You'll be a good psychologist."

"Thanks. Would you like to dance?"

Catherine nodded. "Um-hmm."

Catherine told me she looked forward to her Wednesday evenings with the veterans. Once she and a partner even won the "fast dance" contest.

She and I continued talking about her difficulties separating herself from another person. One day she asked, "Am I obligated to you? Am I coming because I am sick? I mean, if you'll excuse me, I have to be sick to see you."

"Well. It's not exactly the same as with Paul."

"I told you I had to crawl in the mire to be with Cindy. It feels like the same."

"You feel you are degraded seeing me?"

"I have to be sick. I have to depend on you."

"Dependence doesn't have to mean you're sick."

"I think I shouldn't come any more. I can't be insane and a person at the same time."

"Cathy, you're still . . . Don't you think you need some more help? You still count every calorie; you still need your waffles once or twice a week; you still don't feel comfortable with sex; you have pretty serious depressions; you have to memorize your class material because you are having trouble grasping concepts; you still . . ."

"Everyone has a few problems. They're nothing I can't handle."

At that moment, I raised my hands, palms up, in a show of powerlessness. And at the same moment, I thought to myself, *That's it! That's what she needs: to see me powerless. I am powerless. She's in charge.*

"It *is* true that coming to see me is entirely up to you. You can function on your own. I do think, though, that it would be in your interest to let me help you a little longer. What do you think about coming three days a week instead of every day? Perhaps seeing me every day means that too much of you is run through me. There's no time to digest your experiences as part of you."

"Okay. That would be fine. We'll drop Tuesdays and Thursdays."

"I think that would work."

That semester, Catherine received all B's in her course work. "I think I might try for a certificate as a psychiatric technician," she told me. "Los Angeles Trade Tech offers a four-semester course."

"Why a psychiatric technician?"

"I need to work. I don't want to be on welfare. And I know what psych techs do."

"I bet you'd be good at it. Not too many psychiatric technicians have been where you've been. You certainly will understand what someone called psychotic struggles with. What do you have to do to apply?"

"I just have to take a math class next summer at Trade Tech. They're accepting students for the fall of 1975."

Catherine felt oppressed living with Paul. "Why oppressed?" I asked.

"Well, I decided not to go hear Dr. Kelly anymore. I'm going to the Self-Realization Fellowship on Sunset Boulevard instead. Paul keeps telling me that religion is for weak people, so I have to keep it from him. He criticizes me all the time."

"Are you still worried he'll leave you if you tell him what you think?"

"Yes, I am. And I still feel ugly. Paul even told me that my sisters are prettier than I. I took him home to introduce him to Mother."

"He just said that? Right to you?"

"Um-hmm."

Nana had given Catherine enough money to buy a 1973 Ford Pinto, since her Volkswagon seemed to be breaking down so often. Paul asked her if he might borrow it to visit Ronnie, his "female comrade." She had been in an automobile accident and was in the hospital. They had marched in anti-Vietnam War protests together.

"I really don't want you to take it all the way into downtown LA," Catherine said.

"So, Ronnie is in the hospital, and all you can think about is your precious capitalist possession? That's pitiful."

"It's new. Why can't *I* take you to visit Ronnie?"

"Fuck you! You're self-centered and selfish. Ronnie is an old friend. This is a special relationship. There's nothing romantic about it, if that's what you're worried about! I'll be back in a couple of hours."

"Well, okay."

During these months, Catherine developed a friendship with Maria, a fellow student. Maria worked as a housekeeper so she could pay her tuition and send money back to her parents in Mexico. The two women went to the movies, out to eat, and visited. One evening they were talking in Catherine's apartment. "Cathy, I have something to tell you. You're my friend and you need to know. Paul made a couple of passes at me. It has happened more than once. This is not good. I hope you will understand that I can't visit you at your apartment anymore."

"Thank you for telling me. I certainly do understand. What makes me mad is not so much his treating me badly, but his disrespect for you, my friend. We'll just get together at your place."

"How come you didn't get drafted for Vietnam?" Catherine asked Paul one evening.

"My parents filed some sort of request. I'm an only son because my little brother got lost when we were on a camping trip. He was later found dead in a ravine."

"Don't you think you should have volunteered? Someone had to go in your place. You're always talking about how we're all equal."

"Volunteer? To fight for the imperialist dogs? I don't know what I see in you."

Catherine made the dean's list her first semester at Trade Tech. She made straight A's in reading for pleasure, recreational dancing, and elementary medical and surgical vocational nursing. Two more semesters to go. She had heard that she might be eligible for educational benefits based on her father's death in combat. She applied in November and heard in January that she would receive $198 a month, so she withdrew from the Social Security Disability program. "I'm not disabled anymore, anyway," she told me. She was also allowed to work while receiving the veterans' benefits. She obtained a part-time job as a waitress at the Pizza Hut, next-door to Santa Monica College, where she took an evening class in modern dance once a week.

One morning, Paul peered at Catherine across the breakfast-room table. "Why do you need a job?"

"I receive only $270 a month from my benefits to go to school. You're supported by your family."

"You're a slave to bourgeois capitalists."

Catherine looked down at her cup of coffee. "How should I earn some money?"

"You're going to school. The state should support you."

"I'm doing the best I can."

"If you're supporting the system, you don't understand anything!"

Catherine mused to herself, *I am surrounded by the peace of God. That is what Dr. Kelly said. All is well. Divine love is inscribed in my heart and written in my inward parts. I radiate love in thought, words, and deeds. I am radiating love toward all, for everyone represents the love of God. I know and believe that divine love heals me now. Love brings into my experience perfect, harmonious relationships.*

"If you're not going to be around on the weekends, I'm going out. I need to borrow your car," Paul declared.

"I need it to get to work."

"I'll drop you off."

"The last time I loaned you the car you didn't come back when you said."

"Oh, still on the Ronnie thing, are you? Women are always jealous."
Catherine was silent.

"Are you going to loan me your car?"

"I'd rather not."

Paul stomped around, sputtering like a four-year-old. "Well, piss on you!
I'm leaving! I'll be back if you're lucky!"

Catherine told me she thought Paul's behavior was her fault. "I'm bad.
I always say the wrong thing."

"You can't be responsible for his every move," I returned. "Isn't he responsible for anything?"

During the summer break of 1975, Catherine signed up for a drama class
at Santa Monica College one night a week, then quit her job at the Pizza
Hut at the beginning of her final semester at Los Angeles Trade Tech. In
her last semester, she made A's and B's. Her final grade-point average was
3.514, about halfway between A and B.

"I'm nervous about the psych tech license exam," she told me.

"Why? Your grade-point average is high."

"I'm still worried about the exam. I don't trust myself."

Catherine scored sixty-two, not enough to pass. She was allowed three
tries, each one month apart. In February she retook the exam and scored
sixty-five, still not enough to pass.

"I studied hard, Dr. Dorman, but I was nervous. I came up blank. Do
you think my brain is permanently damaged?"

"I don't think it's your brain. Nor do I think this is the same problem
you had at Santa Monica College, where you could process only one word
at a time. You've come quite a way since then. After all, you made pretty
good grades in your courses. You even told me you thought the vocational
nursing and psychology courses were easy. You made one hundreds. I think
you put your finger on it. You were nervous. Perhaps you froze up because
of what happens next, leaving student status?"

"Maybe I can't handle the world. Look at my relationship with Paul. I'm
afraid to say no to him. How will I manage a job?"

"Well, that's true. You have to learn to at least stick up for yourself.
You've been doing it sometimes: He quit asking to borrow your car."

At home, on her knees, Catherine read psalms from the Bible: "I sought the Lord and he heard me and delivered me from all my fears." She did not notice Paul watching her from behind, a smirk on his face and his hands on his hips. "The foxes have their dens and the birds of the air have nests; but the Son of God has nowhere to lay his head." This last psalm made her feel less alone, because Jesus also felt that he didn't belong anywhere.

"What the fuck are you doing with your head bent down? Praying?" Paul snorted. "There's no God. No one is going to save you!" Paul strode over and sat down on the floor in the middle of the room. Catherine got up and stood over him. "I can pray and believe what I want. It makes me feel good."

"Belief in God! You're stupid! Religion is the opiate of the masses. God keeps the masses suppressed."

"You keep *me* suppressed."

"What did you say? I'm trying to liberate you. You don't know anything. You can't learn anything. You can't even pass a stupid exam."

Catherine stood still, looking down. "You're keeping me from growing. Everything I want to do you think is wrong."

"All you want to be is stupid!"

"You're a tyrant!" Catherine raised her leg to strike her foot on the ground, but it landed right on Paul's hand.

"You fucker!" he shouted, scrambling up. "You stepped on my hand!"

"It was an accident!"

Paul shoved Catherine, hitting her with his open palms in both shoulders, knocking her back across the arm of a chair. "You fucker! Why did you step on my hand?"

Regaining her balance, Catherine said, "I told you it was an accident."

"You—"

"I don't want to be here anymore. You've dominated me long enough, Paul. I don't want to live with you anymore."

"What bullshit!"

"I mean it. I've been thinking about it for a long time. You're too self-ish. All you think about is yourself. Your ideas are supposed to be my ideas. I've spent my whole life thinking there was something wrong with me, and I find you, and *you* think there's something wrong with me. I need someone who is interested in my ideas, or no one. You confuse me with all your negativity."

"I'm sorry I hit you."

"I believe you are, but we're going to break up. Nana, my grandmother, gave my sisters and me some land in the desert. Twelve acres apiece. I'm going to sell mine and take a vacation to Hawaii. Maybe I'll move there. Even if I don't, when I come back I want us to be apart."

"When are you going?"

"The real-estate agent said the land should sell right away, in no more than a few weeks. I planned to take my vacation in May, next month. It's your apartment, so I'll move out."

During her next session with me, Catherine said, "I just couldn't take it anymore, Dr. Dorman. His hitting me was just the last straw. I don't know what happened. At first we had some real tender times. Not lately."

"Cathy, it's a lesson about all relationships. I think what happened was that you unwittingly encouraged Paul to dominate you by being too passive. You were always afraid he would leave you, so you let him get away with . . . well, outrageous behavior. Of course, it wasn't all you. He should have known better, or more accurately, someone mature might not have had the need to be so controlling. But when two people go down that path, it's hard to turn things around."

"Ha! Do you know what he did yesterday? He cried and asked me not to leave. It goes to show you, I should have stood up for myself before."

"Sure. It's like everything else you've done. You learn on the firing line."

"You know, Dr. Dorman, I couldn't have done this without you. I could not have been sure if I was right or wrong. I know you never said I was right just to support me, but only if you thought I was really on the right track."

"Well, thanks, Cathy."

"No, I don't mean just with Paul. I feel so different now. I never knew I could be independent. No, that's not exactly right. Do you know those pictures for children, the ones where they draw a line from dot to dot, and when they get back to the beginning, they have drawn a picture?"

"Yes, I do."

"I had no dot for independence. That's why I couldn't think about it."

"You've had to create an 'independence dot' so you can go on with your picture?"

"Yep."

We sat in silence for a while, basking in an unseen glow.

"Dr. Dorman, there's another dot I need to create. I think . . . I think I should be entirely on my own. Away from you. Away from my family. You know how important you've been to me. Without you I would either still be in a mental hospital or in and out of halfway houses. I've talked to a lot of people with schizophrenia, and I know! The drugs, they're probably necessary for some, but those people don't really get better. One of the dots I can now see is that I have a life. All I knew before was avoiding terror. But I think I need to learn to live without you, so I can know me."

"It's time, isn't it?"

"I'm glad you think so. It's the only way I can really get to know myself, isn't that true?"

"Absolutely. I came into your life before you had a self. So in a sense— no, more than a sense—your self and my self have been inextricably bound up. This is the next step for *your* self."

"When I was seven years old, just after Mom married Joe, we lived on Kaneohe, the Marine base in Hawaii, for two years. I remember that as a happy time. You know my land sold? For $12,000. I thought I'd use the money to visit Oahu for a week and see if I like it. I heard you don't need a license to be a psychiatric tech there."

"Well, you might look around and see."

"I'd like to keep my appointments for now, so I can talk to you when I get back."

"That would be fine. We can talk about us then."

Catherine bought a travel guide, *Hawaii on Seven Dollars a Day*, and was off to Oahu. The green necklace that is Hawaii lay 30,000 feet below the airplane window, floating on the gray-blue sea. On her first afternoon there, she wandered among the shops on Kalakaua and Kubio avenues. The next day, she must have walked two miles on the beach, all the way to the Royal Hawaiian Hotel. Twenty-five cents bought her a bus ride all around the island. She found out that Queen's Medical Center was the only major hospital with a psychiatric unit. She telephoned. Yes, they were hiring psychiatric technicians, and no license was needed. "Please apply as soon as you get settled," she was told. She secured a lanai apartment two blocks from the beach on Kiulani Avenue, to begin July 15.

"It's paradise," she told me. "I walked on the beach and said hello to all the tourists. But my parents are nervous. Mother said the cost of living is high and I'll be lucky to get a job. I think they don't want me to go. It's too far away."

"An umbilical cord stretches mighty thin from Los Angeles to Waikiki."

"That's it, isn't it? They're having trouble letting go of me."

"I think so."

Again we sat in silence. I thought to myself: *It has been eight years. She's become part my life. I wonder how I'll do without her?*

"I'll miss you, Dr. Dorman."

"Catherine, I'll miss you too."

"Do you think, if I need to . . . ?"

"The door will always be open." We walked to my office door, shook hands, and lingered for a while. She has large hands, and firm. It was the first time I'd touched her but for that feathery moment in the UCLA hospital long ago.

"Bye, Cathy."

"Goodbye, Dr. Dorman."

Seven

The Limit of My Discernment

You now have seen the torment
of the temporal and the eternal fires;
here, now, is the limit of my discernment.
I have led you here by grace of mind and art;
now let your own good pleasure be your guide.

Dante, The Purgatorio

July 15, 1977: Catherine gazed through the glass roof of the shuttle bus at the tops of the palm trees swaying in the wind. *I wonder if I hurt Dr. Dorman's feelings?* she thought to herself. *Will he be mad at me for going on to bigger and better things? Will he ever want to see me again? Or only if I'm really sick? But . . . I'm not really sick. I'm free and on my own.*

At her apartment, she was met by her landlords, a Japanese couple, and their twenty-one-year-old son, Ray. "Aloha. Welcome to Hawaii," they all said in unison. All three draped a maile lei around her neck. "Perhaps you will become a *kamaaina,* a long-timer," Mrs. Matsumoto said, smiling.

"I'll be glad to show you around," Ray offered. "Restaurants, laundry, things like that?"

"Thanks," Catherine replied. "Thank you all."

The following week, Catherine took a bus to Queen's Hospital to interview for an opening as a psych tech. The personnel manager was impressed that Catherine had completed a course of professional training, and offered her the job. Catherine did not disclose that she herself had been a mental patient.

Her new position was on the inpatient unit, which looked a lot like the one at UCLA—one hall with rooms for men, and another for women. A central glassed in nursing station stood between the two halls. As part of her job, Catherine made sure the patients took their medications. She took this responsibility seriously, but also sympathized with patients' complaints that the medication made them feel "spacey" or dead. More than once, patients asked her, "How do *you* know what it feels like?" She'd reply, "I know." Indeed, three weeks after Catherine started, the head nurse told her that she truly seemed cut out for the work—she developed quick rapport with the patients.

Things at home were going well, too. Lorraine Holloway, who lived on the first floor of Catherine's apartment building, came up one day and introduced herself. She was twenty-nine, two years older than Catherine, and worked as a beautician at the Royal Hawaiian and Moana hotels. The two began spending time together, sometimes meeting after work for "happy hour" at hotel bars along Waikiki beach.

Catherine also spent some weekend afternoons with Ray. She found him to be easygoing, and funny. Eventually, they slept together. She told Lorraine, "Wow! I feel so relaxed with him. It was the first time I ever had an orgasm. Now I see why sex is addictive."

"You bet. That's why I keep going out with my Hawaiian policeman. Are you serious about Ray?"

"Oh no. He's a surfer kid. He likes the blondes on the beach. I'm not that type. But we have fun."

One Sunday a month, Catherine attended services at the Sacred Heart Catholic Church. The choir, all Hawaiians, dressed in native clothing and sang in Hawaiian, accompanied by a ukulele. Catherine told Lorraine that spirituality was important to her but that it would have to take a back seat to her pursuit of adulthood. So she and Lorraine hit the discos and night spots. Catherine still loved to dance and had no trouble attracting partners.

One evening, she danced mostly with a Samoan man, who asked her out. "One date was enough," she told Lorraine the next night, as the two sat chatting in Catherine's apartment. "What a neanderthal. He got drunk and wouldn't leave. I told him I was going to the bathroom, and I telephoned George, who lives next door. He came over and pretended he was from the Honolulu police. Whew! The guy finally left. He was handsome, though."

Just then, the women heard someone shouting Catherine's name in the hall. It was the Samoan. He was drunk, and pounding on every door in the complex.

"Cathy! Catherine! Whatever your name is! Where are you? I know you're in there!" Lorraine and Catherine sat quietly. Doors opened and slammed shut up and down the hall. Finally, silence. Apparently, he had given up and gone home.

"Gee whiz, Cathy. What kind of guy gets your phone number? You went out with a creep. You've got to watch yourself."

"I don't know how to tell who's a creep and who isn't."

"For one thing, you shouldn't smile at everyone. And watch out for the real handsome ones. They're self-centered."

On her days off, Catherine got up at seven o'clock in the morning and strode the mile to downtown Waikiki along the uncluttered beach to Jason's coffee shop. There, she ate her still-mandatory morning sweet roll. This coffee shop had her favorite: an extra-large, sticky cinnamon roll. She would sit alone in the booth, sometimes for an hour or more, absent-mindedly watching the city wake up.

One morning, the only other patrons in the shop were two men. Their loud laughter reverberated through the shop. Unexpectedly, they materialized at the end of Catherine's booth. The taller of the two said, "Uh, hi, I wondered if I might introduce myself?" Catherine looked at him. He was about five feet, eleven inches tall, with a stocky build. A sprinkling of gray frosted his black hair and thick mustache. His light-blue eyes sparkled.

"Sure," she said.

"I'm Clay Morehead, and this is my buddy Jim." Clay's friend nodded.

"We just got in the day before yesterday," Clay continued. "We're here for a month. I work—we work for the government at Kaneohe Marine Base. We—I—was wondering if you would like to drive around the island?"

"Well, no. I don't really know you."

"Oh, we're safe. The government can track me down anywhere."

"I really don't think so."

"How about dinner tonight? Maybe I can call you later?"

"Sure." Catherine gave Clay her telephone number. Clay did call and took her to dinner at the Royal Hawaiian Hotel.

"Whew, this is an expensive place," Catherine said, feeling the white tablecloth and admiring the view of the beach.

Clay smiled. "You have a beautiful tan. Are you from Oahu?"

"No—from California. I grew up in Orange County."

"How long have you been here?"

"Oh, let's see—a little over four months now."

"Well, I live in San Diego." He told Catherine about his job working as a civilian field inspector of military aircraft. As part of his responsibilities, he made the rounds at military bases throughout the western states and Hawaii. He was forty-one years old.

Clay asked Catherine out for the next night, too, and they began spending their mutual days off at the beach. Before long they were seeing each other nightly. They often went to show clubs featuring Hawaiian dancing, where the dancers frequently chose partners from the audience. Catherine thought it sexy that Clay was always picked. Toward the end of Clay's four-week assignment, they spent three days on Maui at the Sheraton Maui Hotel.

"Will you write me when you leave?" Catherine asked during their last breakfast at the hotel.

"Sure." He grinned. "Any chance you'll be coming back to Orange County?"

"I hadn't thought . . . well, maybe."

With Clay now gone, Catherine and Lorraine resumed spending time together. Catherine seemed reluctant to talk with other men who approached, though. At clubs, she would dance freely, then excuse herself and head back to the table.

"You're hung up on Clay, aren't you?" Lorraine asked her one night.

"I'm lovesick. He sent me a few letters and told me how much fun he had. But I don't think it was serious for him. I don't know what he saw in me, anyway." She lowered her eyes.

"Cathy!" Lorraine shook her head and sighed.

"Once I asked him why he went out with younger women, and he said, 'Because they don't have a lot of baggage, and they love having fun.' Does that sound serious? In my letters, I tell him I miss seeing him, but he never says he wants to see *me* again."

After six weeks or so, Catherine finally invited a young man she had danced with up to her apartment, "just for coffee, nothing else." He pulled out a marijuana cigarette and persuaded Catherine to take a puff. At first she coughed—the smoke burned her throat—but she finally inhaled a few times. She sat back in her armchair, waiting to see what would happen next.

Suddenly, the young man stared at her. "You should see the look on your face!" he said. "Are you okay?"

Catherine's eyes were wide open. "My mind—it's separating from my body," she cried.

"Calm down, calm down," he said, patting her nervously on the shoulder. "It'll pass."

"My *mind*."

"Hey, you'll sleep it off." He rose clumsily to his feet. "I've got to go." Catherine watched him, unblinking, as he left.

She sat huddled in her chair. "Help!" she whispered, then listened. *I shouldn't have come here,* she thought. *I'm not going to make it.* She could feel the space inside her that the voices had occupied. She waited for them to speak. But they were mute. The room began to darken. She got up and turned on every light, but it didn't help. She staggered to her bed and lay down. The room spun round and round. She tried to focus her eyes on the ceiling light. The spinning slowed; then she fell asleep.

"Never again," she told Lorraine the next night, shuddering. "Never, never. I know what's down there. I'm not going back."

"Down where? That's just what happens with pot."

"'Just what happens' isn't going to happen to *me*. I almost heard them again."

"Heard who?" Lorraine saw Catherine close her eyes and jerk her head up suddenly. "Cathy?" she asked, peering at her friend's face.

"I'm okay," Catherine said, opening her eyes. "I guess it was—how do you say, a bad trip?"

"Yeah. Certainly *sounds* like it."

About four months after Clay left, Catherine received a surprising letter from him:

Dear Cathy:

I've been thinking a lot about you lately and I'd like to see you again. As you know, ever since my divorce I've been dating around, but I haven't met anyone like you. I feel we connect. You said you weren't sure how long you were going to live in Oahu. I'd like to give us a go. Is there any chance you might be moving back soon?

Regards,
Clay

"Whew," she told Lorraine. "I have to do it. I've never been in love before."

Catherine wrote Clay that she *would* move, probably to Orange County and probably in June, in time for the next psychiatric technician licensing exam. He wrote back that he was living with his friend Jerry near San Diego, but that he wanted to see her every weekend. Catherine gave notice at Queen's Hospital. Nearly every one of her coworkers took her aside to tell her how much they would miss her. The ward would "feel different" without her around, they said. They all had a laugh, too, about the story of Dr. Steve Wing. A staff psychiatrist, Wing preferred prescribing massive doses of drugs and electroshock to even greeting his patients, let alone talking with them. One day the police picked him up in the middle of Ala Moana Boulevard: he was directing traffic in a Superman costume. A squad car took him to the psychiatric ward at Queen's Hospital, where another psychiatrist drugged and discharged him. A month later, he was back on the staff, admitting patients.

Catherine and Lorraine spent one last all-nighter at a disco ending with breakfast at Jason's at four o'clock in the morning. Both wept at the thought of saying goodbye.

"I've learned so much from you, Cathy—about honesty and being real. You are my true friend."

"Imagine what I've learned from *you* in the nine months I've been here," Catherine replied, touching her friend on the shoulder. "Wow! I was like a thirteen-year-old girl. You never said anything about how naive I've been."

In May, Catherine returned to Orange County. She moved back into her old bedroom at Florence and Joe's house. Four weeks after taking the licensing exam, she received notice that she had passed. Immediately, she called all the hospitals in the area to find out which ones had psychiatric wards. She filled out applications at St. Joseph's, where she had been hospitalized ten years ago, and at Hoag Hospital in Newport Beach, and received a job offer from Hoag. Four weeks after starting her new job, she had saved enough money to move into her own apartment in Tustin, about ten miles away.

The same mix of patients were admitted to Hoag as at Queen's Hospital: young patients who had suffered a psychotic break, women and men in their late fifties and sixties who suffered from "psychotic depression," and a sprinkling of individuals not easily classified. Catherine worked the three-to-eleven shift and was relieved that her duties excluded dispensing medication. She did have to oversee the rigid routine of "activities" the patients were expected to attend, as well as the craft shop and outings to nearby Balboa Island and the beaches.

One day, Catherine recognized one of the nurses. "Carole Iverson?" she asked. "You don't recognize me. I'm Cathy Penney. You used to work at UCLA, right?"

"Catherine! You're working here?"

"I sure am."

"I can't believe it. I mean . . ." Carole stopped, awkwardly.

"Oh, it's okay."

"No one thought you'd get better. You look wonderful. I really mean it, Cathy. I'm working here part-time. When do you work? Let's get together. And you know, Eleanor Sorensen is working here too. Do you remember her from UCLA? Wait till I tell her. Maybe we could all get together after work. I want to know how you got all the way here."

"Sure. Let's do. I work four days a week but my schedule varies."

Catherine also ran into Dave Sheffield, my old fellow resident who had accused me of being unethical for not prescribing medication. Catherine told Carole that when she went up and introduced herself to Sheffield, he was "flabbergasted" and wanted to talk with her about her recovery. But he never contacted her.

During these months, Catherine saw Clay almost every other weekend. She worked some weekends, and he told her he had to travel on some other weekends. At first he would drive up from San Diego for the evening, and they would go out for dinner or dancing. Gradually he began spending weekends at Catherine's apartment, then she began driving to visit him at times. Clay lived in Chula Vista, California. His friend and housemate, Jerry, was also a field inspector based out of North Island Naval Air Station on Coronado Island. When Catherine drove to visit Clay, he rented a motel room on Coronado. When she went out to bars and dance clubs with Clay, Jerry, and their friends, most of whom had retired from the military, she was often the only woman.

Just before Christmas, Florence asked Catherine if she and Joe could meet Clay. Catherine arranged the visit for an early Sunday morning, before Joe could start drinking.

"How ya doin'?" Joe stood at the open front door as Catherine and Clay walked up. "I'm Cathy's father. Just call me Joe."

Clay introduced himself to Florence, and Joe said to him, "I hear you keep the mechanics honest."

"I try to, sir. I try. I understand you did some flying? What did you fly?"

"Aw, just A-1's and H-34's." Joe waved his hands.

"Search and rescue, eh," Clay answered.

"Yep. Wouldn't let me near the F-8 Crusaders. I hear your life depends on one hydraulic screw jack. A single piece of metal in those babies keeps you from bein' a smokin' hole in the ground! I'll bet you're peepin' at those?"

"I sure am. And you have to throw away the wing after 800 hours, too."

"You don't say?"

Catherine and Florence walked off into the kitchen, leaving the men talking about how fast you could land an F-8 on an aircraft deck. Clay swore it had to be 140 miles per hour or you'd end up "looking like burnt toast crumbs." The two men drifted into talking about what color paint served best as camouflage. "Dark blue on top and white on the bottom," Joe observed. "That way the Nips can't see you from above *or* below." After Clay and Catherine left, Florence told Joe that she thought Clay was "nice."

One morning Catherine left a voice message on my answering machine: "Hi, Dr. Dorman. This is Cathy Penney. I'm living in Tustin and I'm working as a psychiatric technician at Hoag Hospital in Newport Beach. Everything is pretty good, but I'd like to talk with you about some old feelings that have come up. Here's my phone number." It was definitely her voice. She had given her first and last name. Did she think I'd forgotten her? I sat back and watched an internal movie of Catherine huddled and rocking at UCLA. This work I do—it's a strange profession. I see people, then they disappear. I don't hear from or about most of them ever again. Perhaps they associate their bad experiences with me and want to leave it all locked away. Maybe that's the way it's meant to be. I can be only a part of someone's life. Sure. That's definitely the way it's supposed to be. But that day, I realized with some excitement that I would get to meet the new Cathy.

A few days later, she appeared at my office. "Well, it's good to see you, Cathy." I beamed.

"You too, Dr. Dorman."

"You look good. You're so brown."

"I spent a lot of time on the beach in a swimsuit. I once thought that was sinful. I want to tell you about Hawaii, but something is bothering me that I want to talk to you about first. I'm starting to feel like I'm losing me. It's about my new boyfriend, Clay. I mean, he's very kind and affectionate. I care a lot about him. But I feel like I did with Paul—that I have to suppress me. I'm too ready to do things Clay's way. If he says, 'Let's go out with Jerry and Sam,' I say, 'That's fine.' I don't ever think about where *I* might like to go. That makes me depressed."

"Cathy, these old states of mind are hard to shake. You can't change the past. You *can* supersede your old self by building a new identity on top of the old, which you certainly are doing. But the past remains, like an old, but not completely cold, ember buried within. Things can fan it into flame from time to time. We've talked a lot about how negative feelings are a challenge to you. The challenge will be to declare yourself to Clay in spite of your negative feelings. In fact, be prepared. Declaring yourself will fan these negative feelings, the old you, even more."

"You know, Dr. Dorman, of course I know that. That's exactly what I did time after time in Hawaii. I knew I had to walk into, not away from, my bad feelings. I guess I've been kind of overwhelmed. I've never felt as close to anyone as I do with Clay, except for my mother."

Catherine made two more appointments with me, each a week apart. In the second session, she wanted to talk more about the specific difficulties she had with Clay. For example, how should she tell him she wanted to see more of him, or ask him to join her with her friends for a change? She spent the third session telling me about how happy she was that she had decided to spend nine months in Hawaii.

At Hoag, Catherine, Carole, and Eleanor frequently went to happy hour after work. On the weekends that Catherine did not see Clay, the three women went to the Airport Hotel bar, which had a small dance floor. There was no shortage of men asking for Catherine's phone number. Both Carole and Eleanor encouraged her to date other men, since Clay seemed content with their every-other-weekend arrangement. Catherine did go out to dinner with several—and even had a few "overnight liaisons" as she called them.

One evening, at dinner with Clay, Catherine turned restlessly in her chair. "I've been thinking," she stammered. "We've been dating for eight months now, ever since I got back from Hawaii. I feel like we're just marking time. I mean—I don't want to hurt your feelings or anything, but we should be seeing more of each other."

"Hmm," Clay said, glancing out the restaurant window.

"What do you think?"

"Maybe we should."

"I feel like I'm sliding into an old, comfortable place: just to be glad I'm wanted is a real bad place for me. It's like I'm giving up me. I've felt that before. I'm starting to get depressed. I want to be honest with you, Clay. On weekends when you're away I—well, I've had some dates."

"Dates?" His eyes snapped back from the window to her.

"It's just . . . I'm not sure about us. You were so positive in your letters. You wanted me to come back from Hawaii but now we don't ever talk about us."

"You've had dates?"

"Um-hmm."

"Have you . . . ?"

"Yes, I did. I feel guilty about it."

"How many times?"

"Twice."

"Twice?" He sat back in his chair and let out a loud sigh. Catherine put her hand on his forearm.

"It's just—I have to know I'm not just a passive nobody."

"I think we should move in together," Clay said abruptly.

"You do?"

"We'd have to make arrangements. I don't think Jerry would mind if I moved out. We could rent a house in Coronado. It would be a long way for you to drive to work, though."

"I'm so glad you feel that way, Clay! I could get a job in San Diego. I'm not so happy at Hoag anyway. I've been working on the pediatric ward. I hate the way the doctors drug the little kids. Twelve- or thirteen-year-olds won't behave, so the doctors put them in the hospital and give them Thorazine or Mellaril. I'm not even supposed to sit and talk with them, just make sure they take their medications and stay quiet. The kids all want to talk to me anyway."

"You wouldn't mind looking for a job in San Diego?"

"No. I'd like us to live together, and I need a new job."

So, Clay rented a tiny house on Coronado, not far from the Coronado Hotel. Fifty years before, Coronado had been a second-home community. People built small one- or two-bedroom homes on small lots. Now, with land values high, the homes served as permanent residences. "Quaint and atmospheric," Catherine called their house. She was happy. And Clay seemed genuinely excited about their living together. The two went shopping for undersized furniture. Jerry helped them move in his dilapidated truck. Clay even said they would get married "down the line."

They agreed to share all expenses. Right away, Catherine found a job working at Hillcrest, a County of San Diego inpatient treatment hospital.

But she hated her new job. The nursing supervisor told her not to spend time talking with patients. Instead, she had to make sure the patients didn't spit out their medications. She found the atmosphere cold and mechanical. Two weeks after she started the job, the nursing administrator told her she wasn't the right "type." That was fine with Catherine. However, psychiatric-technician jobs were not plentiful, and it took her two months to find another position—a weekends-only part-time stint at the Southwood Adolescent Treatment Facility.

The following spring, in1980, Florence called Catherine to tell her that a letter had arrived. It was addressed to Catherine from a "Mrs. Clay Morehead." Clay was away on a field trip. Catherine immediately drove to Tustin. Florence handed her the unopened letter. Catherine read it aloud:

Dear Catherine Penney:

Let me introduce myself. I am Clay's wife. WIFE. Yes, you are living in SIN. We have four lovely children: Barbara, age 18, Sally, age 16, Sandra, 10, and 14-year-old Clay Jr. They are torn up because they only see their father a few hours two weekends a month. You have used SEX to steal my husband. You are a HOME BREAKER. Matrimony is HOLY. God punishes evil Jezebels like you. You will taste the fires of HELL. Leave your scheming ways. REPENT. Ask OUR LORD JESUS CHRIST for forgiveness.

Melissa Morehead

Joe and Florence sat gaping at Catherine. "Cathy, you know I'm a dyed-in-the-wool Catholic," Joe said. "I believe in the sanctity of marriage. But I think his wife was wrong writing you that letter. When you met Clay, he was living apart from her for five or six years. I know you're happy with Clay. You're a good person, Cathy. I hope you two can work the thing out."

"What do you think, mother?" Catherine asked, turning to Florence.

"Well, I agree with Joe. You know, Clay makes a good living. It's good security."

"Clay told me in Hawaii that he was divorced. I never would have gone out with him if I'd known he still was married. It isn't right. I'm having some feelings of being bad. I'm glad you both don't think I am."

"No way," Joe said.

That night, Catherine handed Clay the letter as he walked through the door into the kitchen. "I received this from your *wife*," she said.

He glanced down the letter. "I'm sorry, Cathy. I should have told you. We *are* legally separated. It's been six years now. She wants half of my retirement if we divorce. I can't stand the thought." He sagged into a chair and dropped the letter onto the table.

"It's not right that you didn't tell me," Catherine said.

"I know. You're a moral person. I thought you wouldn't go out with me."

"I wouldn't have. Well, maybe I would have in Hawaii. But I wouldn't have come back. . . . And you told me you have to go to work every other weekend. You go to visit your children?"

"Yes. I pay child support, too." He looked up at her and added, "I'm always on time with it."

"Well, Clay, what are you going to do? Are you going to go ahead with your divorce?"

"Yes. I always planned to."

"But you haven't done anything about it."

"I know. I will."

A sense of being trapped filtered up through Catherine's being. *I don't want to be alone,* she thought to herself. *If I push him, he'll leave.* She bowed her head and began preparing dinner.

Over the next two months, Catherine and Clay went on as before. He visited his children, and she marked time at Southwest. They spoke rarely, and when they did, it was with exaggerated politeness. Catherine began visiting her mother and Cindy more frequently. "Keep on him," Cindy counseled her one day when the two sisters were having tea at Cindy's home. "He'll kill you with inaction. He hasn't done anything for six years. He won't now if you don't kick some butt."

"Cindy, I don't want to lose him. He just doesn't want to give up half of his retirement."

"Money? This isn't about money. This is California. He knows she gets half. He could have settled all this years ago. Six years he's been gone, and his wife is writing you hate letters?" Cindy rolled her eyes. "Look. He doesn't want it to be final. She knows that. He's got her just where he wants her, begging and pleading."

"I think you're too hard on him."

"*Somebody* should be. Like *you.*" Cindy got up and began slamming tea cups onto a platter. "You're too much like mother," she snapped. "You still see mother as a victim. She's *not* a victim. She's passive—she still can't stand up to Joe. She never sees what's going on. You were over the edge. Why did she wait so long to get you some help?"

"Well . . ."

"Oh, look at you—you're still defending her. She's doing the same thing with Michael. When he was seventeen, he slashed his chest over an argument with his girlfriend, and he was failing everything in school. What did she do? Nothing. Nothing until a teacher called, then she took him to a clinic. You'd think she'd have called Dr. Dorman. No. She took him to a clinic."

"You always fought, Cindy. That was good for you."

Cindy sat back down and put her head in her hands. "I guess I shouldn't be talking like this to you."

"I'm glad you feel you feel you can talk to me," Catherine said. "It makes it easier for me to talk to *you.*"

Cindy shoved her hair back from her face. "Cathy, since we're talking about family, I should tell you about Nana. You know, she's pretty sick. I think she's going to die soon. And this weird thing with Uncle Frank has come up. Nana would have done anything for him—you know, her only remaining son. All Uncle Frank knows how to do is drink and not work. I guess he knows he's a nothing. But according to Nana he's the only thing that remains of his brother, our father. Now that Nana is bedridden, she even calls Frank 'Chester.' She signed over her house to Uncle Frank and Aunt Peggy." Cindy clenched her fist. "Then that stupid bitch Peggy told Nana she had dementia and took control over her Social Security money. And that's not all. She told Nana it was sinful for her to do her yoga—but that's exactly what's kept Nana alive! Peggy told her she should read the Bible, too. You know the worst? Nana never said a word—not a peep. She's going to die a martyr to our sainted father." Cindy paused, then scrutinized Catherine. "You'll die too, Cathy, if you do the same thing with Clay."

"He has some goodness. He's kind and not judgmental."

Cindy sighed. "Gee, Cathy. I'm sorry for going off on you. I have a big mouth sometimes."

"You're not shy about saying what you think. I could use some of that myself."

Several times over the next several weeks, Catherine visited Nana, who had recently fallen and broken her arm. She had "bedsores to the bone," Catherine told Cindy. Catherine could not bring herself to criticize Aunt Peggy, so when she visited Nana, who now drifted in and out of consciousness, she sat in silence, feeling guilty and helpless. Soon, Nana died.

The next day, as Catherine sat in the living room staring at the wall, Clay put his arm around her and asked, "You're real sad about your grandmother, aren't you?"

Catherine nodded.

"Do you want to talk about her?"

"There's not much to say, Clay. I'm grief stricken. I've lost part of me." Tears coursed down Catherine's cheeks. She hugged Clay. "Thanks for asking." Clay patted her head. "I should have done more for her," Catherine whispered. "I'm too passive."

In the fall of 1980 Catherine announced to Clay that she had decided to resume her education. She needed a nursing degree in order to have more job options. At Southwood, she was qualified only to see to it that patients took their medications.

Southwood had three different units—one for children ages five through nine, another for those ten through twelve, and one for teenagers thirteen through eighteen. One registered nurse worked each shift on each unit. Some licensed technicians like Catherine also worked there. However, the rest of the staff consisted of unlicensed personnel—usually college students studying psychology and a few interns satisfying work requirements for their Marriage, Family, and Child Counselor license.

At Southwood, disruptive children were brought to a technician for approval to medicate. Catherine thought that the technicians used medication in lieu of commonsense, simple interventions such as disciplining an unruly child. Some children even requested medication, claiming bragging rights with their peers. The doctors who had to write the orders to medicate did not want to be bothered with frequent phone calls from the hospital, so they usually wrote "prn" ("as needed") on the orders. The mental-health workers complained to the charge nurse that Catherine was giving them a hard time about approving prn medication requests, and eventually kept their distance from her. Looking at the medication log for Monday through Friday, Catherine saw that many children—even as young as five and six—were routinely approved for medication as often as every four hours.

"The whole thing is ridiculous," she told Clay. "The parents can't control their children, so they take them to a psychiatrist. The psychiatrist doesn't know what to do, so he recommends hospitalizing the kids. In the hospital no one knows what to do with them, so they control them with medication. I get five dollars an hour for trying my best."

Catherine was still working only on weekends so that she could take courses and study during the week. She stepped up her education efforts, signing up for anatomy and physiology courses at San Diego City College. These courses were required for admission to a school that granted the registered nurse, or R.N., degree.

Catherine said no more to Clay about his relationship with his wife. And Clay, trying to keep the status quo, hardly spoke to her for the next two months. She studied, kept house, and prepared meals. Clay visited his children every other weekend as before. Every few months, he also spent an extended time, often several weeks, at military bases in Yuma, Arizona, or Point Mugu, near Santa Barbara. Catherine would sometimes drive to join him for a day or two. "A settled life," Catherine called it. In a letter to Cindy, she confided that she was afraid to bring up the problem of his divorce again, because Clay might leave.

Two years crawled by, during which Catherine completed the R.N. prerequisites. Her grade point average was 3.6—all A' s and B's, and high enough to ensure admission to an R.N. program. But there was a three-year wait at San Diego City College, the only school in the area offering a two-year course leading to the R.N. degree. "I can't wait three years," she told Clay. "I just can't. I called and there's no wait at the College of the Desert in Palm Springs."

"Palm Springs?"

"I have to do it, Clay. It's important that I do this for me."

"How long would it take?"

"Two years."

"That's a long time. What would we do?"

"We can visit each other. You can come to see me, or I'll come down here or see you at the base."

Clay shuffled off to the couch. "I guess we could manage."

"Oh thanks, Clay. I know you don't like it, but it's only two years. I have to continue my education."

"I know," he said. He picked up the remote and turned on the TV.

Catherine was accepted into the associate in nursing degree program of the College of the Desert, to begin in the fall. She would stay in the trailer that Nana had willed Florence, in nearby Desert Hot Springs. A rickety town of one-story houses with sand-and-cactus front lawns, Desert Hot Springs was home to mostly retired people. The town boasted natural hot springs: One was on the tumbleweed- and rock-strewn property where the trailer court was located.

Catherine applied for and received a Pell grant, a federal subsidy for adult returning students, and a student loan from the college. Florence paid the space rent for the trailer and the utility bills. Once school started, Catherine also began working on a per-diem basis two to three days a week as a licensed psychiatric technician at Coachella Valley Hospital in Palm Springs.

As they discussed, Catherine and Clay saw each other every second or third weekend. She often drove to Oxnard or Santa Barbara when Clay was on assignment there. Once, when he was working an extended stay in Santa Barbara, he sent her the key to his motel room, since he would be at work on the Friday afternoon she was to arrive. Catherine left Palm Springs early and arrived at the motel at nine o'clock in the morning. She let herself into his room. Pocketing the key, she glanced around the room—and then froze. Two coffee cups, one with red lipstick on the rim, sat on the nightstand.

Strands of long, black hair lay on one pillow on the rumpled bed. A key turned in the lock, and the maid walked in

"Hello. Can I clean up?" the maid asked.

"Sure." Catherine stepped out of the room. After the maid left, she sat in a chair in a corner of the room and waited. She heard another key in the lock at eleven o'clock. Clay walked in and stood dead still when he spotted Catherine.

"Oh!" he said. "I didn't expect . . ."

"I got an early start."

"That's good. It turns out I don't have to work this afternoon."

"Well, I got here before the cleaning lady was here."

"You . . . you did?"

"Um-hmm."

Clay looked around the room and then back at Catherine. "I thought we might go to the botanical gardens?"

"Um, Clay . . ."

Clay busied himself looking through his luggage.

"Clay, I saw two coffee cups when I came in. One had lipstick on it. Have you been seeing other women?"

"No."

"Then what were two coffee cups doing here? And I saw black hair on the pillow. Did you have sex with someone?"

"Cut it out, Cathy. Nothing happened."

"But . . ."

"If you want to go to the botanical gardens, we'll go. I'm not going to argue with you."

"Well . . . okay."

The silence between them felt as thorny as the cacti that they dutifully appreciated in the botanical garden. It deepened as the day wore on. The next night, they had dinner with one of Clay's coworkers and his wife. Catherine spent most of the evening on the couch with a pounding headache. Clay said not a word to her.

The next day, Catherine called Cindy and told her what had happened. "He *what?*" Cindy exclaimed over the phone. "He just said 'nothing happened'? You just stood there?"

"I didn't want him to get angry. He looked angry."

"If you had walked in and saw his bare ass waving in the breeze above another woman, he would have said nothing was happening. What's wrong with you, Cathy? Why didn't you force it?"

"Well, I told you. I just don't want him to leave."

"Wow. You'll pay for this. Now he sees he can go after every skirt in town because you're afraid of him. I'll bet he's been doing just that all along. You're not with him on most weekends, especially when he's on one of his out-of-town assignments. Jesus! I know you don't want to lose him, Cathy, but you *have* to say something. It just makes me so angry."

During the summer, school was not in session. Catherine, therefore, moved back to San Diego and lived with Clay again. He had given up the house in Coronado for a small one-bedroom house. "Dumpy," Catherine called it. Clay maintained he couldn't afford more.

Back at school in the fall, she studied diligently. In the evenings she visited several neighbors who lived in the trailer park, many of whom were "snow birds"—winter visitors to the desert. Together, they would watch the blood-red desert sunsets. She also often swam in the hot mineral-springs pool that bubbled just steps from her trailer. At times, she talked with her neighbor Helen, who had worked as a makeup person "to the stars," and Wilbur, a former cameraman, both now retired.

On weekend evenings, she often joined her friend Alice, a fellow student, at local discos or at Zelda's, a male-stripper club. At Zelda's, Catherine thought Alice was pretty wild, stuffing dollar bills into the strippers' jock straps. Catherine did have two dates with a young man her age who was visiting from Alaska. After dancing they stayed up late into the night talking. She told Alice she was going to "remain loyal" to Clay, but was sad to see the young man leave. Florence, Cindy, and Theresa visited from time to time on Sunday mornings; the three women would head to the Las Palmas Marriott Hotel for its famous brunch.

Catherine graduated in June 1984, with nearly a straight-A average. Florence, Cindy, and her husband, Allen, and Helen, Wilbur, and Clay all watched her march up to the podium in her white nurse's cap to receive her degree. She glowed as her family and friends offered congratulations and hugs.

"Are you coming back?" Clay asked Catherine.

"Do you want me to?"

"Yes."

So it was done. Catherine would move back "to see how it goes," she told Cindy.

Clay was working on a field job during June, so Catherine lived alone in the house and studied for her registered nurse licensing exam. She took the test in July, and then settled in for the long wait—the results would not come in the mail until October. She had no idea whether she had passed. Eager for work, she lined up some private-duty nursing jobs through an agency. As her first job, she worked as a live-in caregiver for an eighty-eight-year-old, wheelchair-bound woman in Julian, a small tourist town set among apple orchards in the hills one hour east of San Diego. Catherine made sure her charge took her heart medications and ate properly. After six weeks, another nurse took over. Her second job, lasting five days, entailed taking care of an emaciated, sixty-eight-year-old woman dying a painful death from breast cancer.

"Caring is the most important thing in life," she told Clay. "You know what makes it hard to be there? A picture on her nightstand of her wedding."

Clay and Catherine were having a late breakfast one October morning when the letter came from the licensing board. She ripped it open. "I passed!" she shouted to Clay. "I passed! When I took the psychiatric technician exam I was so uptight. That's why I failed both times. This time I was more confident!"

"Honey, you've really worked hard. You do deserve it. Let's go to that Spanish restaurant you like, what's the name? El Matador? Let's order champagne."

"Okay, let's do. Thanks, Clay."

Armed with her R.N. license, Catherine obtained a job at National City Hospital, located in a rough waterfront suburb of San Diego. Small-time drug dealers lounged on the sidewalks near the hospital, watching under hooded eyelids for cars creeping to a stop, then ambling to the passenger-side window to clinch the deal. The hospital was part of the county regional system for patient care. If someone in the area was unruly, or had psychotic episodes, a relative, neighbor, or friend could call the psychiatric emergency team responsible for the area. A mental health worker and some aides would arrive on the scene. If the team judged the individual as "dangerous to himself or others," or unable to care for him- or herself, doctors could hospitalize the person against his or her will.

Since Catherine was now making a better salary, she and Clay could afford to move to a nicer home. Catherine offered to loan Clay $5,000, all that remained from the sale of Nana's land, to make the down payment on a double-wide trailer. They agreed that each would pay half of the mortgage and household expenses. They found a trailer for sale for $40,000 in Lakeside, at the eastern edge of San Diego. They went ahead and moved into their new two-bedroom home in November.

During these months, Catherine did not visit her parents often. She felt "too much of the old stuff" around Joe. He had purchased a long-distance tractor-trailer rig and was drinking as heavily as ever. He told Florence he didn't drink on the road, but she didn't believe him. He still called Florence "the old slew" in front of everybody, and couldn't resist criticizing his daughters' hairstyles and clothing: "Why'd you go and cut it all off?" he'd bluster. "Are you a lez now?" Or, "For chrissakes, you can damn near see through that top. You advertising the merchandise?"

Catherine did visit Cindy at her new Spanish-style mountaintop aerie. The house overlooked the town of Laguna Beach, with its art shops jammed with tourists during the summer and gently curving beach framing the ocean beyond. Allen, Cindy's husband, had inherited his father's clothing manufacturing business.

"Is he still fucking you over?" Cindy asked.

"Oh, Cindy. Things are better."

"I'll bet he never admitted anything."

"No. I never brought it up again. He just had to let off his excess sexual energy."

"Right. I've never heard *that* one before. You sound like Edward Kennedy. He had just been 'picnicking' in the middle of the night when he flew off that bridge and killed Mary Jo Kopechne.

"Well, things are better."

About a month later, Clay and Catherine attended a party in Coronado given by one of his friends. Out of the crowd, a tall Lauren Bacall look-alike headed toward them, swinging her arms. She wore an ankle length, clingy, green silk dress and iridescent green three-inch high heels.

"Well, I dee-clare, Clay," she cried. "Honey bun, it's been a long time." Clay wrapped his arms around her and kissed her on the lips.

"Hi, Amanda. Amanda Van Egdom, this is Catherine Penney."

"Pleased to meet you," Catherine said.

"I'm pleased to meet you. You're Clay's new lady friend?"

"We live together."

"Live together! I dee-clare. How the world has changed." Clay grinned and moved off to join his coworkers.

"Talk to you later, Amanda," he called over his shoulder.

"Well, I do hope so, honey bun." Turning to Catherine, Amanda said, "Well, deary, you'll have to tell me something about yourself. Like where'd you meet Clay?"

"In Hawaii. He was on a field trip." Catherine eyed her lush figure.

"Oh, I know all about his field trips. Now deary, you might like to know a little about your darling. You already know what a handsome brute he is. That thick hair. Those bedroom eyes. Even that bushy mustache is cute on him. Or-din-ar-i-ly I really don't like mustaches, though. They just get in the way, if you know what I mean."

"Well, he is . . ."

"Oh, deary. He certainly *is* handsome. I should know. I'm sure he'll tell you. We used to date when he was married to Melissa. I mean when he was still living with her. He wrote me love letters. I still have them. They are precious."

"When he was . . .?"

"What a man. Deary, I mean what a *man*! Not to be crude or anything, maybe you don't want to hear this, but I'm sure you know he can go on and on for hours. And always at the ready. That's what I call a real magic wand, if you know what I mean. And you know, deary, you have to keep an eye on a man like Clay. Just a tip. Oooh my, there's Carla Moreni. Would you believe? Another one of Clay's ladies. Three of us in the same room! Would you believe? Ta ta."

"Who is Carla Moreni?" Catherine asked later as she and Clay drove along on the graceful curve of the Coronado Bay Bridge, above the cruisers and destroyers moored in San Diego Bay.

"Oh, someone I used to take out," he laconically replied.

"I overheard her say her husband is an invalid."

"Yep. Quadriplegic. A surfing accident just after they got married. I knew them then."

"When did you take her out?"

"Oh, about two or three years after I moved out."

"Did you have sex with her?"

"Yep. Cathy, what's this about?"

"Well, she was married and her husband was an invalid!"

"So what?"

"Didn't that mean anything to you?"

Clay stared straight ahead and stepped on the gas. A dark, angry silence filled the car.

Later that week, Catherine visited Cindy again. "Maybe you should call Dr. Dorman," Cindy said as they lunched on her patio in the sky. "You don't look so good. It reminds me of the time before you got sick. You're quiet and you look down at the floor a lot. Have you lost weight?"

"No, but I'm depressed about Clay. I thought things were okay, but he doesn't talk to me. And he's gone even more now—two to three weeks at a time."

"On assignments, right?"

"Yeah."

"Sounds phony to me. His old girlfriend, the one you met at the party, what did you tell me she said? That he needs a lot of sex?" Cindy shook her head. "Wake up, Cathy."

All through the rest of 1986 and into February 1987, Catherine busied herself with flamenco and drama classes, friends, and work. She still didn't visit Joe and Florence. Florence had gotten a job as a secretary at the University of California in Irvine, much to Joe's displeasure. "How come you're never home, old lady?" he'd mumble. "God dammit, where's my dinner? You're always out with those hens."

"I can have friends," Florence retorted. "I leave dinner for you." Whenever Catherine did visit or call, she found her mother preoccupied with bingo and bridge parties, luncheons, and talking on the phone. Clay was still spending two to three weeks a month out of town, and she felt lonely.

"Clay, I miss seeing you," she told him on one of the rare nights he was home.

"Oh, Cathy, cut it out. You know I have to work."

"But you never worked away this much before."

"I can't help where they send me. Hey, what do you think about going out with Hal and Rosemary tomorrow night? There's a bluegrass group at the Dirty Potato."

"Umm . . . okay," she said, avoiding his eyes.

"Just okay?"

"Okay."

Things took an awkward turn for Catherine at work, too—starting with something that happened during a "shift-change" meeting. At the hospital, nurses working on each unit met, at each shift change, with the nurses just arriving, to advise them of problems and patient status. "Problems" were usually patients who disrupted the unit. At one of these meetings, Catherine said, "I think we're too concerned about patients disrupting the unit and not enough about the patients themselves. Jesus Rosas is an example. He was shouting at everyone, 'Go away. Leave me alone or I'll kill you.' The staff wanted to give him an injection of Haldol to quiet him down. But he never assaulted anyone. I asked him why he was yelling and he told me he wanted the voices to go away."

Darlene Wisner leaned forward. Thin and wizened, she had worked as a nurse on the unit longer than anyone else. "But Cathy," she said. "We can't have someone going around shouting."

"Darlene, I'm not advocating his shouting . . ."

"I think you are. Let me tell everybody what happened. He's a difficult and agitated patient. We followed the rapid-tranquilization protocol. I'll review that. Fifty milligrams of Thorazine, given intramuscularly every two to four hours, and the use of the seclusion room, with restraints if necessary. Thorazine, Mellaril, and Haldol are the usual antipsychotic medications we use. Mr. Rosas resisted medication."

"He saw three staff members surround him. They grabbed him and came at him with a needle!" Catherine said.

Darlene squinted her eyes. "I prefer not to be interrupted, Cathy. You can say what you want when I'm finished. Anyway, as I said, Mr. Rosas resisted. He started swinging at us and increased his shouting behavior. So I ordered five-point restraints and placed him in the seclusion room. Some of you girls are relatively new to the unit. Five-point restraints are leather cuffs on his hands and feet as well as a strap around his lower abdomen to keep him immobile on the bed. That is necessary for patients in a psychotic storm. We need to get such patients into a subdued state as soon as we can. It's for the sake of the patient's health. Now, Cathy, what did you have to say?"

"I just think we have to pay attention to the human side of things. Jesus has been in the seclusion room nearly three days. He has been sleeping in his own urine. We've been discouraged from going in there because he's supposedly dangerous. But he has been nearly knocked out for least two days. He can't resist. He's a wet noodle. I asked other staff to help me change the sheets and to get him a fresh gown, but no one would go in there with me."

Darlene smirked. "Let us go on to discuss the other patients. I'll be happy to engage in a dialogue about handling difficult patients with any of you, whenever you want."

The group broke up. Catherine walked out with Sheila Walker, a psychiatric technician who had worked on the unit nearly as long as Darlene. "The old bitch. If she ever had a heart, it turned to stone a long time ago."

"Ha! Sheila, you tell it like it is!"

"Yeah. For the health of the patient, my ass! The real reason they're put in restraints and doped up is so the staff won't have to bother with them. The nut house. A nice, quiet place. That and because they're so afraid they'll get sued. You're the only one, besides yours truly, who talks to the poor souls. Mark my words, Cathy. It's getting worse. One of these days, they'll have a pill that'll *really* make them tranquil—turn them into walking zombies. Give no trouble to anybody. Didn't somebody write a book about that? *1984!* Yeah. Well, you're seeing it. You heard it here."

"I worry when I say things."

"Nah. You say things just fine. Speak up, girl. What do you think they'll do? Fire you? The pay's lousy and there are no benefits. They'd be doing you a favor."

Jesus Rosas couldn't stand on his own when he was released from the seclusion room, which was really just a padded cell with quilted plastic over soft foam walls, a hard gurney in the middle of the room, and a toilet in a small water closet. Nurses had to push him about in a wheelchair for the next two days. He refused to take oral medications so the nurses gave him Haldol by injection. By his second week in the hospital, he looked ashen and had developed a fever, rapid heartbeat, and labored breathing. The attending psychiatrist occasionally peeked into Jesus's room through the unbreakable window in the door on his daily rounds. More often, he just read the nurses' notes in the chart or asked them, "How's Mr. Jesus doing?"

"Resting comfortably" would come the reply.

At shift changes, Catherine repeatedly reported that Jesus looked sick. Finally, she said, "I try to talk with him, but I can't get him to respond. He hasn't eaten for three days. I think we should notify the doctor." That evening, Jesus, now comatose, was transferred by ambulance to the intensive care unit of a nearby medical hospital. He was diagnosed with untreated neuroleptic malignant syndrome. When he returned, his chart stated, "DO NOT USE HALDOL WITH THIS PATIENT."

Disgusted, Catherine put in an application with the County of San Diego Department of Mental Health. They had good health and retirement benefits. Her references, but for Darlene's, were excellent. She had received two Certificates of Major Recognition. One was "for her excellent case presentation of a difficult patient and her open, candid, appropriate willingness to share nondefensively her attitudes and feelings to achieve better patient care." Another was "for helping return a potentially violent patient to the unit without the use of force." In October, she learned that a position as staff nurse at Hillside, an inpatient facility, had opened. She applied and was accepted.

Four months later, in February 1988, Jesus Rosas was brought to Hillside. In the admissions room, he kicked and karate chopped into the air around him. "Take that! Stay away! I'll kill you!" Without speaking to him, the admitting psychiatrist ordered an injection of Haldol.

Catherine approached the attending psychiatrist in the nurses' station. "Dr. Spurgeon, I know this patient from National City Hospital, where I used to work. He is extremely allergic to antipsychotics, particularly Haldol. He developed neuroleptic malignant syndrome and almost died."

"Ms. Penney, neuroleptic malignant syndrome is extremely rare. I doubt if what Mr. Rosas experienced was that."

"I was right there."

"The nurses tell me he's disrupting the unit. He's at high risk for violence. He needs to be medicated."

"I know him. He's been this way before, many times, and he's never been violent."

"Ms. Penney, I want him medicated."

Again, when Jesus saw the nurses coming at him, he kicked and fought. He was again pinned to a gurney, his arms and legs shackled. Catherine insisted that someone monitor his vital signs every thirty minutes. When she came to work the next morning, she told her supervisor she was worried that Jesus might develop neuroleptic malignant syndrome. That night, he again became short of breath and was transferred to University Hospital. Several days later he came back with a red tag attached to his chart: "NO ANTIPSYCHOTICS." He spent his days in the seclusion room in four-point restraints, not strapped to the bed, but with restraints at his ankles and wrists. His screams could be heard down the hall. Catherine was the only nurse who looked in on him. The rest peered at him through the tiny window in the door. On one of Catherine's visits, she noticed that his skin was breaking down under the restraints, and she notified the charge nurse. The nurse did nothing, so Catherine contacted the patients'-rights office. A representative investigated, and the office immediately told the nursing staff that Jesus must have restraint-free intervals. If restraints proved necessary, the nurses must provide a skin care treatment consisting of antibiotics and a soft restraint lining. Since this meant more work for the nurses, Catherine received more than a few icy stares.

Two months later, Ella Lincoln, another patient whom Catherine knew from National City, was admitted to the hospital. Ella, too, had experienced a severe reaction to injected Haldol—in her case a twitching so violent that her physician thought she might suffer a seizure. He ordered the Haldol stopped. That evening, Ella walked up and down the halls swinging her arms in a circular motion, repeating over and over, "Don'tcha know it? Don'tcha know it? I know it. I know it. Don'tcha know it?" This went on into the night, and the psychiatrist on call finally ordered a Haldol injection.

"I know this woman, doctor," Catherine said. "She's extremely allergic to Haldol, so we discontinued it. She is also on two different medications for high blood pressure."

"What? Allergic? Do you think you can handle her until we get her records?"

"I think that would be best, doctor."

"Okay, I'll write an order for her records."

A week later, the records still had not arrived. Meanwhile, Ella hardly slept or ate, and she refused oral medications. The psychiatrist told Catherine it was "unsafe" to wait any longer, and he ordered Haldol.

"I won't give it," Catherine told him.

"You won't? I'm ordering it!"

"I have a right to exercise my clinical judgment."

"All right! I'll get someone else to do it!"

Toward the end of Catherine's shift, Ella stood in the middle of the hall shouting something unintelligible at the top of her voice. Technicians took her to the seclusion room and placed her in four-point restraints. At two o'clock in the morning, a nurse looked through the little window in the door. Ella lay motionless in a pool of urine. Forty-five minutes later, when she looked exactly the same, the nurse entered the room to discover that Ella wasn't breathing. An ambulance took her to the intensive care unit, where she was pronounced dead.

The next day, the staff members and the psychiatrist in charge held a debriefing. "My concern," Catherine told the group, "is that no one heeded the information I gave the doctor and the nursing staff. At shift change, I said she should be checked every fifteen minutes."

"We just don't have the staff to do that, Catherine," the psychiatrist retorted. "You know that."

"We shouldn't be handling such a patient if we don't have the staff. Ella's death was preventable." The temperature in the room seemed to drop thirty degrees.

The doctor sat upright. "I don't think so, Ms. Penney. I talked to the pathologist this morning. Ella didn't die from neuroleptic malignant syndrome. She aspirated on her own vomit."

Catherine met his eyes directly. "But that's a complication of neuroleptic malignant syndrome."

"No, I don't think so," he said. "We all feel terrible, but these things happen. I hope nobody takes on blame for this."

Catherine walked out of the meeting room with Stephen Childress, another nurse. "I feel terrible, Steve. She's dead!"

"I don't know what else you could have done. You can't twist their arms to check on patients. I wish I had been on yesterday."

Catherine bowed her head. "I can't be the only one, besides you, who sees what's going on! That doctor's in charge. He's supposed to take responsibility."

"He's the worst of the bunch. He shifts the blame back to the patients. And he's a bigot, too. I'm black, but I'm no black activist, Cathy. Ella was black and look how he treated *her*. I was once in a weekly meeting where he said, 'You people,' looking straight at me. What do you say, want to get a drink?"

"I need one," she said, with a grateful smile.

Catherine and Stephen had drinks each day after work, following their conversation about Ella. She began realizing that she found him attractive. Maybe it was his steady, soft voice, or his direct gaze. She could have a real conversation with him, too, not like all the dancing around with Clay.

At the end of one shift, Stephen and Catherine walked out together again. "Hey, Cathy," he suddenly said. "When are you off? This sounds like a line, but I own a small stable out El Cajon way. Maybe you'd like to come? Do you ride?"

"Horses?"

"Ha ha. Yes. Horses."

"I've never . . ."

"I have some gentle riding horses. I'd be happy to teach you."

They both had Friday off. Stephen picked Catherine up at nine o'clock in the morning, and they headed east on Interstate 8 toward El Cajon. Off the interstate, they drove through horse country—white-fenced houses with divided fields and smaller ranches along the peaceful, two-lane road. The gently rolling land was covered with tall, yellow, parched grasses. The bright blue sky directly above faded to a soft yellow in the distance, over pale orange hills dotted with green bushes. Stephen slowed the car as they passed a wooden rail fence, and turned into a dirt driveway under a wooden sign that read "Childress Ranch."

"This is it, my sprawling ranch. Really, it's only five acres. See that little house over there?" he asked, pointing to a clapboard shack. "That's where Ned, my caretaker and horse expert, lives. Never met a man who could read a horse like Ned. Did you know you can talk to a horse? Well, Ned certainly can. I mean talk—and the horse listens and talks back. Yes, sir! Pricks up his ears and whinnies at you. Ned knows just what they're saying. He knows if they need to get out and run, be rubbed down, or just hear someone talk to them. If you want to, you can have your virgin ride, if you don't mind my saying it that way, on Eagle. He's a gentle gelding. Mares are too hard to ride, too twitchy, so I keep only geldings."

"What's a gelding?"

"A castrated stallion."

"Oh."

They walked into the barn, which had four stalls. The horses grunted and snorted in anticipation. Ned, a thin man with a sun-soaked, deeply wrinkled face, approached.

"Hey, Ned, how's it?" Stephen said.

"Hey," Ned replied.

"This here's Cathy. Cathy, Ned."

"Howdy, m'am."

"How do you do?"

"Cathy has never ridden a horse, Ned. I'm going to put her on Eagle and let her get used to the saddle." Stephen opened a door to a wooden shed on the opposite wall, lugged out a saddle, and hoisted it up on Eagle, who craned his head back to have a look. Then, Stephen looked at Catherine. "Let's give it a try, okay?"

"Sure."

Stephen cinched the saddle and helped Catherine mount. He then fitted the horse with a halter and lunge line, led Catherine out into a fenced pen, and gave her the reins. "Hold the reins in one hand," he told her. "And just sit comfortably. I'll give you a chance to get used to it. Scared?"

"Not a bit!"

"Just balance yourself comfortably. Don't flop your legs! Rest them gently against his sides, and keep your heels down. You can trust the horse. He knows if you trust him. Having fun?"

"Oh, this is great! Pretty soon I'll be Annie Oakley. Or maybe I can be a Spanish rider."

Stephen showed Catherine how to squeeze her lower legs up against the horse's sides to get him to walk forward, and how to turn him right or left and stop him with the reins. She rode at a slow walk several times around the pen—then dismounted with a huge grin on her face.

Afterward, Stephen fixed lunch for Catherine in his ranch house, a one-bedroom frame home. Then they walked his property. He was proud of it—a piece of old California in the hands of a black man. He told her the West had a tradition of black cavalrymen, and he was descended from one of them.

Back home, Clay was gone for longer and longer periods of time. He left his phone number with Catherine, but they rarely talked. Catherine began accompanying Stephen to his ranch once or twice a week. She had really learned to ride, and they started exploring the countryside on horseback. One day, they brought along a picnic lunch. Stephen hobbled the horses next to a small creek and spread a blanket under a gnarled oak tree. After lunch they both stretched out on their backs and looked up at the sky dancing through the tangle of black branches and dark-green leaves. Stephen propped himself up on one elbow, leaned over, and lightly kissed Catherine on her lips. She put her arm around his neck and kissed him back. He softly rolled against her side and put his arm under her neck. She rested her head on his chest. They lay there, watching the purple shadows of the tree creep across the ground.

Catherine began spending nights with Stephen. He had told her he was separated from his wife, and Catherine told him she thought Clay was avoiding her. One June day, three months after their intimate picnic, they sat at breakfast at Stephen's kitchen table. He prepared scrambled eggs with salsa and black beans, and laid them out with locally baked cinnamon toast on flowered cotton place mats.

"Stephen," Catherine said. "I think I'm avoiding something. I feel guilty. This is beautiful. You're beautiful. You've been so kind. I mean besides teaching me to ride like a pro. I was scared, but I didn't tell you."

"I think I knew."

"I bet you did. Well, you never let on, and you let me learn at my own pace. What I'm avoiding is that I need to face up to my relationship with Clay. Being with you has made me wake up, to see how it feels to be treated like a woman. I now know that my relationship with Clay is probably over. And Stephen, maybe you're in the same boat. I don't mean to be saying something I shouldn't, but you may need to face up to your relationship with your wife. I can tell, you're still in love with her."

"Cathy, you are one honest woman. I guess that's what I've learned from you."

At this point, Clay had been gone for two months. Catherine left messages for him at the Old West Motel in Yuma. But he did not call. *That's it!* Catherine thought to herself. *I'm leaving.* She called her friend Rosa and asked if she could stay for a few days until she figured out what to do, and then packed her clothes.

At that moment, the door rattled. Clay walked in—nearly tripping over her two suitcases. "What's this?" he snapped.

"Clay, I'm leaving."

"Without saying anything to me? What's going on?"

"Clay! I've tried and tried to call you. You never answer! You used to go away for a week, now it's months. You never answer me directly. You're always evasive. You've been sleeping with other women. I can't go on like this."

He sighed and slumped against the door. "Well, we should give it another try," he said, his voice low.

"Are you willing to try counseling?"

"No. It didn't help my marriage. In fact it made things worse. Those people talk a language I can't understand anyway. We'll work it out."

Clay said he had no out-of-town assignments the next month. During the next four weeks they both seemed to be walking on eggshells. *Get some guts*, Catherine thought to herself. *You have to say something to him.* That evening, Catherine braced herself. "Clay, I have to talk with you."

"What about?"

"I care about you deeply, but I can't keep living like this. You promised, the first year we were together, that you would go ahead with your divorce. Are you going to do that?"

"As long as she holds out for half of my retirement, I won't."

"I just can't keep living like this. You're gone most of the time."

"I've been here for a month now."

"I know, Clay. But you're gone even though you're here. I'm not really here either. Just my body is."

Clay narrowed his eyes, just like he always did when preparing for battle. "What do you want to do about it?"

"I think it would be good if I went to the desert and got a job there for a while, until you get your divorce."

"If you go to the desert, then that's it; it's over between us." Clay sat down and took off his shoes. Then he snatched them up and walked off into the bedroom.

The next day, he left for a two-day job at El Toro Marine Corps base. Catherine called Hillside and said she would be off sick for two days, and then drove to Palm Springs. The next morning, she went to Coachella Valley Hospital in Palm Springs and applied for full-time work. Back at the Desert Spa trailer park, one of her neighbors, an old widower who had been threatening to move back to the city with his children for years, offered to sell her his single-wide mobile home. He told her she could make payments and he would charge no interest.

One week later, Catherine received a call from the human-resources representative at Coachella Valley Hospital offering her a job. Clay was standing right next to her when the call came. "I'll take it, of course. Thank you very much. In two weeks? November twenty-eighth? Yes. That would be fine."

Clay's eyes were so narrowed all Catherine could see was rage. "What about me?" he cried. "You're going to the fucking desert and leaving me with payments here? Well, go! But I expect you to continue giving me half."

"But . . ."

"No fucking buts. You agreed to half the expenses when I bought this thing."

"Well, okay. I'll meet my obligations. But what about the five thousand dollars I loaned you from my grandmother's estate? You promised to pay me back. You've never mentioned it."

"I'll give you your fucking money back. You're a real bitch, Cathy. A real bitch. You don't think of anybody but yourself!"

Catherine's face turned pale. *He is more important,* she thought to herself. *You can set yourself aside, turn the other cheek. He's hurting so.* She shook herself, and fixed her eyes on him.

"I know you are hurting, Clay. But I have always gone along with how you see things. I think now I have to pay attention to me. You know, all in all, I'm glad I've had this experience with you. I have learned how to love, how to accept love, and now I'll learn how to let go."

"Well, just go!" He stalked out the door, slamming it behind him. Catherine heard his truck engine roar to life, and a spray of gravel hit the side of the house as he sped off.

Eight

SWEET NEW GRASS

See there the sun that shines upon your brow,
the sweet new grass, the flowers, the fruited vines
which spring up without the need of seed or plow.

Dante, The Purgatorio

FLORENCE HAD SOLD NANA's trailer after Catherine had graduated and moved back to San Diego. Catherine did buy the mobile home from her neighbor for $6,000, with nothing down and $125 a month. She enjoyed her peaceful solitude. The desert was magical, especially at night, when the moon was full and the mesquite looked black against the shimmering desert floor. For her, the silence connected the earth with the stars above. During the day, roadrunners pecked at her screen door, and quail families marched in single file through the tumbleweed and cacti.

But she felt uneasy, too. She kept waking up at night blanketed by sadness tinged with terror. Somewhere deep within her, a fissure opened. Her hard-won strength, her integrity, her self, began to drip down through that crack. An ancient black mud oozed up through the same crevice. She knew immediately what it all meant. *I'm lost. It's my fault. I'm bad. I'm wrong, hopeless.* One night, she sat on the edge of her bed. The fissure led down to the depths of her soul, where her old self stirred. Had she not been climbing the mountain of Purgatory? Had she not seen the stars? Indeed, she had. But the old part of herself took the form of the King Demon, with his hairy chest and three heads clearly visible above the ice. The Emperor of the

Universe of Pain opened his eyes and lazily fluttered his three sets of bat-like wings, unleashing a freezing wind. His lips, smeared with human blood, twitched and then he spoke: "You! I am not so far away." Numbness spread throughout Catherine's body. She felt a pull—down, down. "I will not!" she cried. "I will not go back there!" *Dr. Dorman told me to be prepared,* she thought to herself. *He said that an ember of my old self remains. I am not bad. I am not helpless. I must use my new self.*

On November 28, 1988, Catherine began working on the psychiatric unit at Coachella Valley Hospital. The hospital had the local Medi-Cal contract, which meant servicing people who could not afford insurance. There were a lot of people being admitted—people who had sunk to the bottom of the well. All patients deemed "5150"—dangerous to themselves or others—or who could not take care of themselves were brought to the hospital's emergency ward. Those who had insurance, private or Medi-Cal, were admitted. The others were shipped off to Riverside County Hospital, sixty miles away.

A few months after Catherine started her new job, she called Cindy to tell her how things were going in general. When she told her about her continuing connection with Clay, Cindy's voice boomed through the receiver. "You're doing what? You've been out of there five months and you're *still* paying half of Clay's mortgage? For God's sake, *why?*"

"Well, I promised him I'd pay half of the expenses."

"Cathy, you gave him an ultimatum: commit or else. He took the 'or else.' It was his choice. He can't have it both ways. The real question is, Why can't you see that?"

"Cindy, you're right. It's just that I'm always afraid I'll hurt someone's feelings."

"Yeah. All the while, he's fucking a dozen women and rubbing your nose in it. How about that for hurting someone's feelings?"

Catherine was silent for a moment. "I'm going to call him."

"Does that mean you're going to end it?"

"Yes. It's done. Thanks, Cindy."

"You're welcome."

Over the next several weeks, Catherine left messages on Clay's answering machine to call her back, but received no reply. Finally, she left another:

"Clay, this is Cathy. I wanted to talk to you in person, but . . . Our agreement that I pay half was based on the fact that we were together. So, I'm not going to continue sending you money. And you must send me the $5,000 I loaned you. It's only fair. Clay, we were together for nine years—you owe me the consideration of returning my phone call." Catherine never heard from him.

To rebuild her social life, Catherine joined the Desert Singles. The group met every Friday for happy hour at Reuben's, a restaurant and bar in Palm Desert, just down the road from Palm Springs. "I'm going to experiment," she told a girlfriend she met through the group. When she dated a man who wanted exclusive rights, Catherine moved on. Palm Springs abounds with golf resorts, all with bars, and some with dance clubs. Catherine went with her friends and met vacationing golfers. Early in 1990, she started dating Don Highton, a sixty-year-old retired police officer she met at a Desert Singles dance party. Don's military language and bigotry reminded Catherine of Joe. However, he seemed respectful, even charmingly deferential, and always took Catherine to the best restaurants. Don was impotent "because of my abdominal aneurysm," he told her. When they had been seeing each other for about a year, things shifted. Don grew more controlling, expecting Catherine to be at home when he decided to call, and to be available for evenings when he wanted to go out. She stopped seeing him. She then dated Knute, a seventy-year-old man who agreed to "just be friends." They enjoyed dinner, movies, and plays, but after three months, Knute began talking of marriage.

No more dating, Catherine thought one evening, sitting outside her front door. She watched a coyote lope through the trailer park, stop, nose the ground, and then move on. *I need to become more intimate with Cathy. No one is going to make me happy unless I'm happy with myself.* She signed up for a yoga class, and a friend lent her a book on Buddhism. "As you think, so you become," she read. "If you think great thoughts, you will become great. If you think low thoughts, you will become low. The higher the thoughts, the greater the freedom." Catherine began practicing meditation. She particularly embraced the idea that individuality resides only within. *No one determines me but me,* she thought to herself. Catherine attended some gatherings of Sikhs and read about Guru Ram Das, his Golden Temple and the Sacred Space, the true and separate self within.

She gathered some women friends around her. Some were coworkers; others, members of Desert Singles and her yoga classes. She needed to stay current with the latest developments in nursing in order to keep her license as a registered nurse. So she took a cruise with some friends from Los Angeles to Ensenada, Mexico, with part of each day devoted to medical and nursing lectures.

Catherine also joined the local chapter of the National Alliance for the Mentally Ill. The group billed itself as an advocacy organization for those who suffered from mental illness, primarily schizophrenia. Catherine detected an Alcoholics Anonymous bias of accepting that schizophrenia is an illness that one just "has," and that can only be managed with drugs, never cured. A local newspaper, *The Desert Sun*, sent a reporter to a group meeting to collect interviews for an article to be published during Mental Health Awareness Week. Catherine was the only interview volunteer. The piece appeared in the October 1990 *Desert Sun*:

OUT OF THE SHADOWS
Mental Illness Stigmas Fade

The ritual was the same every day and night for six months after her release from the hospital.

Cathy, a schizophrenic patient, would look into the bathroom mirror and say, "You are a beautiful person. You have a right to be here."

Eighteen years later, she's now a registered nurse in a local psychiatric unit helping others who suffer like she did.

"Just making it out of schizophrenia is like coming out of hell," said Cathy, who requested confidentiality. "For seven years I was psychotic. I'm not going to deny that. But since then I've been able to be on my own, have a job, and have relationships. My life is rich and beautiful. . . .

"We all have at one time or another felt depressed or despair," Cathy said. "The feelings are the same for the mentally ill. It's just a matter of degree, and being able to cope. I think it's denying part of our humanity not to recognize this."

After the article appeared, Catherine told some of her coworkers she was the Cathy in the article. "A big mistake," she confided to a friend. "Emma Conrad, you know, my unit nurse manager, has started scrutinizing my decisions. She never asked me before why I didn't give an as-needed medication. Now she's quizzing me."

Six months later, in the spring of 1991, Catherine submitted a poem that was published in *The Journal*, a publication of the California Alliance for the Mentally Ill that featured first-person accounts of psychosis. Her poem was titled "Excerpts from My Journal of Madness," and showed her full name as the author, Cathy Penney, R.N.:

> Limitless, spaceless, timeless, like the deep, the deep deep. Where no sun shines, no light exists, where creeping creatures slink to and fro, going nowhere, purposeless, lifeless, only there because nothing is left. Living off one another, devouring each other! Only they don't die, or dissolve, they are just digested and come back in other forms, haunting—taunting—terrorizing. . . .
>
> Help, I'm colliding! I've got to catch my mind—it's straying! It's gaining speed. I'll never catch it. Oh, my God, my God, what will I do? I'm slipping, I'm going to lose hold! Oh Lord, there's nothing there! I'm going to fall—fall—but to where?
>
> . . . I'm dying. I can feel it, slowly. It hurts, I wish it would hurry up. The escape; the final solution. Oh, glorious death, how I desire you. I have waited for you. Now you are here and I can lie down, have peace until the voices raise me up again.

A one-sentence biography accompanied her poem: "Cathy Penney, R.N., continues on her psychotropic medication as she now works in a psychiatric hospital in Southern California, is a CAMI [California Alliance for the Mentally Ill] member, and the spokesperson for the needs of persons with neurobiological disorders."

Catherine immediately wrote an erratum letter, which was published in abbreviated form and with an editorial addition as a "Correction" in the next issue:

In volume 3, number 2, the biographical sentence erred when it said that "she continues on her psychotropic medication." Cathy, a valued CAMI member and effective advocate, writes that, although she was on Thorazine and Stelazine for 8 months in 1967, she has not been on any medication since. She credits her recovery from a neurobiological disorder to "excellent treatment and follow-up care," and adds, "As a psychiatric nurse I see how important it [medication] is for many people. My particular situation shows that there are some people who suffer from severe mental illness that do respond to other treatment and therapy."

Most of the members of the National Alliance for the Mentally Ill had a relative who was psychotic. Many of them were the parents of a schizophrenic. Struck by Catherine's normal demeanor, they urged her to speak at the statewide convention in July 1991, at the Hotel Del Coronado—a stone's throw from where she used to live with Clay. She was to tell her story of recovery to show that treatment works. During her address, Catherine described her slide into madness and her struggle to rejoin the world. When she finished, she reached for a glass of water placed in front of her. The moderator jumped up and said, "Thank you, Cathy, for sharing your wonderful story." He turned to the audience and continued, "See how psychotropic medications make her thirsty."

"Excuse me," Catherine interjected. "Except for a few months twenty-five years ago, before I really got any treatment, I have not been treated with any medications. There are other . . ."

The moderator interrupted her. "Yes. Well, are there any questions from the audience?" Hands raised, and a woman rose. "Jerry, you are the moderator, of course. But there are many of us interested in the fact that Catherine is not on medication and that her psychiatrist spent time with her. We all seek that for our children. There are many of us, I know, who have questions we'd like to ask her."

"There's no more time for questions." Jerry replied. " Perhaps at our next conference."

At Coachella Valley Hospital, tensions over whether to force patients to take medications rose. They came to a head in the case of Earleen Jones, a prostitute who was periodically brought to Coachella for various unruly behaviors. Earleen, known to be a "difficult patient" because of her cursing and resistance to being restrained, was once again brought to the emergency room by police. She had been walking down Palm Canyon Boulevard at four o'clock in the morning, shouting at the heavens, "Fuck you, fuck you all! Get your fucking hands off me, you fucking cowards! The devil will pay you back. You'll see. He'll roast your balls for breakfast!"

The law said that doctors could prescribe medication only in an emergency—defined as an individual's being a danger to others or to him- or herself. As two officers dragged Earleen into the admissions department, the emergency physician exclaimed, "Shit, shut her up! Give her Haldol by injection and ship her out. Up to the nut house." The hospital employed security personnel—burly men in white coats—for the purpose of restraining supposedly dangerous patients. Two such creatures grabbed Earleen's arms. She responded by turning up the volume of her invectives and kicking furiously at the orderlies. It took six people to hold her down. Finally, she was ushered to the ward, a security officer at each side. By this time, she was quiet and calmed down, and actually appeared sedated. Emma Conrad, the nurse manager, ordered Earleen taken immediately to the seclusion room and put in restraints. When Earleen saw four people, two women and two men, coming at her, she shouted, "What are you doing?" The team dragged her toward the seclusion room. "Don't take me there! I haven't done anything wrong! Let go of me, you white sons of bitches! I've got rights! Let me go!"

Policy dictated that patients in the seclusion room wear only a hospital gown, just in case they had a weapon hidden. Emma ordered Catherine and a male aide to help get the gown on Earleen. Once again, six people wrestled with Earleen, trying to strip off her clothes, while she thrashed back and forth like a giant fish in a net. Finally, there she was, stark naked except for her sanitary napkin. The aides managed to get a hospital gown on her and strapped her to the bed. Catherine staggered to the bathroom and vomited. Earleen kept shouting and thrashing, so Emma ordered Catherine to give her another injection of Haldol, and again in one hour, then again in two to four hours.

At the end of one hour, Earleen was still shouting. Catherine told Emma, "It's an as-needed order, and she doesn't need another shot so soon."

"What? Listen to her. She's entirely out of control."

"She's in restraints," Catherine said. "She was quiet when she arrived on the ward."

"Don't you question me. You're always questioning medication orders. I'm going to make sure she doesn't pose a threat to other patients and staff. You know what rapid tranquilization is, Cathy: medicating someone in a psychotic rage. These people need to sleep. They aren't even aware of how much this will help them. I'm *ordering* you to give her another injection of Haldol."

Catherine drew up fifty milligrams of Haldol into a syringe and entered the seclusion room with another nurse. Earleen twisted her mouth like a terrified child. "Oh please, please don't give me another shot. I can't stand being drugged. Please. I'll keep quiet. I will."

Catherine walked out and told the charge nurse, who was just under Emma, "This is not an emergency. She said she would quiet down." The charge nurse ordered her to give the injection anyway.

"I have to consider Emma's order as well as my duties under my nursing license," Catherine replied. "Earleen is not a danger to others or to herself. She is refusing medication, which is her right. We have pushed her into this state."

"Are you refusing to give the medication?"

"Yes, I am."

Another nurse gave Earleen repeat injections every three hours. Catherine was assigned the task of checking Earleen's pulse and respiration rate every fifteen minutes, as well as looking for skin breakdown under the restraints. By now Earleen was so doped she had urinated on the bed sheets, which had also darkened with menstrual blood. Catherine asked for help so she could change Earleen's clothing and linen. Two nurses volunteered.

"No way," Emma said. "Leave her be. Earleen is unpredictable. She's only been calm for a half-hour. I don't want my nursing staff put in harm's way." Emma placed a formal criticism in Catherine's personnel file, accusing her of endangering a patient and the staff by refusing a direct order.

Catherine had been talking to her friend Joyce, another nurse on the unit, about patients'-rights violations. Joyce had worked at the hospital for nineteen years. She was to retire in one more. "It's always been this way," she told Catherine at lunch. "They want to protect their precious *private* patients, the ones that pay, from the 'crazies.' They define 'emergency' and 'being dangerous' as inconveniencing either the private patients or the staff."

"Emma Conrad thinks I'm a troublemaker," Catherine said. "She's watching me. There's a good reason for my paranoia."

"Cathy, anyone who opposes Emma is a troublemaker. And I hear what goes on when you're not here. The whole ward knows about your 'history,' they call it—having been a patient yourself. I overheard the old bitch tell Ursula that people like you shouldn't work in mental health. Your 'history,' she says, colors your objectivity. Ursula, the ever-obedient sycophant, stood there nodding. If someone told Ursula to jump into a tank of feeding sharks, she'd dive right in."

Catherine refused to give medication by injection to other patients who resisted oral medications or who could not give consent, such as a twenty-year-old, severely retarded woman. She also informed patients that they had a right, by law, to refuse medication. One day, Catherine noticed a patient twitching and grimacing, and wrote in the chart that she thought he was having a reaction to injected medication. She talked to the patient's psychiatrist, a man who trusted Catherine's judgment, and he discontinued the order. Catherine's friend, Joyce, overheard Emma mumbling under her breath that she was going to get rid of Catherine. A few weeks later, Catherine attended a meeting during which Emma asked who was going to be on duty during the weekend. Upon hearing that Catherine was scheduled, Emma said, " Oh great. We'll have the inmates running the asylum." At another staff meeting Emma talked about using "creative charting" to get around "stupid, liberal patients'-rights rules." Creative charting meant declaring a patient dangerous when that was not the case, to justify injections of medication, the use of restraints, and the seclusion room.

In May, Emma wrote Catherine up again, this time for refusing to force medication on a male patient who had punched a psychiatric technician during a previous hospitalization. But on this admission, the same patient came in calm and composed, and voluntarily. Emma materialized, seemingly out of thin air, and said to him, "You're going into seclusion. There's no more discussion."

"You bitch," he replied. "You better not touch me." Emma summoned security personnel, who dragged him off, kicking. Catherine told the charge nurse he did not appear dangerous. Emma wrote Catherine up again, to document her "poor nursing skills." "Patients need to know who's calling the shots," she told Catherine. "Giving them medication is for their own good; their illness blinds them to this, so it's up to us to see they take their medication."

Jesse Starke was another patient admitted to the unit from the emergency room, brought there by the police because he had been panhandling in the tourist area. "He's been here before, and his records indicate he's unpredictable," Emma observed. "He needs to be in seclusion so we can observe him."

Catherine looked at Emma. "He's calm."

"Young woman, don't you contradict me! He is known to refuse his medication." Nothing written in the chart indicated that Jesse, when admitted this time, had walked leisurely onto the ward and said, "Hi again, guys." Nor did anyone offer him oral medications. The only note in the chart, written by Ursula, read, "Patient hostile and combative and a danger to staff and other patients. Dr. Smith called and ordered Haldol."

The next morning, Dr. George Smith walked by the seclusion room, opened the peep window in the door, and saw Jesse rhythmically rolling from side to side as best as his arm and leg restraints would allow. The doctor renewed the medication orders. That afternoon, Jesse was released from the seclusion room, a beaten man who could barely walk. Catherine was medication nurse that day and was ordered to give him yet another injection of Haldol. When she approached, Jesse cried, "Please, please no more." She squirted the Haldol into the toilet and then wrote in the chart that she had administered the drug. She told Jesse to call the county office of patients' rights. The number was posted, as required by law, next to the patients' public phone. "I can't do it," he moaned. "God knows what they'd do to me."

Catherine called the hospital patients'-rights representative herself. An investigator showed up the next day and looked over Jesse's chart. Catherine then called the California office responsible for investigating patients'-rights abuses. In addition, she contacted Julian Wright, the attorney for Protection and Advocacy Incorporated, a federally funded patients'-rights organization. He asked Catherine to send him written documentation, with other witnesses if possible. Catherine began going through the charts. Her friend Joyce, as well as Joanne, another nurse, agreed to act as witnesses.

On June 3, 1992, Catherine received a formal disciplinary notice titled: "Nursing assessments, therapeutic interventions, adherence to Unit Standards of Care are not performed at a proficient level." Emma Conrad and charge nurse George Slater accused Catherine of being "unable to promote medication compliance with some patients, and she advised us that the patients had refused medication. It was further noted that in other cases, Ms. Penney had failed to notify physicians of the need to order prn [as-needed] medications." The notice continued:

> The failure of a clinical nurse to perform at a proficient level compro-
> mises patient care. In the case of inability to correctly assess the patient
> for medication, it additionally endangers other patients and staff by in-
> creasing the potential for acting out behavior directed at others. The
> repeated inability of Ms. Penney to favorably respond to long-term
> coaching, for other than short periods of time, is a great concern. It pro-
> hibits her assignments to charge nurse, and/or case manager, two areas
> of performance expected of clinical nurses, limiting her value as a staff
> member, and making it necessary for other clinical nurses to work longer
> in these assignments. . . .
>
> Ms. Penney has been coached for at least a year re her inability to
> properly assess patients for the need for chemical intervention, as well
> as her lack of ability to form therapeutic relationships with the patients
> that promote medication compliance. Each time she has marginally
> improved to a proficient level of performance, but is unable to main-
> tain that improvement. . . . Ms. Penney repeatedly demonstrates the
> inability to maintain a proficient level of performance in these areas.

Catherine wrote a rebuttal:

> . . . I will not force or coerce a patient to take medication, especially if
> that patient has refused to sign a medication consent form or has with-
> drawn his consent to receiving antipsychotic medications by stating such

intentions to me or any other member of the treatment staff. See welfare and institutions codes 5325, 6000, and 6004.

What I do, as I've stated before, is to encourage the patients to take their medications and to talk to their doctor if they have any questions or concerns about their medications. [Just] because a patient is considered to have a high potential for acting-out behavior does not, legally or ethically, or in my view, justify taking away that person's right to informed consent. And, it certainly does not make it right to medicate such a person against his or her will with intramuscular antipsychotic medications, as opposed to offering p.o. [oral] medications first.

Pacing about the unit, using profane language at times, slamming a door, or being delusional, confused, or refusing to follow directions does not constitute an emergency condition: That is not a sudden marked change in the patient's condition so that action is immediately necessary for the preservation of the life or the prevention of serious harm to that patient or others, justifying medicating the individual with, and I stress, IM [intramuscular] psychotropic medications against his will.

As a health care professional, I feel other interventions can be utilized in these cases, such as a one-to-one, giving the person some space, some time out in his room away from stimuli. These interventions, however, are rarely utilized, and medicating individuals is the intervention that is most widely promoted and encouraged regardless if that person has consented or not to taking such medications. . . .

According to welfare and institutions code #5326.5(D), a person confined shall not be deemed incapable of refusal of proposed therapy solely by virtue of being diagnosed as mentally ill, disordered, abnormal, or mentally defective. . . .

Implementation of appropriate interventions involves more than using medication just as a means of chemical restraint. I utilize talking with a patient, and allowing time out or some space for a patient; however, I have been approached in a very negative way by a few of the case managers when I have attempted to do [so]. The medication issue is always brought back. I am informed that it is my job to medicate patients the case managers feel need to be medicated, without allowing time to assess the individual myself or to have some input into the decision as to why he or she needs the medication. The fact that the patient's behavior is bizarre becomes the justifiable cause to medicate against the patient's consent. I have been in nursing fifteen years, seven years as a licensed psychiatric technician and eight years as a registered nurse, and never in all those years has my integrity and my clinical judgment as a nurse professional been so attacked. Never have I been so insulted by a fellow nursing professional. In those years as an R.N., I have functioned as a charge nurse and as a nurse team leader involved in team treatment, [and in] planning and assisting patients in reaching specific treatment goals while they are in the hospital. . . .

I have never worked under a more unprofessional or unfair system of management in my life.

During the next several weeks, a Protection and Advocacy Incorporated representative visited the unit to investigate. He found some patients' charts missing. Catherine received two more disciplinary warnings. One was for a minor insulin-dosing error she made and correctly recorded. Emma issued a second formal disciplinary warning on June 26, 1992, recommending a three-day suspension. After her suspension, Hank Graham, the human resources director of the hospital, placed Catherine on indefinite administrative leave because conditions on the ward had become "too hostile." All the while, the state, county, and Protection and Advocacy Incorporated were investigating patients'-rights abuses.

On October 1, Julian Wright sent the following letter to Hank Graham:

Dear Mr. Graham:

Protection and Advocacy Inc. ("PAI") is the independent agency which is mandated by state and federal law to protect and advocate for the rights of persons with mental illness who are in facilities providing care and treatment.

PAI has the authority to pursue administrative, legal, and other appropriate remedies or approaches to ensure the protection of the rights of such persons. California Welfare and Institutions Code ("WIC") § § [sections] 4900, 4902; U.S.C.A S § 10801 et seq.

Over a significant time, and increasingly over the past several months, PAI has received reports from a substantial number of creditable sources alleging an ongoing and pervasive pattern of extremely serious violations of psychiatric patients' rights within Coachella Valley Hospital's psychiatric unit and its emergency room.

If these charges are well founded, as they appear to be, the hospital would be subject to a variety of possible legal sanctions, including civil liability, revocation of its designation and authorization to evaluate and treat persons detained involuntarily (see WIC § § 5326.9 and 5404), as well as possibly jeopardizing its JCAHO [Joint Commission on Accreditation of Healthcare Organizations] accreditation for failure to comply with applicable standards concerning implementation of patients' rights.

Several of these alleged violations were investigated by the Riverside County Patients' Rights Program, and various changes were recommended by that Program as a result of its investigation. (See the report to the unit's Medical Director dated July 1, 1992, and letter to its Manager of Psychiatric Services dated June 17, 1992.)

While there have apparently been some changes made in the unit's written policies in response to those recommendations, we have been advised that many of the practices have remained essentially unchanged.

The information we have received concerns allegations of abuses and rights violations in three distinct areas:
I.   Medication practices;
II. The use of seclusion and restraint;
III. Provision of advocacy services.

I. Medication Practices

The assertions made in connection with medication practices can be briefly summarized in the following nonexhaustive list:
1. Patients are forcibly administered antipsychotic medication on an emergency basis despite the absence of a legally defined emergency, after which charted entries are fabricated so as to reflect these nonexistent emergencies. We have been advised that prospective psychiatric inpatients are often forcibly medicated as a matter of course (as

well as being restrained) in the emergency room during the pre-admission process—before there has even been an appropriate psychiatric evaluation.

2. Patients are not provided with statutorily required information concerning antipsychotic medication, including their right to refuse it in the absence of a legally defined emergency or a legal determination of their incapacity to refuse such medication following a hearing held for that purpose. See WIC S 5332.

3. So-called "PRN" [as-needed] orders are commonly used to legally circumvent the requirements of an emergency or obtaining informed consent. Such orders, according to our sources, typically authorize around-the-clock intramuscular administration even to patients in seclusion or restrained or calm, already heavily sedated, or even asleep.

4. Patients who refuse medication and are viewed as "management problems" (usually because they are verbally abusive or use profanity) are involuntarily medicated in disregard of the requirements of WIC § 5332 cited above.

II. Seclusion and Restraint

A similar nonexhaustive listing of alleged seclusion and restraint abuses is as follows:

1. There is an almost total disregard of the legal requirement that less restrictive interventions be attempted before the inclusion of seclusion and restraint. See 22 CCR § 70577 (j) (1). Rather, these measures are impermissibly used as punishment for such "infractions" as exercising a right to refuse medications or for purposes of control or staff convenience. See 9 CCR § 865.4(a).

2. We are told that not infrequently the mere use of profanity, noncompliance with nursing staff directives, or "a history of violence" is sufficient to trigger a seclusion order, rather than protection from imminent injury as required by law. See 22 CCR § 70059. It is also noteworthy that, according to our information, seclusion and restraint are more frequently imposed on Medi-Cal patients than on others for the purpose of "protecting" patients with private insurance. False

(otherwise known as "creative") charting, we are told, often accompanies such practices, in order to legitimize them.

3. "Takedowns" are customarily accomplished with the assistance of untrained male security guards who may then participate in disrobing female patients.

4. We are also advised that seclusion and restraint are prolonged for highly questionable periods; orders are often written covering up to twenty-four hours, which generally means that the patients involved will serve that full term even if the behavior that precipitated the order had ceased much earlier. (It is our understanding that in one documented case, a developmentally disabled woman, whose psychiatric detention was itself of dubious validity, was kept in continuous seclusion for sixty-three hours—not because she was dangerous, but rather, according to the chart, because she was "agitated when around others.")

5. We are told that some patients in seclusion and restraint—especially the significant number labeled as "problem patients"—are often denied such "amenities" as routine bathroom (or even bed pan) access and water, not to mention such nursing care as required range-of-motion exercises, and periodic checks of vital signs, etc., in violation of state regulations. In addition, it is our understanding that the required fifteen-minute observations occur through an outer door only. See 22 CCR § 70577 (j).

6. According to our sources, patients who no longer meet the legal criteria for seclusion and restraint are routinely required to enter into illegal "contracts" unrelated to the behavior for which they were secluded or restrained, including purported waivers of their right[s] to refuse prescribed medications, including PRNs, before being let out.

III. Provision of Advocacy Services

Problems in this area first came to PAI's attention as a result of a complaint made by a patient on the psychiatric unit.

We learned from that patient—and it is undisputed—that a hospital employee named George Ellsworth, who plays a key role in the patient-admission process, routinely serves as the patient's "advocate" at the legally required certification-review hearings (also known as probable-cause hearings or Gallinot hearings). See WIC § 5256. It is at such hearings that the question of the hospital's right to continue to hold the patient against his will is resolved. Therefore, under basic principles of constitutional due process, the patient, whose fundamental right of personal liberty is at stake, must be represented by an independent attorney or advocate.

An independent advocate is one who "has no direct or indirect clinical or administrative responsibility for any recipient of mental health services in any mental health facility, program, or service for which he or she performs advocacy activities." WIC § 5500 (d). This essential requirement of independence from the provider of mental health services was recently underscored by a statement of legislative intent to that effect in WIC § 5510, subsection b. Accordingly, the Legislature has mandated a system whereby advocates are appointed, or their services are contracted for, by the local mental health director, WIC § 5500 (e), and pursuant to which they are provided with knowledge of due process proceedings by the State Patients' Rights Office for the specific purpose of providing representation to patients at administrative hearings. WIC § 5512 (h).

Thus, Mr. Ellsworth must immediately cease all activities as patients' advocate at these hearings and be replaced forthwith by an independent advocate designated by the county mental health director in accordance with applicable law.

It is also our understanding that there will be a JCAHO survey of the facility in the near future, and we would appreciate your advising us of the exact date of its scheduled commencement, and of the date set for input by interested parties.

Absent proper resolution of the issues raised in this letter, we will have no choice but to take appropriate legal action to achieve that result and to advise JCAHO and the Medicare and Medi-Cal authorities. Mr. Ellsworth must immediately cease all activities as patients' advocate at these hearings and be replaced forthwith by an independent advocate designated by the county mental health director in accordance with applicable law.

It is our understanding that Mr. Ellsworth is also impermissibly usurping the county patients'-rights advocate's duties in dealing with patients' complaints. Indeed, we understand that patients' right to contact the county advocate and this agency are being denied in violation of the law. These practices must also be terminated at once.

As to the illegal medication and seclusion and restraint practices referred to in this letter, we must insist upon prompt verifiable assurances that such practices are not occurring, or if they are, that they will cease immediately.

To address the issues referred to in this letter, we request a meeting with you at your earliest convenience.

Absent proper resolution of the issues raised in this letter, we will have no choice but to take appropriate legal action to achieve that result and to advise JCAHO and the Medicare and Medi-Cal authorities of the alleged conduct which, if confirmed, would violate professional and Accreditation standards and Certifications.

Very truly yours,
Protection & Advocacy, Inc.
Julian Wright
Staff Attorney

Catherine next received a letter from Coachella's director, Hank Graham, dated October 16. The letter stated that her administrative leave would end, and she would be assigned "to a nursing position other than in the psychiatric unit." She was offered a job in social services, discharge planning, or utilization and review, effective October 22, 1992. She accepted the position in utilization and review, scrutinizing hospital records to make sure they met with all regulations. Graham assured her that "when everything calms down," she would be reassigned to her old position. But on February 13, 1993, the day after her forty-third birthday, she received a notice that her position in utilization and review was being eliminated. Moreover, there was no longer a position available for a registered nurse on the psychiatric unit. She was "laid off."

Catherine immediately contacted a lawyer and filed an action alleging wrongful termination. She also signed up for, and began to receive, unemployment benefits. She did some volunteer work at a local hospice and applied for work at the County of Riverside Department of Mental Health, as well as at a small, private psychiatric hospital. She also filed a grievance stating she was promised first priority for her old position. Her grievance was denied. She then appealed, noting that a nurse who had been working on a per-diem basis was hired full-time.

At the urging of the California Nurses Association, Catherine filed an affidavit with the National Labor Relations Board stating that she was fired for being a whistle-blower. She told the agent who interviewed her that she had also been discriminated against because she was known to have agitated for union representation for the nurses. Back in 1990, the hospital had opposed organizing efforts by some nurses and distributed an antiunion flyer. At a staff meeting on the psychiatric unit, Emma had asked Catherine, "Why are you supporting the union?" Catherine told her that she felt the nurses needed a voice in the interest of fairness. The nurses voted against organizing at that time.

In 1992, before she was laid off, Catherine had met with two Teamsters' representatives to see whether the union would support her in her efforts to eliminate patient abuses. She also talked with them about renewing the effort to lobby the nurses to vote for unionization. Soon, another nurse who was outspoken in his support for unionization was fired from Coachella. Catherine told other nurses that, with a union in place, such arbitrary decisions by management would be more difficult. Another vote on whether to unionize was scheduled just after Catherine returned from administrative leave. The union won by just three votes—Catherine's and those of two per-diem nurses. But the hospital challenged those votes, arguing that the per-diem nurses were part-time and Catherine was no longer working at the hospital. The National Labor Relations Board investigated and ruled against the hospital.

Meanwhile, Catherine's attorney negotiated an $80,000 settlement with the hospital. Director Graham objected, on the grounds that Catherine had failed to mention on her employment application that she had been a patient in a psychiatric hospital. Twenty-five thousand dollars was all he would authorize. Catherine's attorney urged her to accept. The agreement specified that Catherine could not work with any agency, clinic, or organization that was in any way connected to or had a contract with Coachella Valley Hospital. Most medical clinics, as well as Riverside County, had such contracts, which meant that she would have to leave the desert. And, she would be prohibited from talking about any of her experiences at the hospital. "I will not sell out," she told her attorney.

Catherine told Cindy she felt saddened and lost, and that she had even considered calling me. Instead, she would "do something positive for myself." She decided to search for "spiritual meaning."

At Christ of the Desert Newman Center, a Catholic church in Palm Springs, Father Thomas addressed his flock. "Everyone is welcome to receive the sacrament here," he intoned. "God does not deny his grace to anyone. Divorce, abortion, prostitution, homosexuality, anger, or even blasphemy does not exclude you from His grace. Life is about joy, not sin. We celebrate the positive, the beautiful, which is in all of us. Let us read from Psalm 114: 'Return, oh my soul, to your tranquility. For the Lord has been good to you. For He has freed my soul from death, my eyes from tears, my feet from stumbling. I shall walk before the Lord in the lands of the living.'"

Catherine began attending services regularly at the Newman Center. She also joined the women's liturgical dance group at the church, a free-form modern dance performed each Sunday in honor of "the positive spirit of Jesus." And she began attending lectures at the Palm Springs Church of Religious Science.

She received unemployment benefits for two months. In May 1993, she found a job three days a week as a per-diem nurse at Canyon Springs Hospital, a small, private psychiatric facility. She worked as a staff nurse, medication nurse, and charge nurse every other weekend. In October, the Riverside County Department of Mental Health hired her to work with a psychiatrist who ran the Prolixin clinic. Prolixin is an antipsychotic medication given by injection. She was "not thrilled" with the job of giving long-acting injections to patients who refused oral medications. But her new supervisor assured her that the patients were carefully screened so as to ensure the medications were necessary. She learned that she would become eligible for another position with the county, as soon as one was available.

As part of her job, Catherine was offered overtime work at, of all places, the emergency room at Coachella Valley Hospital. Her role was to certify the need for involuntary hospitalization. Coachella apparently was no longer using one of its own employees to do that job. She also had to authorize transportation for those without any form of insurance to the county hospital in Riverside.

One of Catherine's friends from the psychiatric unit at Coachella Valley told her that the hospital had come under severe criticism for inadequate policies in the emergency room and poor practices in the psychiatric unit—practices that had violated health and welfare codes regarding patients' rights. Moreover, some of the charts Catherine had cited in her complaint never did turn up. The California office of patients' rights had enjoined the emergency room from medicating patients without informed consent and ordered it to document specifics of patients' dangerousness before giving medications without consent.

Violations of practice on the psychiatric unit took the form of inadequate documentation, medication of patients for the convenience of staff, use of medication for verbal threats rather than the required physical threats, and unusually long stays in the seclusion room. The staff could no longer take away a patient's clothing—with the exception of potentially dangerous objects like belts. The practice of disrobing patients in the seclusion room was deemed an assault on their dignity. Physicians were required to cease "as needed" orders for medication by injection unless the doctor saw the patient once every twenty-four hours. Many of the psychiatrists had not visited their patients during their entire seclusion room stay. Restraints were not to be used except in cases of physical danger. The hospital was also ordered to give patients'-rights classes to all employees. One problem that remained unaddressed was the use of creative charting—falsifying documentation to justify the use of forced medication. Also, Emma Conrad was given the option of resigning or she would be fired. After her resignation, her computer was missing. Catherine told Joyce that she was glad to see that her efforts had paid off—patients were assured of their rights. She had not lost her job in vain.

In January 1994, a social worker in charge of handling the needs of indigent older adults got married and left the area. Catherine's supervisor at the county wanted a registered nurse to take over the job, since the older adult population suffered all sorts of physical illness. Indeed, cardiovascular disease or Alzheimer's disease led to mental problems as well. Catherine got the job. As registered nurse case manager in Older Adult Services, she was responsible for the caseload west of Palm Desert: the cities of Palm Springs, Cathedral City, Rancho Mirage, Thousand Palms, Sky Valley, and Desert Hot Springs. Another nurse managed the territory east of Palm Desert. She and Catherine shared the services of a licensed clinical social worker.

Catherine loved her new job. Rather than working in an office, shuffling paperwork, she visited clinics, old-age homes, and hospitals. She even went to her old psychiatric unit at Coachella Valley to investigate cases of elder abuse, and saw to it that the county or private agencies provided medical and social services. She also accepted invitations to speak about her experience as a mental patient, with the blessing of her supervisor. She spoke frequently at community meetings sponsored by the county to help remove the stigma from mental illness. Catherine's supervisor often referred public service groups looking for information to Catherine. Catherine felt complimented when a media company paid her to critique and advise on scripts for a local television production on schizophrenia.

In November 1994, Catherine sat in the one remaining seat at a lecture on Buddhism in modern life. David McGregor, in the adjoining seat, offered to buy her coffee afterward. Fifty-nine years old and retired from the Canadian Secret Service, he had also served as an officer in the British navy. He spent the winters in Palm Springs and the summers in Canada and taught Tai Chi to seniors. And he was a Buddhist. Catherine thought him "male and spiritual." The two saw each other nearly every evening and spent many weekends walking and hiking in Joshua Tree National Park.

"A pretty nice life," Catherine told Cindy. "I can be myself at work and I'm appreciated for that, and I'm myself with David, and he appreciates me. No bullshit."

"You really like this guy?"

"Yep. I feel it's a mutual thing. I mean, he respects me and I respect him."

"Are you thinking about the big M?"

"Oh, I know he wants to be married. Little hints are all over the place. He talks about the future as 'we'll do this' or ' we'll go there.' You never know."

Catherine and David exchanged letters—love letters—during the five months when he was back in Canada. He spoke of the spiritual quality of devotion and self-discovery through union with another. He returned to Palm Springs in October 1995. The two read American Indian writers and attended lectures on Eastern philosophy and religion. Catherine particularly liked a passage from the book *Black Elk Speaks*, a biography of a Sioux holy man: "Hear me Four Quarters of the world—a relative I am! Give me the eyes to see and the strength to understand, that I may be like you. With your Power only can I face the winds." Before he left for Canada in the spring, David hinted that he intended to ask Catherine to marry him when he returned to Palm Springs.

Meanwhile, Catherine was becoming very active in the affairs of the community. She often talked to groups about how cost-effective treatment eschews one-on-one, human contact with mental patients. She also accepted an invitation to sit on the board of the Regional Access Project Foundation, a nonprofit public-benefit corporation that distributed tax monies through grants for mental health needs. She had won a reputation all over the valley as an articulate speaker and advocate for those with mental problems. During the summer and fall of 1996, she wrote of her experience in both prose and poetry, and read her works to groups interested in schizophrenia:

Morning Song

I have ventured toward the light of a thousand dawns
and plunged the depths of night-time eternal raging seas.
The hallowed shores of destinies' sweet embrace
have thrown me into savage places
as well as have lifted me up
into the most lofty heights
where heaven and hell intermingle
dissolving into foggy mists,
and fierce fire-breathing dragons
adorned with angel's wings
whisper songs of enchantment
enticing me into the lands that have no voice

so therefore cannot sing.
Today I saw a white-breasted bird
sail across the gray ocean sky
and oh, thought I,
what sweet, beautiful music
there is in uninhibited flight.

Catherine also began to make solo interpretive dance appearances, often to express a particular emotion, at various venues: senior centers, churches, and once at a gathering called "Ceremonial Sounds: A Celebration of Spring with Gongs, Tibetan Bells, Shaman Drums, Rattles, and Catherine Penney as featured dancer."

David returned to Palm Springs in October. The two enjoyed their walks in the desert, and talked about the absence of spirituality in the modern world. One evening, in the spring, about a month before David was to again leave for Canada, he and Catherine sat together on her couch. He produced a single long-stemmed red rose. "It represents my love for you—singular," he said. "I want you to be my wife. We are united in the earth, the water, the air, the fire, and the ether. We can live together everywhere."

"David, how could we live together? In Canada? My job . . ."

"Life is in the interior, not the exterior. We can share the same space. I can afford a good life for us. I don't want you to work. I want us to devote ourselves only to each other."

"You know I love you, David. Marriage . . . I must think."

"Of course. Search your soul."

Agony. Should she? Give up work? Give up independence? A union of souls. Is that real?

David said nothing until one week before he was to leave. "What do you think, Cathy, about us? About marrying me?"

"I can't, at least I can't make that decision now. I feel . . . too much pressure. I have to live with this for a while."

"You must follow your chakras. They are yours alone."

Three months later David wrote that he was engaged to someone else.

Catherine began an affair with Xavier Rosti, a psychiatrist working at a county clinic. "The wild-man doc," as his colleagues called him, was not a big man, but with his striking night-black hair and mischievous, sparkling green eyes, he was "viciously attractive," Catherine told one of her friends. He was part psychiatrist, part city councilman, and part boxing referee. He and his wife lived apart in an "open marriage." Catherine and Xavier spent a weekend in Las Vegas and an evening at his home where he "whipped up" veal marsala fit for gourmets. They had front-row seats at "fight night" at the Springs Casino, run by a local American Indian tribe. "The guy's got a hell of a testosterone level," she told her girlfriend. Catherine's affair with Xavier lasted three months. She felt that open marriage was not moral, and that she couldn't expect anything further from him.

Several months previously, I had received a letter from Catherine telling me of her community involvement and asking if I minded if she identified me as her psychiatrist. Three years before, she had served on a panel of "survivors" of schizophrenia at a meeting of the International Society for the Psychotherapy of Schizophrenia, held in Washington, D.C. Many in the audience wanted to know my side of Catherine's story, and the society asked her to come again. The 1997 meeting was to be held in June, in London. These gatherings attracted 750 to 1,000 therapists from around the world, who made presentations on schizophrenia. I talked with Catherine about my reluctance to involve myself in her out-there-in-the-world life. I did not want to compromise her or any patient's developing autonomy. She rightly assured me she had already developed her autonomy. We agreed to give a joint talk. Catherine would discuss her experience of therapy, and I would discuss mine.

I drove to Palm Springs to meet her before the conference. We arranged to have breakfast at my hotel. We shook hands, and held it for a time. She had a confident smile. She walked and tossed her head in a different way. She was a woman. "Well, Cathy, it's just so good to see you."

"Well, Dr. Dorman, it's good to see *you*."

She caught me up on her life, and we talked about limiting our presentation in London to "what worked" in her therapy, from both points of view. On the opening night of the conference, I met her at a pub across the street from the Queen Elizabeth Conference Centre and bought her a beer. We felt easy and relaxed, two adults, friends, sitting and discussing beer. I happen to regard English beer as the best in the world, better than the German brew. No one can match a good glass of English bitter, served at room temperature in an English pub.

At the conference, we were assigned a small room with only twenty-five seats, and our talk was scheduled for five o'clock, the last meeting time of the day. *All this way to talk to only twenty-five people?* I thought to myself. *Groups. They are all the same. They scratch each other's backs. I'll bet the same few people give the major papers at each meeting.* I located the lady responsible for room assignments. She told me, in that "just so" way peculiar to the English, that it was not at all proper to object, since the rooms had already been assigned. "Just the way it is," she said. But, demonstrating the fairness that also characterizes the English, she found me at three o'clock in the afternoon to tell me that a large room down the hall had become available owing to a speaker's illness.

As we sat in the room giving our talk, about 300 people crowded in. When we finished the audience rose to its feet and applauded. An interesting question-and-answer session followed the address. I was not used to seeing so much interest in the schizophrenic's experience, or in therapy, and found the whole event very energizing. Afterward, Catherine said it was her turn to buy *me* a beer. Of course.

To this day, Catherine continues to speak to community-activist groups about everything from her experience as a former mental patient to issues having to do with care of the elderly. She is a panel member of the Riverside County CARE program, funded by the county Department of Public Social Services and the county Office of Aging. There, she coordinates programs and trains caregivers to handle elder abuse. She still works for the county of Riverside, seeing to the needs of the older, indigent population. Catherine and I met in Los Angeles to talk to UCLA undergraduates taking a course on schizophrenia. We met again in Palm Springs to tape a program on schizophrenia for a series aired on Discovery Health Channel.

February 12, 2000: Catherine's fiftieth birthday. She and Cindy sit on Cindy's patio, sipping jasmine tea and nibbling birthday cake. In the distance the ocean sparkles with the flashing reflections of the afternoon sun. Just a few umbrellas dot the town beach below; the tourist swarms will be back soon enough. "My, Cathy, have we gotten old already?" Cindy asks.

"I don't feel old. I'm just hitting my stride."

"You are! You really are. So who's the latest? Are you seeing anyone?" Little "smiling wrinkles" appear at the outer corners of Cindy's eyes.

"Um-hmm. I am."

"Well, tell."

"Ed. I met him last October at a lecture on world religions and spirituality. The one empty chair was right next to him. That's the second time that has happened to me. Maybe the spirits are trying to tell me something."

"Probably. But what are they trying to say? Stay away from the last chair? Or stay away from the guy sitting *next* to the last chair?"

Catherine laughs. "Or, I have a surprise for you, miss. Sit down here!"

"Is he a who or a what?"

"Well, after the lecture was over, he invited me to have coffee at Starbucks, across the street. He's attractive, but I was a little distant because I couldn't tell how old he was. Fifty? Sixty? He was a teacher and writer, then he retired and sold real estate. He bought plenty for himself. We exchanged addresses and phone numbers, and four days later he wrote. Then he called and invited me up to Santa Rosa. I told him I didn't know him well enough for that, so he flew down to Palm Springs. I intended to keep it platonic."

"But Plato failed you?" Cindy grins.

"I failed Plato. Ed is intelligent, and he has a good sense of humor. We have a lot of the same interests: Native American spirituality and Buddhism. And ta da! He's single. I found out he's sixty-seven—and I'm still attracted to him."

Cindy leans back in her chair. "Elder abuse, that's what it is."

"Ha! I suppose so. No, I'm real kind to him. He sent me airfare and I visited him in Santa Rosa for four days. We went everywhere: to Sonoma, Bodega Bay, and Fishermen's Wharf in San Francisco. We hiked, too. It's such beautiful country up there. I flew to Phoenix once, too. We drove to Sedona. Talk about beautiful—all those red rocks pointing up to the sky. The whole country is like an outdoor cathedral. That weekend he decided to move to Palm Springs. I went looking for condos for him and found one. He flew down, took one look, and bang! It was done."

Cindy puts her cup down, and plants both feet on the floor. "Are you living together?"

"Oh no, no, no. I like it just the way it is. He's in his place and I'm in mine. In fact, I think it'll stay that way. He's helping me look for a house, too. Just maybe, I've found one. You know, he was married once, but only for six months. That was just a long date. He's really a bachelor. It makes it better. Just friends. Good friends. My dearest companion. I meet him at Jamba Juice in the mornings. Sometimes I'll stay over at his place, and we go together for juice with wheat grass. Then we go to Brodsky's Bagels, and we each have half a bagel with cream cheese. We share one coffee. He's not supposed to drink too much coffee. We read the newspaper and discuss the world. He comes to my flamenco lessons. We walk in Indian Canyon and drive to Idyllwild. I guess I'm going on and on?" Catherine looks at Cindy, who gazes lazily at the sky. "We have a loving bond built on mutual trust. It's such a good feeling to truly care about another person—with no strings attached. I think the most important thing about a relationship is to be honest about your feelings, not just to the other person, but to yourself as well."

"Whew! Cathy, I envy you. I really do. I've always been the wise one, the big sister. Now *I* have a big sister."

Nine

LORD OF YOURSELF

. . . here your will is upright, free, and whole,
and you would be in error not to heed
whatever your own impulse prompts you to:
lord of yourself I crown and mitre you.

Dante, The Purgatorio

IT IS UNCOMMON FOR schizophrenics to recover fully. Indeed, most of them live out their entire lives in sheltered environments. Nearly all regularly take medications that suppress the most severe horrors, such as hallucinations, suicidal thoughts and feelings, and repeated hospitalizations, but do not result in a cure. Their options for building personal relationships with others and for constructing meaningful work lives are limited.

Why has Catherine achieved such a rich and full life? And what can her story teach us about schizophrenia? Current psychiatric theory does not allow for cure, and might say that Catherine's experience represents merely an isolated or aberrant case—one that proves little about schizophrenia. However, to be valid, a scientific theory must account for all examples. What if we were to use Catherine's story to look at the larger problem of mental illness in a whole new light? Widening the lens through which we view mental illness can expose some startling insights—not only into why Catherine has recovered, but also into how individuals suffering from other supposedly hopeless conditions might live satisfying and productive lives.

According to a 1998 article by R.V. Bijl in the journal *Social Psychiatry and Psychiatric Epidemiology*, 48 percent of Americans and 41.2 percent of the Dutch will suffer from mental illness during their lifetimes. The article reports that 23 percent of the Dutch and 29 percent of Americans have had a mental illness in the previous twelve months. Moreover, women are more than one-and-one-half times more likely than men to experience multiple occurrences of mental illness, both during their lifetimes and in the previous twelve months. Sixteen-and-one-half percent of the women in this study reported having suffered a mental illness in the previous month.

What do these shocking numbers mean? How can nearly fifty percent of the population be abnormal? To answer that question, we might well take a look at what "normal" means. Normal generally refers to an average, or mean of observed quantities. "Average" means the usual state. Therefore, one cannot propose that half of a group is abnormal. Yet once any definition is established, future generations regard that definition as inviolable. The above figures argue strongly that we need to look at how normal and abnormal mental states came to be defined.

THE HISTORY OF MENTAL-STATE DEFINITION

The process of defining mental states extends back to the earliest eras of human civilization. For instance, as early as the time of Hammurabi, the Babylonian king who ruled around 1750 B.C., society called upon priests to cure individuals who were thought to be possessed by madness. The physician-priests of Babylon appealed to the gods through incantation, sacrifice, and prophecy based on astrology.

The Greek physicians at the time of Aristotle (384–322 B.C.) tried to understand the irrational mind and regarded madness as a divine gift. Oracles, usually women who went into seizure-like trances, offered the wisdom of madness to supplicants at sites throughout the ancient world. Examples include Miletus and Patara on the western coast of modern Turkey, and Cumae, near Naples, Italy. At Cumae, one can still explore the room in the cave where the "sibyl" sat and prophesied. Though madmen spoke the thoughts of the Gods, the general public shunned them—they were spat upon in the ancient Greek marketplace.

After Aristotle, "dogmatic rationalists" in ancient Greece regarded irrationality as an error of judgment. If the error were corrected, one would not be bothered by passion. E. R. Dodds, a professor of Greek history, described this approach in his book, *The Greeks and the Irrational*, as "leaving a mind untouched by joy, sorrow, untroubled by hope, or fear, passionless pitiless and perfect." The goal was freedom from undue emotion.

Up through the Middle Ages, people regarded the insane as messengers of the devil. They were beaten, mocked, and tortured. If apprehended, they were housed with criminals. The Bethlehem Hospital for the Insane in London was founded in 1247. Conditions at Bethlehem were horrible: the inmates were chained, poorly nourished, and often left to rot in their own excrement. In the thirteenth century, in Gheel, Belgium, an institution devoted to the care of "disturbed children" was established. Physicians known as "alienists" cared for these unfortunates.

Things took a more hopeful turn in the eighteenth century in Europe. Phillipe Pinel is an apt example. The son of physicians and a physician himself, in 1745 Pinel served as physician-in-chief at the Salpêtrière Hospital for Insane Women in France. In the spirit of reform that defined that era, he unchained the madwomen under his care and directed they be given humane treatment. He regarded his charges as sufferers of a physical malady, a lesion in the central nervous system.

Because physicians were in charge of the insane, they persisted in viewing madness as an illness. Even those who attempted to understand the importance of psychological phenomena to the development of extreme mental states used a medical model. Franz Alexander and Sheldon Selesnick, in their book, *The History of Psychiatry*, write that J. E. D. Esquirol, a student of Pinel, defined hallucinations as "sensory impressions . . . that do not exist and . . . are entirely the products of the mind." Esquirol defined illusions as "false impressions based upon a misinterpretation of an actual sensory stimulus."

It was perhaps Esquirol and his book, *The Mental Maladies*, published in 1838, that set the stage for the German psychiatrists who elaborated on Esquirol's classification system in the nineteenth century. The German psychiatrist Karl Ludwig Kahlbaum talked about types of abnormal behavior marked by "symptom complexes" that followed a course. Johann Christian Heinroth, another psychiatrist, made forty-eight different diagnoses. So many classification systems arose that, as the historian Gregory Zilboorg wrote, "the composer Berlioz was prompted to remark that after their studies have been completed a rhetorician writes a tragedy and a psychiatrist a classification."

Emil Kraepelin, whom we met in Chapter 3 and who coined the term *dementia praecox* to describe what we now call schizophrenia, was the most influential late nineteenth-century classifier of so-called mental illnesses. His student essay to the medical faculty at Würtzburg was titled, "On the Influence of Acute Diseases on the Origin of Mental Diseases." He described syndromes—behaviors and types of thinking that were curable and incurable—and attempted to predict their outcome. His classification system was published as a standard textbook of psychiatry, which swelled to two volumes totaling 2,425 pages in the ninth edition, published a year after his death in 1927. Kraepelin's exhaustive descriptions of dementia praecox and manic depression as the two major psychoses still form the basis of the current classifications system of mental illness. According to Zilboorg,

> The Kraepelinian system was a true triumph . . . because it brought about fulfillment of the age-long ambition of bringing mental disease into medicine, carrying it in through the front door, so to speak, bringing about a complete union of psychiatry and medicine. . . . Kraepelin established the fact that mental disease, like any other disease . . . is a disease running a regular course. He also took it for granted that, like any other disease, it is due either to a defective organ, or to heredity, or to improper body economy, or to metabolic changes, or to internal secretion—endocrine conditions. He thus brought the physiological laboratory into psychiatry and psychiatry into the laboratory. [p. 460]

Within the medical establishment, however, some physicians insisted that psychological phenomena played a major role in the development of diseases that should thus be described entirely in psychological terms. Physical complaints lacking an organic basis were deemed to be "hysterical," that is, originating in the uterus, and regarded as imaginary. J. M. Charcot, in Paris, studied hysterical sufferers using hypnosis and produced, through suggestion, a replication of their somatic complaints. Sigmund Freud, a neuropathologist by training, studied under Charcot in 1885. He then used

Viennese neurologist Josef Breuer's method of hypnosis, which involved listening to the hypnotized patient rather than making suggestions. Freud finally let his patients talk without hypnosis and concluded that a structure within the mind not accessible to consciousness existed—the unconscious. He then began to study and describe the unconscious, concluding that sexual drives in the form of specific "complexes" strongly influenced our behavior. This belief prevails among psychoanalysts even today.

So, we now have two competing theories about what actually drives human thinking, feeling, and behavior. One theory (held by psychoanalysts) points to psychosexual drives contained within the unconscious, a *structure* within the brain. The other (held by psychiatrists) points to *illness* within the brain. Psychoanalysts and psychiatrists alike refer to their own systems of "psychopathology," or disease of the mind.

Psychiatrists are steeped in the tradition of describing behavior or feeling states as "symptoms." Psychoanalysts, who emerged from psychiatry, hear in their patients' utterances symptoms of disturbed oedipal and other conflicts, which to them prove their existence. Psychiatrists, who believe that physical processes in the brain explain the mind, now claim center stage. Modern psychiatrists see themselves as scientists using scientific methods, and thus are convinced that the constructs—or ideas—that they build through scientific inquiry closely match reality. But, as the philosopher Ludwig Wittgenstein warned, we must be mindful of how our constructs are arrived at, lest we regard them as reality itself.

THE *DIAGNOSTIC AND STATISTICAL MANUAL OF MENTAL DISORDERS*

Modern psychiatry began with the reform of mental institutions that unfolded from 1650 to about 1800. During that time, psychiatrists were not considered members of the fraternity of physicians, since they "merely" took care of the insane. Psychiatrists of the late eighteenth and nineteenth centuries subsequently sought to prove that psychiatry used the same principles of diagnosis and disease as the rest of medicine. Twentieth-century American psychiatrists elaborated on their predecessors' classification systems.

The resulting system reached its zenith with the 1952 publication of an official manual of mental diseases, the *Diagnostic and Statistical Manual of Mental Disorders* (*DSM*), published by the American Psychiatric Association.

The *DSM*, now in its fourth edition, is the most comprehensive example of mental-state definition that has ever existed. But it is also an example of the very problem of how we define abnormal and normal. The manual uses the phrase "mental disorders" rather than "mental illnesses" in its title, but the word "diagnostic" gives its bias away. What but an illness does one diagnose? Unlike diagnostic manuals in the rest of medicine, the *DSM* lists only descriptions of feelings and behaviors—not physical changes. Each description refers to a different mental illness. The problem is that the book describes disease entities without providing any evidence; that is, it *implies* the existence of disease. In orthopedics, by contrast, a particular fracture of the wrist bones is diagnosed as a Colles fracture. One can see the characteristic fracture on an x-ray. Moreover, the fracture is nearly always produced by a fall on outstretched hands, and there is characteristic pain and swelling. The *DSM* states only that physical changes "may be associated" with the mental disorder in question. "May be associated" is not the same as clear-cut objective evidence, or cause and effect. Despite popular belief to the contrary, there is no credible evidence of physical lesions in the brain for any of the 374 mental illnesses listed in *DSM*—with the exception of mental retardation, intoxication, and in some demented states such as Alzheimer's disease or stroke, about twenty examples. Compilers of the *DSM* arrive at descriptions of the mental illnesses by "consensus," a fact they declare at the beginning of the manual, under the title "Cautionary Statement." They achieve this consensus by polling psychiatrists. Moreover, the authors want to have it both ways: on the one hand, they know they are listing theories or opinions; on the other hand, they call these opinions mental illnesses (disorders) with the weightiness that attaches to a medical diagnosis.

Paula Caplan, a former consultant to those who created the *DSM*, and a research psychologist, in her book, *They Say You're Crazy*, describes how the *DSM* authors arrived at decisions regarding who is abnormal. She traces the thinking of the committee responsible for the *DSM*, and laments the fact that it included ordinary feelings—such as premenstrual emotionality in women—as signs of mental disorder. Caplan also points out that women, because they are seen in American culture as more emotional than men, are disproportionately labeled mentally ill. She argues that the *DSM* is neither responsible nor scientific, but often just political. Consider that homosexuality was delisted in 1974 after protests by the gay-rights movement. Self-defeating personality disorder was deleted when feminists opposed it. How can supposed facts of medicine be changed by political protest?

Other obvious problems in the *DSM*'s classification system arise from the personal values of the classifiers. Take fetishism, for example, a diagnosis with code number 302.81. Three criteria must be met to make the diagnosis:

A. Over a period of at least six months, recurrent, intense sexually arousing fantasies, sexual urges, or behaviors involving the use of nonliving objects (e.g., female undergarments).
B. The fantasies, sexual urges, or behaviors cause clinically significant distress or impairment in social, occupational, or other important areas of functioning.
C. The fetish objects are not limited to articles of female clothing used in cross dressing (as in transvestic fetishism) or devices designed for the purpose of tactile genital stimulation (e.g., a vibrator). [p. 526]

We are thus told that being aroused by contact with female undergarments or other "nonliving objects" is cause for being declared abnormal, as is cross dressing, another mental illness (transvestic fetishism). The *DSM* committee has created a "thing"—fetishism—by naming it, and providing "proof" in the form of criteria that it exists. This is circular reasoning at its worst.

The *DSM* defines another disorder, hypoactive sexual desire, as "persistently or recurrently deficient (or absent) desire for sexual activity. The judgment of deficiency or absence is made by the clinician, taking into account factors that affect sexual functioning, such as the context of the person's life" (p. 496). With this "mental illness," we are left to wonder what "deficient" sexual fantasies are, how the "judgment of the clinician" is made, what "factors" affect sexual functioning, and what "context" means. We are not informed as to what constitutes "clinically significant distress," nor are we told how to define "impairment" or "other important areas of functioning."

Psychiatrists have extended their domain by trying to include the entire range of human variation in their system of medical diagnosis. Shyness, for example, has become social phobia. Disruptive children are labeled as suffering from oppositional defiant disorder. Millions of children who need to be taught restraint and personal discipline are designated as suffering from attention-deficit/hyperactivity disorder—and drugged. A proposed diagnosis, minor depression, might very well include all of us. The list goes on and on.

THE *DSM* AND SCHIZOPHRENIA

We now think of mental illnesses as facts supported by a prestigious professional group, the American Psychiatric Association, and its official-looking manual. Thus, investigators now look for the physical basis of these facts in the brain. But the logic behind the idea that so-called mental illness necessarily means that a brain abnormality exists is as specious as the logic of declaring that mental illness exists because of agreement among psychiatrists.

Let us look at the criteria in the *DSM* for the diagnosis of schizophrenia. I have omitted some additional "exclusion" criteria in the list below, because they do not apply to Catherine's situation:

A. Characteristic symptoms: Two (or more) of the following, each present for a significant portion of time during a one-month period (or less if successfully treated):
(1) delusions
(2) hallucinations
(3) disorganized speech (e.g., frequent derailment or incoherence)
(4) grossly disorganized or catatonic behavior
(5) negative symptoms, i.e., affective flattening, alogia [not speaking], or avolition [not moving]

Note: Only one Criterion A symptom is required if delusions are bizarre or hallucinations consist of a voice keeping up a running commentary on the person's behavior or thoughts, or two or more voices conversing with each other.

B. Social/occupational dysfunction: For a significant portion of the time since the onset of the disturbance, one or more major areas of functioning such as work, interpersonal relations, or self-care are markedly below the level achieved prior to the onset (or when the onset is in childhood or adolescence, failure to achieve expected level of interpersonal, academic, or occupational achievement).

C. Duration: Continuous signs of the disturbance persist for at least six months. This six-month period must include at least one month of symptoms (or less if successfully treated) that meet Criterion A (i.e., active-phase symptoms) and may include periods of prodromal [before the active phase] or residual symptoms. During these prodromal or residual periods, the signs of the disturbance may be manifested by only negative symptoms or two or more symptoms listed in Criterion A present in an attenuated form (e.g., odd beliefs, unusual perceptual experiences). [p. 285]

Catherine certainly met the criteria for a diagnosis of schizophrenia, but a difficulty arises right off in the definition of terms. Delusions (Criterion A-1) are defined as "erroneous beliefs." According to the *DSM*, "Persecutory delusions are the most common: The person believes he or she is being tormented, followed, tricked, spied on, or subjected to ridicule" (p. 275). Catherine's experience of being tormented was hardly an erroneous belief. But to the outside observer who could not see a tormenter, her belief was erroneous. Such an observer, who cannot understand the life experience of the patient, might well decide that the patient was delusional. The *DSM* tries to correct this problem by saying, "The distinction between a delusion and a strongly held idea is sometimes difficult to make and depends on the degree of conviction with which the belief is held despite clear contradictory evidence" (p. 275). What contradictory evidence was there that

Catherine was not as tormented as she felt? Catherine was also strongly convinced that she was bad, even evil, but these feelings, too, were not erroneous beliefs. She based her conclusions, in part, on the fact that she heard voices to kill members of her family and me.

Catherine did hear voices, which qualified her as suffering from hallucinations (Criterion A-2). But her voices were not just hallucinations—meaningless symptoms; they spoke the rage she dared not acknowledge. Her speech was "disorganized" (Criterion A-3) only to an outside observer who could not determine the nature of her internal logic. The *DSM* says, "Because mildly disorganized speech is common and nonspecific, the symptom must be severe enough to substantially impair effective communication" (p. 276). Catherine's silences were not "impaired" communication. They communicated her need to protect herself. Her catatonia (Criterion A-4) was also not just another symptom. It was her attempt to shut herself down in order to survive experiences that overwhelmed her.

Catherine's emotional flatness, rigidity, lack of ability to experience pleasure, and seeming unresponsiveness (Criterion A-5, negative symptoms) meant a poor prognosis. Underneath, Catherine did not have "a diminution of thoughts that is reflected in the decreased fluency and productivity of speech," the *DSM*'s definition of "impaired thinking." A description of what an observer *sees* is limited to what the observer *looks for*. She thought and felt too much, if anything. The *DSM* does address the problem of differentiating "poverty of speech," or alogia, from unwillingness to speak. The manual vaguely suggests that this is a "clinical judgment," to be arrived at by "observation over time and in a variety of situations." It makes no mention of the importance of just asking the patient or trying to understand his or her world.

The same hazy definitions and failure to acknowledge the individual's internal experiences apply to all *DSM* diagnoses. Take major depression and dysthymia, the so-called mood disorders. The manual states: "The episode must be accompanied by clinically significant distress or impairment in social, occupational, or other important areas of functioning" (p. 320). "Clinically significant" means according to the judgment of the observer, and has led to the term *clinical depression*, now in widespread use. The problem is that a "diagnosis" is rendered based on the superficial description of a few feelings relating to sadness. Since a diagnosis means an illness, the suffering individual is left with the impression that his or her sadness is abnormal.

SURGERY AND DRUGS: CHASING DISEASE-CAUSING STRUCTURES IN THE BRAIN

Influenced by *DSM*, researchers have searched the brain for specific sites corresponding to schizophrenia and other diagnoses. Antonio Egas Moniz, a Portuguese neurosurgeon, received a Nobel Prize in 1949 for his discovery of the structures in the brain—the prefrontal lobes—that supposedly cause schizophrenia. He performed prefrontal lobotomies on monkeys and noticed that they became calm. He then moved on and operated on schizophrenics. Thomas Szasz, in his book *Schizophrenia: The Sacred Symbol of Psychiatry*, quotes Moniz's reasoning: "If we could suppress certain symptomatic complexes of psychic nature by destroying the cell-connecting groups, we would prove definitely that the psychic functions and the brain areas that contributed to their elaboration are closely related. That would be a great step forward as a fundamental fact in the study of psychic functions on organic basis" (p. 92).

It is mind-boggling that the Nobel committee failed to appreciate Moniz's reductive reasoning. Elliot Valenstein, in his book *Blaming the Brain*, addresses the problem:

It is probably impossible today to find any scientist who believes that a mind can exist without a brain like some free-floating, disembodied soul. This does not mean, however, that the mind can be understood by studying the properties of any of the molecular components of the brain. A reductionistic approach that studies only the properties of organs, neurotransmitters, cells or atoms cannot understand consciousness and thought. Mental activity emerges from the integrated action of more than 20 billion brain cells (some of which are influenced by as many as 10,000 synaptic connections). Moreover, it is impossible to understand consciousness and thought without considering the psychosocial context that not only shapes the content of thought, but also the physical structure of the brain. Mental activity (normal or disordered) simply does not exist at a molecular level. *We must use methodologies that are appropriate to the level at which a phenomenon exists.* [p. 139, author's emphasis]

The experience of the soul, the self, and the human spirit cannot be reduced to organic elements. John Horgan, author of *The Undiscovered Mind*, calls this an "explanatory gap." T. M. Luhrmann, author of *Of Two Minds*, goes to the heart of the matter: "To say that mental illness is nothing but disease, is like saying that an opera is nothing but musical notes" (p. 266).

In a similar way, researchers have used drugs to alter the functioning of supposed structures causing schizophrenia. Eve C. Johnstone has spent twenty-five years studying schizophrenia from a biological perspective at the University of Edinburgh. In her book *Schizophrenia: Concepts and Clinical Management,* she writes that we still do not understand brain function. But psychiatrists continue to argue that because psychotropic drugs affect neurotransmitter chemistry, mental diseases like schizophrenia *must* exist. The absurdity of this argument is obvious: Just because you can target a given feeling or experience, say hallucinations or depression, with a drug proves only that you can affect brain chemistry. It does not prove that a chemical abnormality exists that the drug corrects. Just about everything alters neurotransmitter chemistry: psychotropic drugs, sadness, happiness, fear, an individual's will, his or her spontaneous thoughts, excitement, cocaine, and marijuana, to name a few. Moreover, just looking at physical processes, any mental state is an emergent phenomenon, a result of the dynamic interplay between brain elements, not a static phenomenon lodged among a few anatomical sites.

But with the conviction that the mind and the brain are one, the die was cast. Psychiatry was not going to be deprived of its chance to become a legitimate medical specialty by identifying real diseases of the mind located within the structures of the brain. Moniz's own words were prophetic:

I arrived at the conclusion that the synapses, which are found in billions of cells, are the organic foundation of thought. Normal psychic life depends upon the good functioning of the synapses and mental disorders

appear as a result of synaptic derangements. . . . All of these consider-
ations led me to the following conclusion: it is necessary to alter these
synaptic adjustments and change the patterns chosen by the impulses
in their constant passage so as to modify the corresponding ideas and
force thought into different channels. [Szasz, p. 91]

Despite Moniz's certainty that surgery had calmed his lobotomized patients'
thoughts, one of them burst into his office and shot him through the spine,
paralyzing him.

Human beings are made up not only of consciousness and thought, but
also of unconsciousness and emotion—and all is in constant flux. What I
feel or think at one moment can change at the next moment, influenced by
what occurred the previous moment and influencing what occurs the next
moment. To declare that someone suffers a chemical imbalance freezes any
such moment into a "thing," a certainty. The one-way view that neurotransmitters produce and regulate behavior ignores both the complexity of a
moment and the evidence that experience also affects neuronal function.
According to Elizabeth Bates, director of the Center for Research in Language at the University of California at San Diego, language in babies' brains
is organized differently than it is in adults "because the experience of language itself helps create the shape and structure of the mature brain." One
analysis showed that breast-feeding improved intelligence scores; another
showed that psychotherapy influenced serotonin levels in the brain. Even
the gross structure of the brains of identical twins is different, and life experiences can turn genes on and off. Exposure to stress, too, can produce
long-lasting brain changes. How might the high levels of continual stress
many mental patients experience over years and years affect the brain? The
chemical-imbalance theory is hopelessly simplistic.

All this is not to exclude genetic or biological influences on behavior or
feeling. A new mother recently told me that her little boy, a toddler, took
dolls and lined them up head to toe, then gleefully clapped his hands and
shouted, "Choo choo!" I do not remember the source but I once read of an
experiment where researchers watched a group of little boys and girls play
with blocks. The boys stacked the blocks and knocked them down; the girls
built a circle and sat in the middle. I do not wish to promote gender stereo-

typing, but I do want to show that genetic and biological influences are part of our makeup. Some children seem passive at birth, others more active; some are gregarious and others not so; some have talent for music or art, others a predilection for mathematics.

THE PERSISTENCE OF THE "BROKEN BRAIN" BELIEF

Biological influences form a "tapestry with the environment," to quote biologist Jerome Kagan, in John Horgan's book. "Every competent biologist," Kagan said, "knows that nature [biology] and nurture [environmental influences] are woven together so tightly that they cannot be easily unraveled, even in organisms much simpler than humans" (p. 163). A genetically wingless fruit fly, for example, will develop wings if the temperature in the laboratory rises by ten degrees. Male sheep raised by female goats sexually prefer goats. The female ring dove will not lay eggs unless a male is around. Grizzly bears must be taught to fish and polar bears raised in captivity do not learn how to survive in the wild. As many parents know, relatively uninhibited or inhibited infants at birth may not retain these characteristics. "Some extremely shy infants become outgoing adolescents and some happy babies become sullen introverted teenagers," writes Horgan (p. 164). It is also known that the longer immigrants stay in the United States, the more they experience physical and mental problems. Children who have close relationships with their day-care givers have higher academic scores. Biology is not destiny; then again, neither is the environment.

Valenstein says that "no biochemical, anatomical or functional signs have been found that reliably distinguish the brains of mental patients" (p. 125). Nevertheless, researchers continue to claim that schizophrenics suffer from "broken brains." We can sometimes find anatomical and chemical differences between the brains of different people, but we cannot say what has caused those differences—and what, in turn, these differences cause. One of my patients recently asked me about the "fact" that the brains of schizophrenics "light up" when viewed with special imaging techniques. She then opined, "I guess my brain would light up too if I were under as much stress as is a schizophrenic."

The public firmly believes that depression and schizophrenia stem from chemical imbalances within the brain. We are increasingly told that not only are mental problems due to brain abnormalities, but that our very personalities are biological phenomena. *U.S. News and World Report*'s February 7, 2000, cover declared, "Why We Fall in Love; Biology, Not Romance, Guides Cupid's Arrow." A lead article in the August 25, 1999, *Wall Street Journal* refers to "biological processes by which the disease takes hold," referring to mental disorders. In the June 13, 1999, *Boston Globe*, Madeline Marget wrote sensitively about her schizophrenic son and declared, "One can make two plain statements about schizophrenia: it is a physical disease of the brain, and a person afflicted with it has a serious mental illness."

Public perception is largely shaped by the media, and science reporters are drawn to the latest miracle breakthrough. Often, these reporters are tipped off in advance of publication by the public relations departments of prestigious medical journals. Understandably, reporters are driven by the public's hunger for cures and solutions, but often gross oversimplification results. Joe Palca, president of the National Association of Science Writers, is quoted in a February 12, 2000, *Los Angeles Times* article titled, "Medical Miracles or Misguided Media": "We could probably ignore ninety-nine percent of the science news in a given year, because its intrinsic value won't be known for many years or may not be that great." An example of egregiously irresponsible reporting appeared in *USA Today* on November 8, 1999, in an article by Stephen L. Cohen: "New scientific breakthroughs have reinforced the notion of a biological model of human behavior. . . . It appears that physical pathways in the brain may dictate much, if not all, of human behavior." Yet it would be a mistake to blame just the media. It is certainly a legitimate enterprise to subject the brain to scientific study and to report the findings. Neurobiology is a frontier science and is rapidly expanding. But studying the brain is not like studying other organs.

Nonscientific organizations use these beliefs. The National Alliance for the Mentally Ill (NAMI) posts supposed facts on its Web site; for example, "Just as diabetes is a disorder of the pancreas, mental illnesses are brain disorders . . ." The site proclaims, "Part of NAMI's success has been its ability to influence how Americans think about mental illnesses." Unfortunately, this has been true. NAMI's former director of research, E. Fuller Torrey, is the organization's guru and an advocate for the brain-disorder theory. In his book *Surviving Schizophrenia*, he states, "It [schizophrenia] is a brain disease." He cites evidence that the brains of schizophrenics are different from others. This is equivalent to saying muscle tension causes anxiety, since such tension exists in anxious people. At the end of Torrey's book, he lists the "fifteen worst" books about schizophrenia. Some of them are personal accounts, such as Hannah Green's *I Never Promised You a Rose Garden* and Theodore Rubin's *David and Lisa*. In a book-burning style of personal attack, Torrey declares the authors hallucinatory or muddle-headed. Torrey had also published an earlier book, *Schizophrenia and Civilization*, wherein he documented an increased incidence of schizophrenia with the coming of the Industrial Age. This claim points firmly to environmental factors, but Torrey instead concludes that a virus must have spread during that era.

One would think that NAMI and other advocacy groups would want to explore *any* potential cure for schizophrenia—not just drug treatment, surgery, or other tactics that presume biological cause. What is the point of declaring only one option? In NAMI's case, the motive seems both personal and political. According to an activist group, NAMI received a total of $11.72 million from drug companies between 1996 and mid-1999. The leading donor, Eli Lilly and Company, maker of Prozac, gave NAMI $1.1 million in 1999 alone. NAMI's founders, originally a group of parents and family members of schizophrenics, initially reacted (I should say overreacted) to the then-prevailing notion that parents were at fault. They wanted to shift the blame to biology.

Political motives frequently delay new discoveries. Take the example of John Harrison, an English clockmaker who solved the problem of determining longitude at sea. Before Harrison's invention of a portable clock, ships routinely were lost at sea since the only known way to navigate involved observing the stars. Dava Sobel, in her book *Longitude*, tells how, in 1714, the British Parliament passed the Longitude Act, which promised a prize of several million dollars in today's currency to the person who found a "practicable and useful" means of determining longitude. The difficulty was that vested interests did not favor such a development. Reverend Nevile

Maskelyne's position as astronomer royal at Greenwich depended on existing navigational methods, since Maskelyne promoted a system that employed lunar distance. The astronomer royal used every delaying tactic he could to thwart Harrison's success. Harrison spent forty years fighting Maskelyne before finally gaining his reward.

THE DILEMMA OF DEFINING IMPROVEMENT

Torrey has claimed that seventy percent of patients with schizophrenia improve on drugs. But what exactly is improvement? Nearly all studies on this are limited to changes in clinical rating scales. This means defining change by measuring the presence or diminution of a few feelings and behaviors, usually those used to define the condition in the first place. McKenna surveyed 500 standard-treatment-outcome studies in schizophrenia. He found only two that tried to measure how the afflicted individuals' lives had actually changed. Not surprisingly, the instruments used to measure quality-of-life changes in the two studies were woefully inadequate. How do you measure the quality of a person's life? The only way I know is to ask that person about his life or other experience. Any other measure is necessarily limited. This is another problem with all current measures of improvement: They assess only what can be quantified. How do you quantify, or measure my tears, when I stand in front of a painting by Vermeer?

Studies that examine the treatment of mentally disturbed people are often biased. Most such research is funded by drug companies. In an article in the May 30, 2003 The Times (London), the Health Editor, Nigel Hawkes, wrote, "A review of industry-sponsored research shows that it is four times more likely to come up with results favorable to the sponsor [drug company] than research backed by others." The research is skewed to reflect "good news" and to exclude negative results. Hawkes continues, ". . . the questions asked in drug company trials were carefully chosen so as to be more likely to yield a positive answer." Drug companies design their research to "prove" that the drug being studied affects one or more variables, such as anxiety, sadness, delusions, hallucinations, or frequency of hospitalization. The fact that the drug does affect these variables tells us little about the mental state being studied. For example, studies show that with the use of drugs, the more florid aspects of schizophrenia, such as delusions and hallucinations, may ease, and the frequency of repeat hospitalizations decreases. Such results bring some relief to the families of schizophrenics, but not so much to the sufferers themselves—despite popular opinion to the contrary. Studies not funded by drug companies show that schizophrenics in Third World countries do better long term than their drug-treated brethren in the United States. This suggests that long-term drug treatment may be harmful. Another study, funded by a university in Italy, showed that the long-term use of antidepressant medication (the serotonin reuptake inhibitors) was harmful. The problem of drug company influence is so serious that leading British and American medical journals now require authors to declare whether or not their research was funded by drug companies.

Even Torrey, who denigrates any form of treatment not using drugs as "incompetent," writes that schizophrenia is not a curable disease. He speaks of drug use as "controlling its symptoms." But he says that the use of these drugs is similar to the control of symptoms in diabetes. That is, it allows the patient "to lead a comparatively normal life." This is misleading. "Comparatively normal" means that patients' hospital stays are reduced, they do not hallucinate as actively as before, and they live with slowed thought and muted feeling. Sometimes they can manage limited employment. This is not comparatively normal at all. Eve Johnstone offers a more objective opinion than that of Torrey: "The introduction of newer 'atypical' antipsychotics has provided drugs with less severe side-effects, but their efficacy remains limited and the adverse effects are still a problem. The treatments available rarely produce full recovery, and many patients continue to struggle with considerable psychosocial and vocational disability" (p. 12).

Improvement is thus defined as a diminishing of offensive behavior and feeling. Psychiatrists refer to this as stabilization. Valenstein describes this well: "Anyone who has seen schizophrenics treated with antipsychotic drugs knows . . . they usually show signs of being sedated—often shuffling around the wards and responding slowly both physically and mentally. . . . But upon questioning they usually indicate that the delusional thoughts and the voices are still there" (p. 135). If the drugs are stopped, there is an eighty-percent chance of recurrence severe enough to warrant rehospitalization.

Efforts to achieve improvement have reached sometimes grotesque levels. Mental patients have been subjected to physical treatments from the beginnings of institutional care, but particularly from the nineteenth century to the present. Schizophrenics have had to endure dunking in hot or cold water, being spun in a chair, and being infected with malaria—the fever cure. Indeed, Julius Wagner-Jauregg received the Nobel Prize in 1927 for his fever therapy. Then came the insulin coma cure. An overdose of insulin drops blood sugar so low that the patient becomes comatose. In Austria in 1930, Manfred Sakel reported that thirty-five out of fifty schizophrenic patients were completely cured, and nine showed partial improvement. I am old enough to have observed insulin coma therapy. In 1959, I saw rows of patients strapped to gurneys in the cavernous psychiatric ward of the Larue D. Carter State Mental Hospital at Indiana University School of Medicine. All were connected to intravenous setups. As the insulin dripped into their veins, they began to sweat profusely, a sign of dangerously low blood sugar. Some convulsed as they lapsed into coma. After a few minutes, a glucose solution was run in and they awakened, dazed and amnesic. The whole scene had a sickening, dank, prison feel, the living dead being tortured and led back to their cells. No doubt this treatment caused a change in those patients' brain chemistry, if not the outright death of brain cells, which need sugar to survive. Perhaps that change disrupted their mental states and therefore their behaviors, just as drugs do today.

Some physicians speculated that seizures would cure schizophrenia, and used Metrazol, a drug that induces seizures. In 1938, Italian psychiatrists Ugo Cerletti and L. Bini introduced electric-shock therapy to induce convulsions. Even today, electroshock remains a treatment for depression. The offending brain came under furious attack from Walter Freeman as well, an American neurosurgeon who performed thousands of lobotomies with an ice pick in the 1950s and 1960s. Contemporary neurosurgeons are experimenting with electrodes implanted in the brain, connected by wires to an external stimulator. If the patient feels sad or anxious, he or she just pushes a button, and the neuronal circuit mediating the feeling is blocked. Or patients can undergo surgery, done at Harvard Medical School's teaching hospital, Massachusetts General, and at other university hospitals.

During these procedures, surgeons sever the connections to the cingulate gyrus, a neuronal crossroads carrying brain circuits related to feeling.

As with drug therapy, all of these measures assume that a "broken brain" causes mental disorders. But nothing was broken about Catherine's brain, even though she certainly met all the criteria for severe, poor-prognosis schizophrenia. Catherine's recovery involved more than a reduction in the symptoms of schizophrenia. Today, she is a normal person with a strong identity who takes no medications and has no need of constant support in her day-to-day living by trained professionals or family members. This is *true* improvement.

According to Torrey, Catherine should not have improved. He reiterates the party line regarding psychotherapy and schizophrenia: "Given what we know about the brains of persons with schizophrenia, it should not be surprising to find that insight-oriented psychotherapy makes them sicker" (p. 168). Torrey goes on to say that psychotherapy "should be explicitly avoided," dismissing it as "negligent" and "malpractice." Torrey cites studies of psychotherapy that, under close examination, reveal the use of inexperienced therapists who saw their patients for just half an hour twice a week. Torrey also cites only short-term studies, usually covering treatment periods of less than two years. Finally, he ignores the "Michigan study," done by Bertram Karon, that while also short-term, showed a positive effect of psychotherapy. Catherine would have qualified as "not improved" after three years of psychotherapy if judged by how she looked to an outside observer. And I am sure that she would disagree with Torrey, who said, "Insight-oriented psychotherapies are analogous to pouring boiling oil into wounds because they ignore the chronic schizophrenic's particular vulnerability to over-stimulating relationships, intense negative affects, and pressures for rapid change" (p. 168).

LEAVING THE MEDICAL MODEL

To understand schizophrenia, and for that matter, all mental states, we must leave the medical model. We can then be free to explore the mind without prejudice. For example, we can break apart the diagnostic entity schizophrenia into aspects of human experience that reflect all the complexity that makes up any experience: biological influences, individual and social psychology, the development of consciousness, cognition, language development, anthropology, philosophy, and creativity—to name just a few. If we look at schizophrenia as a part of the human experience, we must take seriously what the schizophrenic says, as opposed to classifying his or her statements and behaviors as pathological or normal.

The actual experiences of sufferers are the road to understanding. The first autobiographical description of the inner experience of madness written in English came in 1436 with *The Book of Margery Kemp*. Dale Peterson has excerpted some passages in his book, *A Mad People's History of Madness*: "Sometimes she [Margery Kemp] heard with her bodily ears such sounds and melodies that she could not well hear what a man said to her at that time, unless he spoke the louder. . . . She saw with her bodily eyes many white things flying all about her on every side, as thick, in a manner, as specks in a sunbeam" (p. 14). Kemp tries to explain hearing voices, and experiencing visions: "By this token, daughter, believe that it is God Who speaketh in thee" (p. 15). But, she rejects this explanation: "She would give no credence to the counsel of God, but rather believed it was some evil spirit deceiving her" (p. 16).

If we listen to schizophrenics, they tell us that they are attempting to make sense of their experiences. Their attempts represent normal human effort, and are not evidence of pathology. Mary Barnes's *The Snake Pit* is another riveting account from Peterson's book. She describes the doctor in the mental hospital as diabolical, the attendants as guards, and electroshock treatment as electrocution. We might dismiss her feelings as delusions, but they are *her* truth. Nor should we ignore artists' accounts of madness. For a sense of the irony and humor of madness, listen to the song "Blow-Top Blues" played by Lionel Hampton and sung by Dinah Washington. Louis A. Sass, in his book *Madness and Modernism*, observes, "Schizophrenics can, in fact, be persons of considerable intelligence and mental complexity. . . . In light of these propensities, it seems unfortunate—and ironic—that the patient's own perspective should be accorded so little attention, that it should often be dismissed either as devoid of significance altogether or as the product of the most primitive and rudimentary forms of mental life" (p. 7).

Catherine was willing to share her account of her madness. As we've seen, the disease model excludes environmental influences, but Catherine's experience, and that of many others, tells a different story:

> My mother always said her marriage to my natural father was perfect. I was supposed to replace him. I think she felt depressed and lonely, too, because her mother and father died. So I think a lot of responsibility was put on me. I became so very protective of her. If I did or felt anything for myself, like feeling lonely or hurt, or if I was mad at her, I thought I had hurt her and she would go away. She was my whole life and I think I was hers. I sabotaged myself to guarantee her loving me. It seems like all my young life I struggled with a feeling of not being entitled to happiness, to have a life. I was always supposed to let the other person have it. I was left with my unhappiness, which I had to brush under the rug. But my unhappiness was there anyway. Without knowing it, I made my mother's reality my reality.

Because of her unusually close relationship with her mother, Catherine failed to develop an identity of her own. She adopted, by fusion, her mother's unhappy identity. Because cognitive and emotional development occur within families, we must own up to the part we play in the development of the individuals within those families. If a passive infant at risk of having trouble establishing an independent identity lands in a family that greatly values independent identity, he will fare much better than if he ends up in a family that does not value independence. If a child with an aggressive mentality who always pushes against her boundaries is reared in a family that can't establish reasonably firm boundaries, she may not learn to differentiate herself. This is not a matter of placing blame. Rather, it is a matter of being willing to examine the contribution of *all* aspects of human existence to all mental states. Indeed, families are not the only social contexts in which human development unfolds. The culture of the larger society, the historical era in which an individual grows up, regional and community beliefs—all this shapes an individual's development, too.

THE LACK OF AN "I": THE ROLE OF SELF-DEVELOPMENT
IN PSYCHOSIS

As for the chain of events leading up to schizophrenia, statistics tell us that individuals who become schizophrenic have difficulty socializing and make poor grades in school. While this is often but not always true, these gross descriptions of behavior do not help us understand why these events take place. I asked Catherine how and why she became insane, and she responded:

> I didn't have any sense of me—myself. Do you remember that time we were invited to speak at the UCLA seminar on recovery from schizophrenia? Afterwards the instructor got up and said my recovery was unusual because schizophrenics don't usually have the ego strength to involve themselves in a therapeutic relationship. That doctor didn't get it at all. Ego strength? I didn't have an ego. My ego developed in therapy. There was no ego in me for life to stick to. All of my life was my mother. So when I got to adolescence I was lost. My life was like sand being blown away little by little until I was left with nothing. The only thing I could do was resort to craziness to have a me.

If one looks to the experience of other schizophrenics, this same theme— the lack of an ego, or self—is repeated again and again. Sigmund Freud's famous patient, Shreber, talked about soul-murder. Catherine talked about having "no nucleus, no central self." A schizophrenic man said (quoted from Jaynes): "Gradually I can no longer distinguish how much of myself is in me, and how much is already in others. I am a conglomeration, a monstrosity modeled anew each day" (p. 418).

This lack of self-development is central to schizophrenia, and to most of the so-called mental illnesses. The experience of one's self is central to the human condition, which is why "mental illness" is but one aspect of human experience. Julian Jaynes, professor of psychology at Princeton University, has tackled the problem of schizophrenia from the point of view of how an "I" develops in the first place. One does not have to agree with his thesis that human beings did not even possess an experience of

"I" until 1000 to 2000 B.C. to appreciate the relevance of his argument that schizophrenics suffer such a lack. As Jaynes explains:

> Another way in which this erosion of the analog "I" shows itself is in the relative inability of schizophrenics to draw a person. . . . They leave out obvious anatomical parts, like hands or eyes; they use blurred and unconnected lines; sexuality is often undifferentiated; the figure itself is often distorted and befuddled. . . . [p. 418]
>
> A schizophrenic not only begins to lose his "I" but also his mind-space, the pure paraphrand that we have of the world and its objects that is made to seem like a space when we introspect. To the patient it feels like losing his thoughts, or "thought deprivation." . . . The effort of this is so bound up with the erosion of the analog "I" as to be inseparable from it. [p. 420]

In the deepest grip of her psychosis, Catherine talked a lot about time standing still. Jaynes has this to say: "Another way the dissolving of mind-space shows itself is in the disorientation in respect to time so common in the schizophrenic. We can only be conscious of time as we can arrange it into a spatial succession, and the diminishing of mind-space in schizophrenia makes this difficult or impossible" (p. 421).

Jaynes also refers to the lack of "I" as responsible for the schizophrenic's inability to give logical answers. There is no "unifying conceptive purpose," he says, since answers to questions must come from a person's mind-space. The schizophrenic tries to tie answers to external circumstances. When the schizophrenic says he is commanded by outside forces, the psychiatrist regards it as a delusion, a falsification of reality, but Jaynes says, "With the loss of the analog 'I,' its mind-space, and the ability to narrate, behavior is either responding to hallucinated directions, or continues on by habit. The remnant of self feels like a commanded automaton" (p. 423).

If we look at people who suffer excessive anxiety, the kinds of disorders described in the *DSM*, we can see similar phenomena. Anxious individuals are afraid, sometimes of even going out of the house. If you ask them what they are afraid of, they may well tell you about external circumstances—that lightning might strike them or that they will become lost while driving. They fear personal catastrophe. This is the same catastrophe that people falling into schizophrenia feel (which psychiatrists call prepsychotic anxiety) as what is left of their mind-space erodes. Schizophrenics react by withdrawing and using what appear to be bizarre explanations to preserve their remnants of self. An anxious person, with more "I" to start with than the schizophrenic, retreats to the safety of four walls instead.

Anorexics experience similar processes. It is difficult, nearly impossible, to persuade an anorexic patient to give up what she calls "control," her rigid dieting. But what is she controlling? Ask any anorexic, and you will get the same answer: the overwhelming anxiety of personal catastrophe. The symptoms of anorexia nervosa usually begin at about the same time in adolescence as do the symptoms of schizophrenia, and for the same reason. It is in adolescence that one needs a reasonably strong sense of self. It is at this time of life that one begins to enter adulthood and the larger world. So it is no wonder that the experience of self-dissolution occurs at this time. Anorexia, excessive anxiety, and schizophrenia are not different diseases. These syndromes reflect different responses to the same problem.

In an effort to outdistance a fragmented, weak, or barely perceptible personal identity, one can try several things. For example, one can adopt an external identity within a group or cause, or withdraw into a narrow existence that puts few demands on self-assertion. Or, one might chemically alter oneself so as not to feel the terror or sadness of a diminutive self. Ironically, that very terror may be all that is left of the authentic self. The fact is that sadness and anxiety are natural reactions to a poorly developed "I."

There is another often-ignored strategy as well: a person's creative attempt to structure his or her bewildering or eroding internal world. In our modern rush to shift responsibility away from ourselves, we skip over what an individual might be doing to bring about his or her own state of affairs. When I talked with Catherine while preparing this book, I asked her opinion about this. She replied, "My becoming crazy wasn't hereditary or physical or chemical, you know. It looked like it happened overnight, which was not true. It took years. No one ever attributed it to *me* doing it!"

Many of Catherine's "symptoms" emerged from her efforts to protect or "fix" herself. For instance, she became catatonic "to get around being violent," and developed rigid dietary rules "because I had to control something.

Everything else was chaos." She told me that thinking itself was overwhelming, so she tried to wipe out thinking by "going down inside myself." Many of her attempted solutions only worsened her confusion and anxiety, which required even more effort on her part to keep things under control. Her "personal construction"—that is, her creative attempt to structure her internal world—began to "leak," meaning that she felt her lack of development, confusion, terror, and rage in spite of her own efforts to erase them. Finally, she was flooded.

The same problem exists for people who complain of depression. It is rare that such individuals do not have a very good reason to be sad—even those who say that the depressed feelings "came out of the blue." Listening carefully, therapists can often discover that depressed patients' feelings are normal responses to events in their internal and/or external worlds. Their fragile selves are "leaking." Such an individual's personal construction, which may be an identity style such as being dominant or passively withdrawing, has begun to fail. He or she then tries to construct new defenses, which also fail. Treating such an individual with drugs just adds another layer of control that does not address the real problem. The agony at his or her core has been left untouched.

THE PRICE OF THE DISEASE MODEL

American psychiatry's campaign to promote itself as a medical specialty has carried a high price tag: It has directed research efforts into nonexistent disease entities; promised drug control of mental problems as treatment; and undermined effective, legitimate social, cultural, and psychotherapeutic efforts to help people navigate these states of mind. Moreover, psychiatric residency programs have gradually curtailed training in psychotherapy. For twenty-eight years, I have supervised psychiatrists in training at UCLA. Supervision consists of a senior therapist meeting with the resident psychiatrist on a regular basis to review his or her work. This is probably the best way to learn psychotherapy, because it rests on a one-on-one apprenticeship. But last year, the assistant to the director of residency training told me that the program was being cut and asked whether I would be interested in teaching in a walk-in clinic. Such clinics focus on crisis management, leaving little or no opportunity to teach psychotherapy skills. "We are shifting our focus to the new era," the assistant told me. "Modern insurance payment programs are based on short-term care."

"No thanks," I replied. "Let me know when you need an experienced therapy supervisor."

As psychiatry has abandoned psychotherapy, schools that teach psychotherapy as part of a degree program in psychology have filled the gap somewhat. But many schools offering a doctoral degree in clinical psychology are heavily influenced by the medical model, which restricts a psychotherapeutic approach. These programs teach students that if a patient is depressed beyond the capacity of his or her therapist to understand, the person must be suffering a clinical depression. He or she is sent off to the psychiatrist for a prescription. There are some top-flight schools. One is the Scarborough Psychotherapy Training Institute in London, led by Heward Wilkinson, the senior editor of the *International Journal of Psychotherapy*. A look through the syllabus reveals a well thought out program emphasizing a humanistic approach with demanding standards leading to a degree in psychotherapy. However, these exceptions cannot overcome the damage that the disease model of mental problems has left behind.

THE EXPERIENCE OF THERAPY

Perhaps the best way to understand the power of therapy is to ask the participants. From my point of view, Catherine's "I" development was central. One does not develop an "I," a unique individual identity, in a vacuum. Part of this development occurs in nature. For instance, I experience my self, my "I," viewing a landscape, smelling a rose, or rolling down a grassy hillside. Another part of "I" development occurs with other human beings. An example is that Catherine identified with the grandmother. She incorporated, or took as a good part of herself, her grandmother's Spanish ancestry. Catherine expresses this through her continuing interest in flamenco dancing. Another example is speaking of my personal experience to another person. I am emphasizing experience, which involves feeling over intellectualization. Of course, my intellect is part of my self. But it is my *experience* of my intellect that is important.

The essence of therapy is the creation of a situation, a relationship, that encourages the process of "I" development. My job was to get to know Catherine, to understand her "I." If my understanding resonated with *her* experience of her self, she might gain some experience that her "I" was real. Catherine told me that in one of our early meetings she "put up an antenna" when I said that perhaps her silence was a way to be "cozy and safe." She contrasted my remark with her previous experience of being diagnosed, therefore judged.

The therapist, of course, is not a blank slate. He is a student of the human condition. When he listens to his patient he will be comparing what he has learned with what his patient says and does. Sometimes, perhaps often, he will recognize a particular dynamic, such as his patient's use of projection or his inability to use metaphor. Most psychoanalytic schools of thought suggest that the therapist adopt a position of "interpreting" a given dynamic, such as saying, "The voices you hear are your own thoughts." The idea is that the patient is supposed to "confront" her hidden or unconscious internal forces. Sometimes such interpretations are called for, and sometimes not. Sometimes what the therapist is interpreting is wrong. For instance, contrary to what I had expected, Catherine did not need to "confront" her anger toward her mother. Her anger disappeared because the origin of her rage lay in her experience of being small and helpless—of having little "I." As she grew, she was no longer angry. Thus, her rage was not about hating her mother; it was a global hatred of her own condition.

The therapist must be "in tune" with his patient. "In tune" means being sensitive to what his patient is experiencing at the moment. For example, I acknowledged Catherine's anger and tried to understand its origin. Catherine corrected me. *She* was concerned about her experience of feeling *bad*, even evil, because of her voices. Being "in tune" with Catherine meant I was obliged to acknowledge her sense of badness (her "I" experience). At the same time, I wanted to show her that despite her rage, she was not evil. In order to experience being not so bad, she would have to accept at least a piece of my "I," my reflection of her. Wilfried Ver Eecke, professor of philosophy at Georgetown University, has studied successful psychotherapy of schizophrenia. He writes about this acknowledgment and addition process as essential in his paper, "A Lacanian Explanation of Karon's and Villemoe's Successful Psychodynamic Approaches to Schizophrenia."

There were three phases in Catherine's treatment. The first was marked by the acknowledgment and addition process referred to above. I acknowledged that Catherine was a person whose true thoughts and feelings could be appreciated. She, in turn, began to appreciate my experience of her, including my efforts to understand the origin of her experiences. The combination added bits and pieces of "I" to her individual self-system until she developed enough "I" to at least partially separate from me.

The second phase, partial separation from me, began when Catherine opened her eyes. She quickly developed a hunger for new experience, *her* experience. It was during this time that she moved into her own apartment—away from the identity of a "sick" person needing others to help her with many of the basic details of living. She began the process of affirming her independent identity. On one hand, during this phase, I acknowledged the truth of her vast insecurity, and on the other a truth she could not know, that growth and development were possible.

Catherine's announcement that she was going to stop therapy marked the beginning of the third phase, the consolidation of her separate identity. It was important that *I* experienced a sudden diminution in my power when Catherine made her announcement. It was the point where *both* of us recognized that we were equals. From that point on, Catherine used me as a reality check. She continued seeing me, albeit less frequently, to help her affirm the reality of her perceptual apparatus. Self-confidence can be defined as the ability to trust one's perceptual apparatus. Finally, Catherine reached a point where she could not go forward without the experience of independence.

I think there has been a post-treatment phase, too. Not really a phase, rather both of us have been permanently changed. We have come to know each other, and we have developed a deep respect and affection for each other. Each of us, her "I" and my "I," has been changed by the other. Training programs for therapists often emphasize the importance of the "neutrality" of the therapist. The therapist's feelings are regarded as "countertransference," an impediment to the progress of therapy. I have found that a great deal is lost if the therapist does *not* feel or experience a change as a result of his relationship with his patient. An essential part of continuing "I" development is the experience of having an effect on another person, and being affected by others.

Thirty-four years have passed since I first met Catherine, and twenty-six years since we ended her psychotherapy. Catherine tells us what she regards as essential:

In Hawaii I heard many psychiatrists say it was the patient's fault when no progress was made. If the doctor doesn't trust himself, he is going to rely on something outside of himself, and tranquilizers seem to be the answer. The last thing a person needs is to have the doctor go along or initiate a false solution. Someone has to be able to stand outside the pit. I'll bet seventy-five percent of all the patients I have ever talked with have said the same thing, but they stay on the drugs because they do not have anything else. I certainly remember threatening to sign out of the hospital because I saw everyone around me getting relief, and there I was climbing the walls. If I had received drugs I might have gotten temporarily out of my catatonic state, but I'd have been back there sooner or later. I've seen patients leave the hospital, then go off their tranquilizers. The decrease in anxiety wasn't initiated by the patient, so when he goes off his tranquilizer or antidepressant, his pain comes back and he still doesn't know how to cope, except by going back on the drug. I think that is demeaning.

When medications are given, I think the doctor is looking for relief from his own anxieties. He sees mental problems as something to fear, something to get rid of. By using tranquilizers, the doctor is just making his patient's problem more inaccessible. He is pushing it out to the boondocks. When the doctor gives drugs, he is really saying the drugs will do it for the person. He is stunting his patient's growth. It tells the patient that he is hopeless, and puts him into a role as a chronically sick person.

The time and effort needs to be taken to get down to the crux of the matter, even though it takes a long time, because in the long run a lot of time is wasted if the proper thing isn't done. I guess this society is kind of superficial—appearances are important and the dirt is just brushed under the rug. As long as everything looks clean.

The doctor assumes that his patient's anxiety is so extreme and terrifying he can't cope. But, you know what? Every human being copes. It might be an odd style, but everybody finds some way. I devised my own way to cope with my anxiety. The doctor can't offer his patient a false way. His patient has to find a way himself, and sometimes he will go through weird and unacceptable ways of coping, but that may be necessary to get to a better place. Because the patient's ways are strange and hard to understand, he is labeled as being unhealthy.

After I changed so much, my aunt said to me, "Golly, you got well overnight." It wasn't overnight. The transition is a process, which begins the moment the doctor sees his patient. If the doctor is smart, he will keep on with someone even though he feels he's not getting anywhere. When I was in the hospital, and afterwards, I was not aware of all the little changes that were occurring. It was the years I was at UCLA sitting there, rocking back and forth. It was the years of what we were doing which gave me a base to change. People just do not suddenly give up their defenses or protections. They are given up little by little, and one day you don't need them anymore. An anorexic, for example, is not going to give up her food habits until she sees there is no reason to keep them any longer, and a drug user is not going to give up overdosing on drugs until he can see a ray of light indicating another way.

The only way I made it was to face head-on what I feared. Now, when I feel down, it is not like a foreign body invading me. I realize that depression and anxiety are parts of me and I don't have to be afraid of those parts. I realize I'm human and there must be a reason I feel bad. Then it is up to me to get out of it. But if you don't feel you have the strength to find your way out, you don't even want out, which is when it becomes frightening. A person has to develop the tools to face up to himself. The *struggle* is the way out. If you eliminate the suffering, you eliminate the awareness of what has to be done. Drugs kill the creative part of the person, the part that has the ability to overcome. The doctor thinks he's getting the person out of pain. I think that is bullshit. People miss finding out what resources they have inside them.

And you know, Dr. Dorman, I got better because you used yourself. You were real, which allowed me to be real. You were not afraid of my craziness or my developing independence. The greatest gift a human being can give is to cultivate another person's unique talents, strengths, and sense of self-worth. Armed with those tools, one can approach life head-on, regardless of what obstacles may come one's way. This has not been so much about conquering schizophrenia, but about honesty and living a life of quality, and meeting the dawn of each new day with great expectation and acceptance.

I cannot treat everyone. I never know, when I begin, who will have the stamina or will to do battle with their demons, or whether they will succeed. Schizophrenics are just as human as anyone else, and treating them is no different. I lent Catherine my strength, so that she might build her self. She did.

BIBLIOGRAPHY

Alexander, F., and Selesnick, S. T. (1966). *The History of Psychiatry*. New York: Harper & Row.

Alighieri, D. (1954). *The Inferno*, trans. J. Ciardi. New York: Mentor.

——— (1961). *The Purgatorio*, trans. J. Ciardi. New York: Mentor.

American Psychiatric Association. (1994). *Diagnostic and Statistical Manual of Mental Disorders, 4th ed.* Washington, DC.

Bijl, R. V., Ravelli, A., and van Zessen, G. (1988). Prevalence of psychiatric disorder in the general population: results of the Netherlands Mental Health Survey and Incidence Study (NEMESIS). *Social Psychiatry and Psychiatric Epidemiology* 33: 587–595.

Caplan, P. J. (1995). *They Say You're Crazy: How the World's Most Powerful Psychiatrists Decide Who's Normal*. Reading, MA: Addison-Wesley.

Dodds, E. R. (1964). *The Greeks and the Irrational*. Berkeley and Los Angeles: University of California Press.

Feather, J., and Feather, L. (1945). "Blow-Top Blues." Lionel Hampton and his septet with Dinah Washington. Decca records no. 23792.

Horgan, J. (1999). *The Undiscovered Mind: How the Human Brain Defies Replication, Medication, and Explanation*. New York: Free Press.

Jaynes, J. (1990). *The Origin of Consciousness in the Breakdown of the Bicameral Mind*. Boston: Houghton Mifflin.

Johnstone, E. C., Humphreys, M. S., Lang, F., Laurie, S. M., and Sandler, R.

(1999). *Schizophrenia: Concepts and Clinical Management.* Cambridge: Cambridge University Press.

Karon, B. P., and VandenBos, G. R. (1981). *Psychotherapy of Schizophrenia: The Treatment of Choice.* New York: Jason Aronson.

Luhrmann, T. M. (2000). *Of Two Minds: The Growing Disorder in American Psychiatry.* New York: Knopf.

McKenna, S. P. (1997). Measuring the quality of life in schizophrenia. *European Psychiatry* 12(suppl. 3): 267s–274s.

Peterson, D., ed. (1982). *A Mad People's History of Madness.* Pittsburgh, PA: University of Pittsburgh Press.

Sass, L. A. (1992). *Madness and Modernism: Insanity in the Light of Modern Art, Literature, and Thought.* Cambridge, MA and London: Harvard University Press.

Sobel, D. (1995). *Longitude: The True Story of a Lone Genius Who Solved the Greatest Problem of His Time.* New York: Walker.

Szasz, T. (1998). *Schizophrenia: The Sacred Symbol of Psychiatry.* Syracuse, NY: Syracuse University Press.

The Times (London). (2003). May 30, p. 4.

Torrey, E. F. (1983). *Surviving Schizophrenia: A Manual for Families, Consumers, and Providers.* New York: Harper Perennial.

Valenstein, E. S. (1998). *Blaming the Brain: The Truth About Drugs and Mental Health.* New York: Free Press.

Ver Eecke, W. (2002). A Lacanian explanation of Karon's and Villemoe's successful psychodynamic approaches to schizophrenia. *Journal of the American Academy of Psychoanalysis* 30(4): 633–643.

Zilboorg, G. (1941). *A History of Medical Psychology.* New York: Norton.